ALL ABOUT HINDUISM

ALL ABOUT HINDUISM

Sri Swami Sivananda

Published by

THE DIVINE LIFE SOCIETY

P.O. SHIVANANDANAGAR—249 192

Distt. Tehri-Garhwal, Uttarakhand, Himalayas, India

Price]   2007   [Rs. 120/-

First Edition: 1947
Second Edition: 1961
Third Edition: 1977
Fourth Edition: 1988
Fifth Edition: 1993
Sixth Edition: 1997
Seventh Edition: 2003
Eighth Edition: 2007

[2,000 Copies]

ISBN 81-7052-047-9
ES5

Published by Swami Vimalananda for
The Divine Life Society, Shivanandanagar, and printed by him
at the Yoga-Vedanta Forest Academy Press,
P.O. Shivanandanagar, Distt. Tehri-Garhwal, Uttarakhand,
Himalayas, India

Dedicated to
All Those
Who Love Hinduism
And Its Sublime Philosophy
And Practise Its Teachings

SRI SWAMI SIVANANDA

Born on the 8th September, 1887, in the illustrious family of Sage Appayya Dikshitar and several other renowned saints and savants, Sri Swami Sivananda had a natural flair for a life devoted to the study and practice of Vedanta. Added to this was an inborn eagerness to serve all and an innate feeling of unity with all mankind.

His passion for service drew him to the medical career; and soon he gravitated to where he thought that his service was most needed. Malaya claimed him. He had earlier been editing a health journal and wrote extensively on health problems. He discovered that people needed right knowledge most of all; dissemination of that knowledge he espoused as his own mission.

It was divine dispensation and the blessing of God upon mankind that the doctor of body and mind renounced his career and took to a life of renunciation to qualify for ministering to the soul of man. He settled down at Rishikesh in 1924, practised intense austerities and shone as a great Yogi, saint, sage and Jivanmukta.

In 1932 Swami Sivananda started the Sivanandashram. In 1936 was born The Divine Life Society. In 1948 the Yoga-Vedanta Forest Academy was organised. Dissemination of spiritual knowledge and training of people in Yoga and Vedanta were their aim and object. In 1950 Swamiji undertook a lightning tour of India and Ceylon. In 1953 Swamiji convened a 'World Parliament of Religions'. Swamiji is the author of over 300 volumes and has disciples all over the world, belonging to all nationalities, religions and creeds. To read Swamiji's works is to drink at the Fountain of Wisdom Supreme. On 14th July, 1963 Swamiji entered Mahasamadhi.

THE UNIVERSAL PRAYERS

I

O Adorable Lord of Mercy and Love!
Salutations and prostrations unto Thee.
Thou art Existence-Consciousness-Bliss Absolute.
Thou art Omnipresent, Omnipotent and Omniscient.
Thou art the Indweller of all beings.

Grant us an understanding heart,
Equal vision, balanced mind,
Faith, devotion and wisdom.
Grant us inner spiritual strength
To resist temptations and to control the mind.
Free us from egoism, lust, greed, hatred, anger
and jealousy.
Fill our hearts with divine virtues.

Let us behold Thee in all these names and forms.
Let us serve Thee in all these names and forms.
Let us ever remember Thee.
Let us ever sing Thy glories.
Let Thy Name be ever on our lips.
Let us abide in Thee for ever and ever.

—*Swami Sivananda*

II

O Thou Invisible One! O Adorable One! O Supreme!
Thou permeatest and penetratest this vast universe from the
unlimited space down to the tiny blade of grass at my feet.
Thou art the basis for all these names and forms. Thou art
the apple of my eye, the Prema of my heart, the very Life
of my life, the very Soul of my soul, the Illuminator of
my intellect and senses, the sweet Anahata music of my

heart, and the substance of my physical, mental and causal frames.

I recognise Thee alone as the mighty Ruler of this universe and the Inner Controller (Antaryamin) of my three bodies. I prostrate again and again before Thee, my Lord! Thou art my sole refuge! I trust Thee alone, O ocean of mercy and love! Elevate, enlighten, guide and protect me. Remove obstacles from my spiritual path. Lift the veil of ignorance, O Thou Jagadguru! I cannot bear any longer, even for a second, the miseries of this body, this life and this Samsara. Give Darsana quickly. O Prabho! I am pining. I am melting. Listen, listen to my fervent, Antarika prayer. Do not be cruel, my Lord. Thou art Dinabandhu. Thou art Adhama-Uddharaka. Thou art Patita-Pavana (Purifier of the fallen).

Om Santi Santi Santih!

III

Sarvesham Svasti Bhavatu
Sarvesham Santir Bhavatu
Sarvesham Purnam Bhavatu
Sarvesham Mangalam Bhavatu

> May auspiciousness be unto all;
> May peace be unto all;
> May fullness be unto all;
> May prosperity be unto all.

Sarve Bhavantu Sukhinah
Sarve Santu Niramayah
Sarve Bhadrani Pasyantu
Ma Kaschid-Duhkha-Bhag-Bhavet

> May all be happy;
> May all be free from disabilities;
> May all behold what is auspicious;
> May none suffer from sorrow.

Asato Ma Sadgamaya
Tamaso Ma Jyotir-Gamaya
Mrityor-Ma Amritam Gamaya

Om Santi Santi Santih!

Lead me from the unreal to the Real;
Lead me from darkness to the Light;
Lead me from mortality to Immortality.

Om Peace! Peace! Peace!

CONTENTS

xiv

8. HINDU YOGA

9. HINDU THEOLOGY

10. HINDU MYTHOLOGY AND SYMBOLS

11. HINDU PHILOSOPHY—I
(THE SHAD-DARSANAS)

ALL ABOUT
HINDUISM

CHAPTER 1

HINDU RELIGION

Silent adorations to *Satchidananda Para-Brahman,* Who is the silent Witness of all minds, Who is the Indweller in all beings, Who has projected this world for His own *Lila* or sport, Who is the support for this world, body and mind and all movements, and Who is the foundation for all societies and their activities.

PURPOSE OF RELIGION

The word Religion comes from the Latin word *religio* which consists of two words, viz., *re* (back) and *ligare* (to bring or bind). That which binds the soul back to God is religion. Religion shows the way for the attainment of God-realisation.

Religion satisfies the deep inward craving in man who is not always content with leading merely an animal existence and wants spiritual consolation, solace and peace. Man cannot live by bread alone. A time comes in the life of many of us when mere worldly prosperity does not satisfy us and we hanker after something more. In the case of many more, trials and tribulations of life turn their attention to spiritual solace.

DISTINGUISHING FEATURES OF HINDUISM

A REVEALED RELIGION

Hinduism is the religion of the Hindus, a name given to the Universal Religion which hailed supreme in India. It is the oldest of all living religions. This is not founded by any prophet. Buddhism, Christianity and Mohammedanism owe their origin to the prophets. Their dates are fixed. But no such date can be fixed for Hinduism. Hinduism is not born of the teachings of particular prophets. It is not based on a set of dogmas preached by a particular set of teachers. It is free from religious fanaticism.

Hinduism is also known by the names *Sanatana-Dharma* and *Vaidika-Dharma.*

Sanatana-Dharma means eternal religion. Hinduism is as old as the world itself. Hinduism is the mother of all religions. Hindu scriptures are the oldest in the world, Sanatana-Dharma is so called, not only because it is eternal, but also because it is protected by God and because it can make us eternal.

Vaidika-Dharma means the religion of the Vedas. The Vedas are the foundational scriptures of Hinduism. The ancient Rishis and sages of India have expressed their intuitive spiritual experiences *(Aparoksha-Anubhuti)* in the Upanishads. These experiences are direct and infallible. Hinduism regards the spiritual experiences of the Rishis of yore as its authority. The priceless truths that have been discovered by the Hindu Rishis and sages through millennia constitute the glory of Hinduism. Therefore, Hinduism is a revealed religion.

A RELIGION OF FREEDOM

Hinduism, unlike other religions, does not dogmatically assert that the final emancipation is possible only through its means and not through any other. It is only a means to an end and all means which will ultimately lead to the end are equally approved.

Hinduism allows absolute freedom to the rational mind of man. Hinduism never demands any undue restraint upon the freedom of human reason, the freedom of thought, feeling and will of man. It allows the widest freedom in matters of faith and worship. Hinduism is a religion of freedom. It allows absolute freedom to the human reason and heart with regard to questions such as nature of God, soul, creation, form of worship and the goal of life. Hinduism does not lie in the acceptance of any particular doctrine, nor in the observance of some particular rituals or form of worship. It does not force anybody to accept particular dogmas or forms of worship. It allows everybody to reflect, investigate, enquire and cogitate. Hence, all sorts of religious faiths, various forms of worship or Sadhana, and diverse kinds of rituals and customs, have found their honourable places side by side within Hinduism and are cultured and developed in harmonious relationship with one another.

Hinduism does not condemn those who deny God as the creator and ruler of the world, who do not accept the existence of an eternal soul and the state of Moksha or state of liberation. Hinduism does not render the upholders of such views unfit to be recognised as pious and honourable members of the Hindu religious society.

The religious hospitality of Hinduism is proverbial. Hinduism is extremely catholic and liberal. This is the fundamental feature of Hinduism. Hinduism pays respects to all religions. It does not revile any other religion. It accepts and honours truth—wherever it may come from and whatever garb it may put on.

There are considerable numbers of the followers of other religions in India. And yet, the Hindus live in perfect harmony, peace and friendship with all of them. Their tolerance and fellow-feeling towards the followers of other religions is remarkable.

Despite all the differences of metaphysical doctrines, modes of religious discipline and forms of ritualistic practices and social habits prevalent in the Hindu society, there is an essential uniformity in the conception of religion and in the outlook on life and the world, among all sections of Hindus.

THE GLORY OF VEDANTA AND YOGA

Vedanta, or the philosophy of the Upanishads, is lofty, sublime and unique. The Western philosophers have paid their tribute to the ancient seers of the Upanishads. They have been amazed at the lofty heights scaled by them. Schopenhauer studied the Upanishads and meditated on the thoughts of the Upanishads just before going to bed. He said: "The Upanishads are the solace of my life and they will be solace to me after my death also."

The Raja-Yoga system of Hinduism is also splendid and unique. The lessons are immensely practical and highly instructive. No system of physical exercise on the surface of the earth can compete with Hatha-Yoga. Kundalini-Yoga is wonderful. Hence the Americans and Europeans are in search of Hindu Sannyasins and Yogins. They visit the Himalayas frequently in quest of Yoga teachers. Some are living under Hindu Yogins as disciples and are practising Yoga. Many Europeans and Americans are even now Hindus by faith and practice, though they are born Christians. They practise Raja-Yoga and Vedanta.

EMPHASIS ON PRACTICE

Hinduism provides spiritual food and Yoga Sadhana for all sorts of people to suit their temperaments, capacities, tastes, stages of spiritual development and conditions of life. It prescribes Yoga Sadhana even for a scavenger or a cobbler to attain God-realisation, while doing his ordinary avocation in the world. Hindu Yoga and Vedanta teachers lay great stress on self-restraint, Tapas, renunciation and practical Sadhana which is best calculated to control the mind and the senses and unfold the divinity or attain Self-realisation. Hinduism is not a religion of mere theories. It is eminently practical. In no religion you will find such a variety of practical Yoga practised and such sublime unique philosophy expounded.

That is the reason why India is the only glorious land of sages, Rishis, Yogins and saints.

Religion is practical aspect of philosophy. Philosophy is rational aspect of religion. The philosophy of Hinduism is not arm-chair philosophy. It is not meant for intellectual curiosity and vain discussion. Hindu philosophy is a way of life. The philosopher of Hinduism seriously reflects after hearing the Srutis, does Atma-Vichara, constantly meditates, and then attains Self-realisation or Atma-Sakshatkara. Moksha is his goal. He attempts to attain Jivanmukti now and here.

Religion is spiritualisation of human life for a Hindu. Religious culture is really the culture of freedom for him. Religion governs all the departments of Hindu life. He must realise the freedom of the soul in every department of life. Religion affords the greatest scope for him for the culture of true freedom. Religion is the only way to him for the realisation of perfect freedom in life.

It is in India alone that every man knows something of philosophy. The cowherd who tends the cattle, the peasant who ploughs the fields, the boat-man who pulls at his oar, sing songs replete with philosophical truths. Even the barber repeats OM NAMAH SIVAYA, SIVOHAM before he takes up the razor. The Paramahamsa Sannyasins, the itinerant monks of Hinduism, have disseminated the highest of Vedanta from door to door. In exchange for a handful of rice, they have distributed from door to door, through religious songs, the priceless gems of Hindu religion and philosophy.

WHO IS A HINDU

In a meeting of the Sanatana Dharma Sabha, Lokamanya Tilak said: "A Hindu is he who believes that the Vedas contain self-evident and axiomatic truths."

The Hindu Maha Sabha has given another definition: "A

Hindu is one who believes in a religion which has originated in India."

"Those who burn the dead are Hindus." This is another definition given by some.

"He who protects the cows and the Brahmins is a Hindu." This is another definition given by some.

Some define: "A Hindu is one who regards India as his motherland and the most sacred spot on earth."

Some others define: "He who calls and considers himself a Hindu is a Hindu."

Some define: "He who accepts the Vedas, the Smritis, the Puranas and the Tantras as the basis of religion and of the rule of conduct, and believes in one Supreme God (Brahman), in the Law of Karma or retributive justice, and in reincarnation *(Punarjanma)*, is a Hindu."

"He who follows the Vedic or Sanatana-Dharma is a Hindu." This is the definition by some.

"He who is a follower of the Vedanta is a Hindu." This is another definition given by some others.

"He who has perfect faith in the Law of Karma, the law of reincarnation *Avatara,* ancestor worship, *Varnashrama Dharma, Vedas* and existence of God, he who practises the instructions given in the Vedas with faith and earnestness, he who does *Sandhya, Sraaddha, Pitri-Tarpana* and the *Pancha-Maha-Yajnas,* he who follows the Varnashrama Dharmas, he who worships the Avataras and studies the Vedas, is a Hindu." This is the definition given by some highly cultured men. This is the only correct and complete definition.

ORIGIN AND SIGNIFICANCE OF THE TERM

That part of the great Aryan race which migrated from Central Asia, through the mountain passes into India, settled first in the districts near the river Sindhu, now called the Indus, on the other side of the river. The Persians pronounced the word Sindhu as Hindu, and named their Aryan brethren Hindus. *Hindu* is only a corrupt form of *Sindhu*.

The Hindu Aryans spread themselves over the plains of the Ganga. Then the Persians gave the name Hindusthan, or abode of the Hindus, to the whole of those districts between Punjab and Benaras.*

The classical name for India which is used in Sanskrit literature is *Bharata-Varsha* or *Bharata-Khanda*, after the name of Bharata who ruled over a large extent of territory in days of yore. Manu's name for the whole central region between the Himalayas and the Vindhya mountains is *Aryavarta*, Abode of the Aryans. Another name for the whole of India is *Jambu-Dvipa*. The Greeks gave the name Indu to the whole of this country. It was on account of this *India* became popular as the name of this country throughout Europe.

Hindu is not a mere name. This name *Hindu* is not only of geographical, but also of national and racial importance. The whole history of our nation from the very beginning is bound up with it. All our ideas and ideals are so intimately connected with it that it is difficult to give a simple definition of it. Poets, prophets and Avataras came to sing the praises and glory of this name. Rishis, sages and saints took their birth to compile the *Sastras* and *Darsanas* for this nation. Heroes and warriors have fought for its honour and laid down their very lives for it. Piety, nobility, generosity, philosophy, religious bent of mind, Yoga, religious tolerance, wisdom, devotion, renunciation, Self-realisation, Ahimsa, Satya and purity are associated with the name 'Hindu'.

THE SPIRITUAL SOIL OF INDIA

India is the sacred land which has given birth to countless sages, Rishis, Yogins, saints and prophets. India is the land

---

* Latest historical researches have now proved that the Aryans did not come from outside India, but were the original inhabitants of India.

---

that has produced many Acharyas or spiritual preceptors like Sri Sankara and Sri Ramanuja; many saints like Kabir, Ramdas, Tukaram and Gauranga Mahaprabhu; many Yogins like Jnana Dev, Dattatreya and Sadasiva Brahman; and many prophets like Buddha and Nanak. Buddha is our flesh and blood.

India is proud of Guru Govind Singh and Sivaji. India is proud of king Bhoja and Vikramaditya. India is proud of Sankara and Kabir. India is proud of Valmiki and Kalidasa. Krishna, Rama and all Avataras were born in India. How sacred is India! How sublime is India! The dust of Brindavan and Ayodhya, the land trodden by the sacred feet of Krishna and Rama, still purifies the heart of countless people. Even Jesus, during the missing period of His life, lived in Kashmir and learnt Yoga from the Indian Yogins. Glory to Mother India!

India is a spiritual country. India never conquered territories or annexed dominions. Military conquest is not her ambition. She wants her children to have *Atma-Svarajya* or Absolute Independence. She does not call upon them to rule over others. She wants them to have conquest over internal and external nature. She wants them to possess brilliant divine virtues, moral stamina and inner spiritual strength born of wisdom of the soul. Ahimsa is her weapon to have the spiritual conquest and the conquest of the minds of others.

People of India have Self-realisation as their goal. They do not, generally, bestow too much attention on material prosperity and advancement. They want Yoga or communion with the Supreme Being. They practise Ahimsa, Satya and Brahmacharya. They wish to enjoy the eternal bliss of the Absolute. They are always ready to renounce worldly possessions in order to possess or realise the inner Atman or Brahman. They will sacrifice anything and everything in order to attain the immortal Atman. They are always spiritual-minded.

India is the sacred land with several holy rivers and powerful spiritual vibrations. The hoary Himalayas attract the people of the whole world. It is a land peculiarly suitable for divine contemplation and Yogic practices. Every country has its own special attractive features. India is the land of Yogins and sages. This is the special attractive feature of India. This is the reason why people from America, England and all parts of the world come to India for the practice of Yoga.

THE FACTS OF HISTORY

India is the most tolerant country in the world. She has a very expansive heart. She includes all nations in the embrace of her love.

The Western nations are the descendents of the original Hindus or Aryans. They might have forgotten their old connections with the Aryans and Hindu culture. They might have forgotten all about their ancestors. But this cannot be effaced from the annals of history. Mother India, the repository of Hindu culture, cannot forget her children beyond the seas. They are always dear to her.

Hindu culture and Hindu civilisation were at their zenith in the days of yore. Greeks and Romans imitated the Hindus and absorbed Hindu thoughts. Even now Hindu culture and Hindu civilisation stand foremost in the world. No religion has produced so many great saints, sages, Yogins, Rishis, Maharshis, prophets, Acharyas, benefactors, heroes, poets, statesmen and kings as Hinduism. Each and every province of the country has produced intellectual giants, poets and saints. Even now India abounds in Rishis, philosophers, saints and high intellectuals. Even now she abounds in sages and great souls.

The Hindus had to undergo severe hardships and tortures. They had to face fierce battles and cruelties and yet they live today. Some mysterious power has preserved them. Some in-

visible force has protected them. That power will protect
them for ever.

REASONS FOR SURVIVAL OF THE HINDU RELIGION

Hinduism is neither asceticism nor illusionism, neither
polytheism nor pantheism. It is the synthesis of all types of
religious experiences. It is a whole and complete view of life.
It is characterised by wide toleration, deep humanity and
high spiritual purpose. It is free from fanaticism. That is the
reason why it has survived the attacks of the followers of
some of the other great religions of the world.

No religion is so very elastic and tolerant like Hinduism.
Hinduism is very stern and rigid regarding the fundamentals.
It is very elastic in readjusting to the externals and non-es-
sentials. That is the reason why it has succeeded in living
through millennia.

The foundation of Hinduism has been laid on the bedrock
of spiritual truths. The entire structure of Hindu life is built
on eternal truths, the findings of the Hindu Rishis or seers.
That is the reason why this structure has lasted through
scores of centuries.

ITS FUTURE

The glory of Hinduism is ineffable. It has within it all the
features of a universal religion. Its Dharmas are universal. Its
doctrines are sublime. Its philosophy is grand. Its ethics is
soul-elevating. Its scriptures are wonderful. Its Sadhanas or
Yoga-Vedantic practices are unique. Glorious has been the
past of this religion; still more glorious is its future. It has a
message to give to a world rent asunder by hatred, dissension
and war—the message of cosmic love, truth and non-
violence, the gospel of unity of Self or Upanishadic oneness.

The more you know of India and Hinduism, the more will
you come to regard and love it and the more grateful to the
Lord will you be in that you have got a taste for practising

Yoga and that you are imbibing the teachings and spirit of Hinduism.

Glory to India! Glory to Hinduism! Glory, glory to the Rishis and the seers who have kept burning the flame of Hinduism with its extreme effulgence and splendour!

CHAPTER 2
HINDU SCRIPTURES
SANSKRIT LITERATURE

Sanskrit literature can be classified under six orthodox heads and four secular heads. The six orthodox sections form the authoritative scriptures of the Hindus. The four secular sections embody the later developments in classical Sanskrit literature.

The six scriptures are: (i) Srutis, (ii) Smritis, (iii) Itihasas, (iv) Puranas, (v) Agamas and (vi) Darsanas.

The four secular writings are: (i) Subhashitas, (ii) Kavyas, (iii) Natakas and (iv) Alankaras.

THE SCRIPTURES
THE SRUTIS

The *Srutis* are called the *Vedas,* or the *Amnaya.* The Hindus have received their religion through revelation, the Vedas. These are direct intuitional revelations and are held to be *Apaurusheya* or entirely superhuman, without any author in particular. The Veda is the glorious pride of the Hindus, nay, of the whole world!

The term *Veda* comes from the root *Vid,* to know. The word *Veda* means knowledge. When it is applied to scripture, it signifies a book of knowledge. The Vedas are the foundational scriptures of the Hindus. The Veda is the source of the other five sets of scriptures, why, even of the secular and the materialistic. The Veda is the storehouse of Indian wisdom and is a memorable glory which man can never forget till eternity.

Revealed Truths Without Beginning or End

The Vedas are the eternal truths revealed by God to the

ALL ABOUT HINDUISM

great ancient Rishis of India. The word *Rishi* means a seer from *dris,* to see. He is the *Mantra-Drashta,* a seer of Mantra or thought. The thought was not his own. The Rishis saw the truths or heard them. Therefore, the Vedas are what are heard (Sruti). The Rishi did not write. He did not create it out of his mind. He was the seer of thought which existed already. He was only the spiritual discoverer of the thought. He is not the inventor of the Veda.

The Vedas represent the spiritual experiences of the Rishis of yore. The Rishi is only a medium or an agent to transmit to people the intuitional experiences which he received. The truths of the Vedas are revelations. All the other religions of the world claim their authority as being delivered by special messengers of God to certain persons, but the Vedas do not owe their authority to any one. They are themselves the authority as they are eternal, as they are the Knowledge of the Lord.

Lord Brahma, the Creator, imparted the divine knowledge to the Rishis or seers. The Rishis disseminated the knowledge. The Vedic Rishis were great realised persons who had direct intuitive perception of Brahman or the Truth. They were inspired writers. They built a simple, grand and perfect system of religion and philosophy from which the founders and teachers of all other religions have drawn their inspiration.

The Vedas are the oldest books in the library of man. The truths contained in all religions are derived from the Vedas and are ultimately traceable to the Vedas. The Vedas are the fountain-head of religion. The Vedas are the ultimate source to which all religious knowledge can be traced. Religion is of divine origin. It was revealed by God to man in the earliest times. It is embodied in the Vedas.

The Vedas are eternal. They are without beginning and end. An ignorant man may say how a book can be without beginning or end. By the Vedas, no books are meant. Vedas came out of the breath of the Lord. They are the words of God. The Vedas are not the utterances of persons. They are not the composition of any human mind. They were never written, never created. They are eternal and impersonal. The date of the Vedas has never been fixed. It can never be fixed. Vedas are eternal spiritual truths. Vedas are an embodiment of divine knowledge. The books may be destroyed, but the knowledge cannot be destroyed. Knowledge is eternal. In that sense, the Vedas are eternal.

The Four Vedas and Their Sub Divisions

The Veda is divided into four great books: the Rig-Veda, the Yajur-Veda, the Sama-Veda and the Atharva-Veda. The Yajur-Veda is again divided into two parts, the Sukla and the Krishna. The Krishna or the Taittiriya is the older book and the Sukla or the Vajasaneya is a later revelation to sage Yajnavalkya from the resplendent Sun-God.

The Rig-Veda is divided into twenty-one sections, the Yajur-Veda into one hundred and nine sections, the Sama-Veda into one thousand sections and the Atharva-Veda into fifty sections. In all, the whole Veda is thus divided into one thousand one hundred and eighty recensions.

Each Veda consists of four parts: the Mantra-Samhitas or hymns, the Brahmanas or explanations of Mantras or rituals, the Aranyakas and the Upanishads. The division of the Vedas into four parts is to suit the four stages in a man's life.

The Mantra-Samhitas are hymns in praise of the Vedic God for attaining material prosperity here and happiness hereafter. They are metrical poems comprising prayers, hymns and incantations addressed to various deities, both subjective and objective. The Mantra portion of the Vedas is useful for the Brahmacharins.

The Brahmana portions guide people to perform sacrificial rites. They are prose explanations of the method of using the

Mantras in the Yajna or the sacrifice. The Brahmana portion is suitable for the householders.

The Aranyakas are the forest books, the mystical sylvan texts which give philosophical interpretations of the rituals. The Aranyakas are intended for the Vanaprasthas or hermits who prepare themselves for taking Sannyasa.

The Upanishads are the most important portion of the Vedas. The Upanishads contain the essence or the knowledge portion of the Vedas. The philosophy of the Upanishads is sublime, profound, lofty and soul-stirring. The Upanishads speak of the identity of the individual soul and the Supreme Soul. They reveal the most subtle and deep spiritual truths. The Upanishads are useful for the Sannyasins.

The subject matter of the whole Veda is divided into *Karma-Kanda, Upasana-Kanda* and *Jnana-Kanda.* The Karma-Kanda or Ritualistic Section deals with various sacrifices and rituals. The Upasana-Kanda or Worship-Section deals with various kinds of worship or meditation. The Jnana-Kanda or Knowledge-Section deals with the highest knowledge of Nirguna Brahman. The Mantras and the Brahmanas constitute Karma-Kanda; the Aranyakas Upasana-Kanda; and the Upanishads Jnana-Kanda.

The Mantra-Samhitas

The Rig-Veda Samhita is the grandest book of the Hindus, the oldest and the best. It is the Great Indian Bible, which no Hindu would forget to adore from the core of his heart. Its style, the language and the tone are most beautiful and mysterious. Its immortal Mantras embody the greatest truths of existence, and it is perhaps the greatest treasure in all the scriptural literature of the world. Its priest is called the Hotri.

The Yajur-Veda Samhita is mostly in prose and is meant to be used by the Adhvaryu, the Yajur-Vedic priest, for superfluous explanations of the rites in sacrifices, supplementing the Rig-Vedic Mantras.

The Sama-Veda Samhita is mostly borrowed from the Rig-Vedic Samhita and is meant to be sung by the Udgatri, the Sama-Vedic priest, in sacrifices.

The Atharva-Veda Samhita is meant to be used by the Brahma, the Atharva-Vedic priest, to correct the mispronunciations and wrong performances that may accidentally be committed by the other three priests of the sacrifice.

The Brahmanas and the Aranyakas

There are two Brahmanas to the Rig-Veda—the Aitareya and the Sankhayana. "The Rig-Veda," says Max Muller, "is the most ancient book of the world. The sacred hymns of the Brahmanas stand unparalleled in the literature of the whole world; and their preservation might well be called miraculous." (HISTORY OF ANCIENT SANSKRIT LITERATURE)

The Satapatha Brahmana belongs to the Sukla Yajur-Veda. The Krishna-Yajur-Veda has the Taittiriya and the Maitrayana Brahmanas. The Tandya or Panchavimsa, the Shadvimsa, the Chhandogya, the Adbhuta, the Arsheya and the Upanishad Brahmanas belong to the Sama-Veda. The Brahmana of the Atharva-Veda is called the Gopatha. Each of the Brahmanas has got an Aranyaka.

The Upanishads

The Upanishads are the concluding portions of the Vedas or the end of the Vedas. The teaching based on them is called Vedanta. The Upanishads are the gist and the goal of the Vedas. They form the very foundation of Hinduism.

There are as many Upanishads to each Veda as there are Sakhas, branches or recensions, i.e., 21, 109, 1000 and 50 respectively to the four Vedas, the Rig-Veda, the Yajur-Veda, the Sama-Veda and the Atharva-Veda.

The different philosophers of India belonging to different schools, such as Monism, Qualified Monism, Dualism, Pure Monism, Difference-cum-non-difference, etc., have acknowledged the supreme authority of the Upanishads. They have given their own interpretations, but they have obeyed the authority. They have built their philosophy on the foundation of the Upanishads.

Even the Western scholars have paid their tribute to the seers of the Upanishads. At a time when the Westerners were clad in barks and were sunk in deep ignorance, the Upanishadic seers were enjoying the eternal bliss of the Absolute, and had the highest culture and civilisation.

The most important Upanishads are Isa, Kena, Katha, Prasna, Mundaka, Mandukya, Aitareya, Taittiriya, Chhandogya, Brihadaranyaka, Kaushitaki and Svetasvatara and Maitrayani. These are supremely authoritative.

May the fundamental truths of the Vedas be revealed unto you all, like the Amalaka fruit in the palm of your hand. May Gayatri, the blessed Mother of the Vedas, impart to you the milk of Knowledge, the ancient wisdom of the Upanishads.

The Upa-Vedas

There are four *Upa-Vedas* or subsidiary Vedas, viz., the Ayurveda, the Dhanurveda, the Gandharva Veda and the Arthasastra, forming auxiliaries to the four Vedas, which mean, respectively, the science of health, the science of war, the science of music and the science of polity.

The Vedangas

There are six *Angas* or explanatory limbs, to the Vedas: the *Siksha* and *Vyakarana* of Panini, the *Chhandas* of Pingalacharya, the *Nirukta* of Yaska, the *Jyotisha* of Garga, and the *Kalpas* (Srauta, Grihya, Dharma and Sulba) belonging to the authorship of various Rishis.

Siksha is a knowledge of phonetics. Siksha deals with pronunciation and accent. The text of the Vedas is arranged in various forms or *Pathas.* The Pada-patha gives each word its separate form. The Krama-patha connects the word in pairs.

Vyakarana is Sanskrit grammar. Panini's books are most famous. Without knowledge of Vyakarana, you cannot understand the Vedas.

Chhandas is metre dealing with prosody.

Nirukta is philology or etymology.

Jyotisha is astronomy and astrology. It deals with the movements of the heavenly bodies, planets, etc., and their influence in human affairs.

Kalpa is the method of ritual. The Srauta Sutras which explain the ritual of sacrifices belong to Kalpa. The sulba Sutras, which treat of the measurements which are necessary for laying out the sacrificial areas, also belong to Kalpa. The Grihya Sutras which concern domestic life, and the Dharma Sutras which deal with ethics, customs and laws, also belong to Kalpa.

The Pratishakhyas, Padapathas, Kramapathas, Upalekhas, Anukramanis, Daivatsamhitas, Parishishtas, Prayogas, Paddhatis, Karikas, Khilas and Vyuhas are further elaborations in the rituals of the Kalpa Sutras.

Among the Kalpa Sutras, the Asvalayana, Sankhyana and the Sambhavya belong to the Rig-Veda. The Mashaka, Latyayana, Drahyayana, Gobhila and Khadira belong to the Sama-Veda. The Katyayana and Paraskara belong to the Sukla Yajur-Veda. The Apastamba, Hiranyakesi, Bodhayana, Bharadvaja, Manava, Vaikhanasa and the Kathaka belong to the Krishna Yajur-Veda. The Vaitana and the Kaushika belong to the Atharva-Veda.

The Smritis

Next in importance to the Sruti are the Smritis or secondary scriptures. These are the ancient sacred law-codes of the Hindus dealing with the Sanatana-Varnasrama-Dharma. They supplement and explain the ritualistic injunctions called *Vidhis* in the Vedas. The Smriti Sastra is founded on the Sruti. The Smritis are based on the teachings of the Vedas.

The Smriti stands next in authority to the Sruti. It explains and develops Dharma. It lays down the laws which regulate Hindu national, social, family and individual obligations.

The works which are expressly called Smritis are the law books, Dharma Sastras. Smriti, in a broader sense, covers all Hindu Sastras save the Vedas.

The laws for regulating Hindu society from time to time are codified in the Smritis. The Smritis have laid down definite rules and laws to guide the individuals and communities in their daily conduct and to regulate their manners and customs. The Smritis have given detailed instructions, according to the conditions of the time, to all classes of men regarding their duties in life.

The Hindu learns how he has to spend his whole life from these Smritis. The duties of Varnasrama and all ceremonies are clearly given in these books. The Smritis prescribe certain acts and prohibit some others for a Hindu, according to his birth and stage of life. The object of the Smritis is to purify the heart of man and take him gradually to the supreme abode of immortality and make him perfect and free.

These Smritis have varied from time to time. The injunctions and prohibitions of the Smritis are related to the particular social surroundings. As these surroundings and essential conditions of the Hindu society changed from time to time, new Smritis had to be compiled by the sages of different ages and different parts of India.

The Celebrated Hindu Law-Givers

From time to time, a great law-giver would take his birth. He would codify the existing laws and remove those which had become obsolete. He would make some alterations, adaptations, readjustments, additions and subtractions, to suit the needs of the time and see that the way of living of the people would be in accordance with the teachings of the

Veda. Of such law-givers, Manu, Yajnavalkya and Parasara are the most celebrated persons. Hindu society is founded on, and governed by, the laws made by these three great sages. The Smritis are named after them. We have Manu Smriti or Manava Dharma-Sastra (the Laws of Manu or the Institutes of Manu), Yajnavalkya Smriti and Parasara Smriti. Manu is the greatest law-giver of the race. He is the oldest law-giver as well. The Yajnavalkya Smriti follows the same general lines as the Manu Smriti and is next in importance to it. Manu Smriti and Yajnavalkya Smriti are universally accepted at the present time as authoritative works all over India. Yajnavalkya Smriti is chiefly consulted in all matters of Hindu Law. Even the Government of India are applying some of these laws.

There are eighteen main Smritis or Dharma Sastras. The most important are those of Manu, Yajnavalkya and Parasara. The other fifteen are those of Vishnu, Daksha, Samvarta, Vyasa, Harita, Satatapa, Vasishtha, Yama, Apastamba, Gautama, Devala, Sankha-Likhita, Usana, Atri and Saunaka.

The laws of Manu are intended for the Satya Yuga, those of Yajnavalkya are for the Treta Yuga; those of Sankha and Likhita are for the Dvapara Yuga; and those of Parasara are for the Kali Yuga.

The laws and rules which are based entirely upon our social positions, time and clime, must change with the changes in society and changing conditions of time and clime. Then only the progress of the Hindu society can be ensured.

Need for a New Law-Code

It is not possible to follow some of the laws of Manu at the present time. We can follow their spirit and not the letter. Society is advancing. When it advances, it outgrows certain laws which were valid and helpful at a particular stage of its growth. Many new things which were not thought out by the old law-givers have come into existence now. It is no use insisting people to follow now those old laws which have become obsolete.

Our present society has considerably changed. A new Smriti to suit the requirements of this age is very necessary. Another sage will place before the Hindus of our days a new suitable code of laws. Time is ripe for a new Smriti. Cordial greetings to this age.

The Inner Voice of Dharma

He who is endowed with a pure heart through protracted Tapas, Japa, Kirtana, meditation and service of Guru and who has a very clear conscience, can be guided by the inner voice in matters of Dharma or duty or moral action. The inner voice that proceeds from a clean heart filled with Sattva is, indeed, the voice of God or Soul or Antaryamin or Inner Ruler. This voice is more than Smriti. It is Smriti of Smritis. Purify your heart and train yourself to hear this inner voice. Keep your ear in tune with the 'voice'.

The Sruti and the Smriti

The Sruti and the Smriti are the two authoritative sources of Hinduism. *Sruti* literally means what is heard, and *Smriti* means what is remembered. Sruti is revelation and Smriti is tradition. Upanishad is a Sruti. Bhagavad-Gita is a Smriti.

Sruti is direct experience. Great Rishis heard the eternal truths of religion and left a record of them for the benefit of posterity. These records constitute the Vedas. Hence, Sruti is primary authority. Smriti is a recollection of that experience. Hence, it is secondary authority. The Smritis or Dharma Sastras also are books written by sages, but they are not the final authority. If there is anything in a Smriti which contradicts the Sruti, the Smriti is to be rejected.

THE ITIHASAS

The Friendly Treatises and the Commanding Treatises

There are four books under this heading: The Valmiki-

Ramayana, the Yogavasishtha, The Mahabharata and the Harivamsa. These embody all that is in the Vedas, but only in a simpler manner. These are called the Suhrit-Samhitas or the Friendly Treatises, while the Vedas are called the Prabhu-Samhitas or the Commanding Treatises with great authority. These works explain the great universal truths in the form of historical narratives, stories and dialogues. These are very interesting volumes and are liked by all, from the inquisitive child to the intellectual scholar.

The Itihasas give us beautiful stories of absorbing interest and importance, through which all the fundamental teachings of Hinduism are indelibly impressed on one's mind. The laws of Smritis and the principles of the Vedas are stamped firmly on the minds of the Hindus through the noble and marvellous deeds of their great national heroes. We get a clear idea of Hinduism from these sublime stories.

The common man cannot comprehend the high abstract philosophy of the Upanishads and the Brahma Sutras. Hence, the compassionate sages Valmiki and Vyasa wrote the Itihasas for the benefit of common people. The same philosophy is presented with analogies and parables in a tasteful form to the common run of mankind.

The two well-known Itihasas (histories) are the epics (Mahakavyas), *Ramayana* and *Mahabharata*. They are two very popular and useful Sastras of the Hindus. The Ramayana was written by the sage Valmiki, and the Mahabharata by Vyasa.

The Ramayana

The Ramayana, the Adi-Kavya or the first epic poem, relates the story of Sri Rama, the ideal man. It is the history of the family of the solar race descended from Ikshvaku, in which was born Sri Ramachandra, the Avatara of Lord Vishnu, and his three brothers. The ideal characters like Rama, Sita, Lakshmana, Bharata and Sri Hanuman that we find in

Ramayana firmly establish Hindu Dharma in our minds. The story of the birth of Rama and his brothers, their education and marriages, the exile of Sri Rama, the carrying off and recovery of Sita, his wife, the destruction of Ravana, the Rakshasa King of Lanka, and the reign of Sri Rama, are described in detail in Ramayana. How a man should behave towards his superiors, equals and inferiors, how a king ought to rule his kingdom, how a man should lead his life in this world, how he can obtain his release, freedom and perfection, may be learnt from this excellent epic. The Ramayana gives a vivid picture of Indian life. Even today our domestic, social and national ideals are copied from the noble characters in the Ramayana and the Mahabharata. The great national heroes stand even today as beacon-lights to guide and inspire the people of the whole world. The lives of Rama, Bharata and Lakshmana provide a model of fraternal affection and mutual service. Sri Hanuman stands as an ideal unique Karma Yogin. The life of Sita is regarded as the most perfect example of womanly fidelity, chastity and sweetness. The Ramayana is written in twenty-four thousand verses by Sri Valmiki.

The Mahabharata

The Mahabharata is the history of the Pandavas and the Kauravas. It gives a description of the great war, the Battle of Kurukshetra, which broke out between the Kauravas and the Pandavas who were cousins and descendants of the lunar race. The Mahabharata is an encyclopaedia of Hindu Dharma. It is rightly called the fifth Veda. There is really no theme in religion, philosophy, mysticism and polity which this great epic does not touch and expound. It contains very noble moral teachings, useful lessons of all kinds, many beautiful stories and episodes, discourses, sermons, parables and dialogues which set forth the principles of morals and metaphysics. The Pandavas obtained victory through the grace of Lord Krishna. The Mahabharata is written in one hundred thousand verses by Sri Krishnadvaipayana Vyasa.

The Bhagavad-Gita

The most important part of the Mahabharata is the *Bhagavad-Gita.* It is a marvellous dialogue between Lord Krishna and Arjuna on the battle-field, before the commencement of the great war. Bhagavan Sri Krishna became the charioteer of Arjuna. Sri Krishna explained the essentials of Hindu religion to Arjuna. Just as the Upanishads contain the cream of the Vedas, so does the Gita contain the cream of the Upanishads. The Upanishads are the cows. Lord Krishna is the cowherd. Arjuna is the calf. The Gita is the milk. The wise men are those who drink the milk of the Gita.

The Gita is the most precious jewel of Hindu literature. It is a universal gospel. The Gita teaches the Yoga of Synthesis. It ranks high in the religious literature of the world.

Arjuna saw before him his dear relatives and teachers in the battle-field. He fainted and refused to fight against them. Then Lord Krishna imparted knowledge of the Self to Arjuna and convinced him that it was his duty to fight regardless of consequences. Afterwards Arjuna gave up his *Moha,* or delusion. All his doubts were cleared. He fought against the Kauravas and achieved victory.

Knowledge of Ancient Indian History and Culture

The Mahabharata contains also the immortal discourse of Bhishma on Dharma, which he gave to Yudhishthira, when he was lying on the bed of arrows. The whole Mahabharata forms an encyclopaedia of history, morals and religion unsurpassed by any other epic in the world.

The Ramayana and the Mahabharata speak to us clearly about the ancient India, about her people, her customs, her ways of living, her arts, her civilisation and culture, her manufactures, etc. If you read these two books, you will come to know how great India once was, and you will be inspired to make her great once more. No other country has produced so many great men, great teachers, great Yogins, great Rishis, great prophets, great Acharyas, great kings, great heroes, great statesmen, great patriots and great benefactors, as India. The more you know of India and Hinduism, the more you will honour and love it and the more thankful to the Lord you will be that you were born in India as a Hindu. Glory to India! Glory to Hinduism! Glory to the seers of the Upanishads! Glory, glory to Lord Krishna, the author of the Song Divine!

THE PURANAS

The Puranas are of the same class as the Itihasas. They have five characteristics *(Pancha-Lakshana)* viz., history, cosmology (with various symbolical illustrations of philosophical principles), secondary creation, genealogy of kings and of Manvantaras. All the Puranas belong to the class of Suhrit-Samhitas.

Vyasa is the compiler of the Puranas from age to age; and for this age, he is Krishnadvaipayana, the son of Parasara.

The Puranas were written to popularise the religion of the Vedas. They contain the essence of the Vedas. The aim of the Puranas is to impress on the minds of the masses the teachings of the Vedas and to generate in them devotion to God, through concrete examples, myths, stories, legends, lives of saints, kings and great men, allegories and chronicles of great historical events. The sages made use of these things to illustrate the eternal principles of religion. The Puranas were meant, not for the scholars, but for the ordinary people who could not understand high philosophy and who could not study the Vedas.

The Darsanas are very stiff. They are meant only for the learned few. The Puranas are meant for the masses with inferior intellect. Religion is taught in a very easy and interesting way through these Puranas. Even to this day, the Puranas are popular. The Puranas contain the history of remote times. They also give a description of the regions of the universe not visible to the ordinary physical eye. They are very interesting to read and are full of information of all kinds. Children hear the stories from their grandmothers. Pundits and Purohits hold Kathas in temples, on banks of rivers and in other important places. Agriculturists, labourers and bazaar people hear the stories.

The Eighteen Puranas

There are eighteen main Puranas and an equal number of subsidiary Puranas or Upa-Puranas. The main Puranas are: Vishnu Purana, Naradiya Purana, Srimad Bhagavata Purana, Garuda (Suparna) Purana, Padma Purana, Varaha Purana, Brahma Purana, Brahmanda Purana, Brahma Vaivarta Purana, Markandeya Purana, Bhavishya Purana, Vamana Purana, Matsya Purana, Kurma Purana, Linga Purana, Siva Purana, Skanda Purana and Agni Purana. Of these, six are Sattvic Puranas and glorify Vishnu; six are Rajasic and glorify Brahma; six are Tamasic and they glorify Siva.

Neophytes or beginners in the spiritual path are puzzled when they go through Siva Purana and Vishnu Purana. In Siva Purana, Lord Siva is highly eulogised and an inferior position is given to Lord Vishnu. Sometimes Vishnu is belittled. In Vishnu Purana, Lord Hari is highly eulogised and an inferior status is given to Lord Siva. Sometimes Lord Siva is belittled. This is only to increase the faith of the devotees in their particular Ishta-Devata. Lord Siva and Lord Vishnu are one.

The best among the Puranas are the Srimad Bhagavata and the Vishnu Purana. The most popular is the Srimad Bhagavata Purana. Next comes Vishnu Purana. A portion of the Markandeya Purana is well known to all Hindus as *Chandi,* or Devimahatmya. Worship of God as the Divine

Mother is its theme. Chandi is read widely by the Hindus on sacred days and Navaratri (Durga Puja) days.

The Srimad Bhagavata Purana and the Ten Avataras

The Srimad Bhagavata Purana is a chronicle of the various Avataras of Lord Vishnu. There are ten Avataras of Vishnu. The aim of every Avatara is to save the world from some great danger, to destroy the wicked and protect the virtuous. The ten Avataras are: Matsya (The Fish), Kurma (The Tortoise), Varaha (The Boar), Narasimha (The Man-Lion), Vamana (The Dwarf), Parasurama (Rama with the axe, the destroyer of the Kshatriya race), Ramachandra (The hero of Ramayana—the son of Dasaratha), who destroyed Ravana, Sri Krishna, The teacher of the Gita, Buddha (The prince-ascetic, founder of Buddhism) and Kalki (The hero riding on a white horse, who is to come at the end of the Kali-Yuga).

The object of the Matsya Avatara was to save Vaivasvata Manu from destruction by a deluge. The object of Kurma Avatara was to enable the world to recover some precious things which were lost in the deluge. The Kurma gave its back for keeping the churning rod when the Gods and the Asuras churned the ocean of milk. The purpose of Varaha Avatara was to rescue, from the waters, the earth which had been dragged down by a demon named Hiranyaksha. The purpose of Narasimha Avatara, half-lion and half-man, was to free the world from the oppression of Hiranyakasipu, a demon, the father of Bhakta Prahlada. The object of Vamana Avatara was to restore the power of the gods which had been eclipsed by the penance and devotion of King Bali. The object of Parasurama Avatara was to deliver the country from the oppression of the Kshatriya rulers. Parasurama destroyed the Kshatriya race twenty-one times. The object of Rama was to destroy the wicked Ravana. The object of Sri Krishna Avatara was to destroy Kamsa and other demons, to deliver His wonderful message of the Gita in the Mahabharata war, and to become the centre of the Bhakti schools of India. The object of Buddha Avatara was to prohibit animal sacrifices and teach piety. The object of the Kalki Avatara is the destruction of the wicked and the re-establishment of virtue.

The Tamil Puranas

Lord Siva incarnated himself in the form of Dakshinamurti to impart knowledge to the four Kumaras. He took human form to initiate Sambandhar, Manikkavasagar, Pattinathar. He appeared in flesh and blood to help his devotees and relieve their sufferings. The divine Lilas of Lord Siva are recorded in the Tamil Puranas like Siva Purana, Periya Purana, Siva Parakramam and Tiruvilayadal Purana.

The Upa-Puranas

The eighteen Upa-Puranas are: Sanatkumara, Narasimha, Brihannaradiya, Sivarahasya, Durvasa, Kapila, Vamana, Bhargava, Varuna, Kalika, Samba, Nandi, Surya, Parasara, Vasishtha, Devi-Bhagavata, Ganesa and Hamsa.

Utility of the Puranas

Study of the Puranas, listening to sacred recitals of scriptures, describing and expounding of the transcendent Lilas of the Blessed Lord—these form an important part of Sadhana of the Lord's devotees. It is most pleasing to the Lord. *Sravana* is a part of *Navavidha-Bhakti*. *Kathas* and *Upanyasas* open the springs of devotion in the hearts of hearers and develop *Prema-Bhakti* which confers immortality on the *Jiva*.

The language of the Vedas is archaic, and the subtle philosophy of Vedanta and the Upanishads is extremely difficult to grasp and assimilate. Hence, the Puranas are of special value as they present philosophical truths and precious teachings in an easier manner. They give ready access to the mysteries of life and the key to bliss. Imbibe their teachings. Start a new life of Dharma-Nishtha and Adhyatmic Sadhana from this very day.

Another class of popular scriptures are the Agamas. The Agamas are theological treatises and practical manuals of divine worship. The Agamas include the Tantras, Mantras and Yantras. These are treatises explaining the external worship of God, in idols, temples, etc. All the Ágamas treat of (i) *Jnana* or Knowledge, (ii) *Yoga* or Concentration, (iii) *Kriya* or Esoteric Ritual and (iv) *Charya* or Exoteric Worship. They also give elaborate details about ontology and cosmology, liberation, devotion, meditation, philosophy of *Mantras,* mystic diagrams, charms and spells, temple-building, image-making, domestic observances, social rules, public festivals, etc.

The Agamas are divided into three sections: The *Vaishnava,* the *Saiva* and the *Sakta.* The three chief sects of Hinduism, viz., Vaishnavism, Saivism and Saktism, base their doctrines and dogmas on their respective Agamas. The Vaishnava Agamas or Pancharatra Agamas glorify God as Vishnu. The Saiva Agamas glorify God as Siva and have given rise to an important school of philosophy known as Saiva-Siddhanta, which prevails in South India, particularly in the districts of Tirunelveli .and Madurai. The Sakta Agamas or Tantras glorify God as the Mother of the Universe, under one of the many names of *Devi.*

The Agamas do not derive their authority from the Vedas, but are not antagonistic to them. They are all Vedic in spirit and character. That is the reason why they are regarded as authoritative.

The Vaishnava Agamas

The Vaishnava Agamas are of four kinds: the Vaikhanasa, Pancharatra, Pratishthasara and Vijnanalalita. The Brahma, Saiva Kaumara, Vasishtha, Kapila, Gautamiya and the Naradiya are the seven groups of the Pancharatras. The

Naradiya section of the Santi-Parva of the Mahabharata is the earliest source of information about the Pancharatras.

Vishnu is the Supreme Lord in the Pancharatra Agamas. The Vaishnavas regard the Pancharatra Agamas to be the most authoritative. They believe that these Agamas were revealed by Lord Vishnu Himself. Narada-Pancharatra says: "Everything from Brahma to a blade of grass is Lord Krishna." This corresponds to the Upanishadic declaration: "All this is, verily, Brahman—*Sarvam Khalvidam Brahma.*"

There are two hundred and fifteen of these Vaishnava texts. Isvara, Ahirbudhnya, Paushkara, Parama, Sattvata, Brihad-Brahma and Jnanamritasara Samhitas are the important ones.

The Saiva Agamas

The Saivas recognise twenty-eight Agamas, of which the chief is Kamika. The Agamas are also the basis of Kashmir Saivism which is called the Pratyabhijna system. The latter works of Pratyabhijna system show a distinct leaning to Advaitism. The Southern Saivism, i.e., Saiva Siddhanta and the Kashmir Saivism, regard these Agamas as their authority, besides the Vedas. Each Agama has Upa-Agamas. Of these, only fragmentary texts of twenty are extant. Lord Siva is the central God in the Saiva Agamas. They are suitable to this age, Kali Yoga. They are open to all castes and both the sexes.

The Sakta Agamas

There is another group of scriptures known as the *Tantras.* They belong to the Sakta cult. They glorify Sakti as the World-Mother. They dwell on the Sakti (energy) aspect of God and prescribe numerous courses of ritualistic worship of the Divine Mother in various forms. There are seventy-seven Agamas. These are very much like the Puranas in some respects. The texts are usually in the form of dialogues between Siva and Parvati. In some of these, Siva answers the questions put by Parvati, and in others, Parvati answers, Siva questioning. Mahanirvana, Kularnava, Kulasara, Prapanchasara, Tantraraja, Rudra-Yamala, Brahma-Yamala, Vishnu-Yamala and Todala Tantra are the important works. The Agamas teach several occult practices some of which confer powers, while the others bestow knowledge and freedom. Sakti is the creative power of Lord Siva. Saktism is really a supplement to Saivism.

Among the existing books on the Agamas, the most famous are the Isvara-Samhita, Ahirbudhnya-Samhita, Sanat-kumara-Samhita, Narada-Pancharatra, Spanda-Pradipika and the Mahanirvana-Tantra.

THE SIX DARSANAS

These are the intellectual section of the Hindu writings, while the first four are intuitional, and the fifth inspirational and emotional. Darsanas are schools of philosophy based on the Vedas. The Agamas are theological. The Darsana literature is philosophical. The Darsanas are meant for the erudite scholars who are endowed with acute acumen, good understanding, power of reasoning and subtle intellect. The Itihasas, Puranas and Agamas are meant for the masses. The Darsanas appeal to the intellect, while the Itihasas, Puranas, etc., appeal to the heart.

Philosophy has six divisions—*Shad-darsana*—the six Darsanas or ways of seeing things, usually called the six systems or six different schools of thought. The six schools of philosophy are the six instruments of true teaching or the six demonstrations of Truth. Each school has developed, systematised and correlated the various parts of the Veda in its own way. Each system has its *Sutrakara*, i.e., the one great Rishi who systematised the doctrines of the school and put them in short aphorisms or Sutras.

The Sutras are terse and laconic. The Rishis have condensed their thoughts in the aphorisms. It is very difficult to understand them without the help of commentaries by great sages or Rishis. Hence, there arose many commentators or *Bhashyakaras*. There are glosses, notes and, later, commentaries on the original commentaries.

The Shad-Darsanas (the six schools of philosophy) or the Shat-Sastras are: the NYAYA, founded by Gautama Rishi, the VAISESHIKA by Kanada Rishi, the SANKHYA by Kapila Muni, the YOGA by Patanjali Maharshi, the PURVA MIMAMSA by Jaimini, and the UTTARA MIMAMSA or VEDANTA by Badarayana or Vyasa. The Darsanas are divided into three pairs of aphoristic compositions which explain the philosophy of the Vedas in a rationalistic method of approach. They are: the Nyaya and the Vaiseshika, the Sankhya and the Yoga, and the Mimamsa and the Vedanta. Each set of Sutras has got its *Bhashya, Vritti, Varttika, Vyakhyana* or *Tika* and *Tippani*.

Sutra

Svalpaksharam-asandigdham
Saravad-visvatomukham
Astobham-anavadyam cha
Sutram sutravido viduh

A Sutra or an aphorism is a short formula with the least possible number of letters, without any ambiguity or doubtful assertion, containing the very essence, embracing all meanings, without any stop or obstruction and absolutely faultless in nature.

The Sutrakara or the composer of the aphorisms is said to be as happy as one would be while getting the first male child, if he is but able to reduce one letter in his abstruse Sutra of far-fetched words and ideas. The best example of the greatest, the tersest and the most perfect of Sutra literature is the series of aphorisms called the *Ashtadhyayi* composed by Panini. Panini is the father of all Sutrakaras from whom all others seem to have borrowed the method of composition.

The Sutras are meant to explain a big volume of knowledge in short assertions suitable to be kept in memory at all times. The six Vedangas and the six systems of Hindu philosophy form the twelve sets of Sutra literature of the world. In addition to these, there are later compositions like the Narada-Bhakti Sutras, the Sandilya-Bhakti Sutras, etc., which also wish to assume an equal form with the famous Sutras mentioned above.

Bhashya

Sutrartho varnyate yatra
Padaih sutranusaribhih
Svapadani cha varnyante
Bhashyam bhashyavido viduh

A Bhashya is an elaborate exposition, a commentary on the Sutras, with word by word meaning of the aphoristic precepts, their running translation, together with the individual views of the commentator or the Bhashyakara. The best and the exemplary Bhashya in Sanskrit literature is the one written by Patanjali on the Vyakarana Sutras of Panini. This Bhashya is so very famous and important that it is called the MAHABHASHYA and its celebrated author is specially called the BHASHYAKARA. Patanjali is the father of Bhashyakaras. The next important Bhashya is the one on the Mimamsa Sutras written by Sabara-Swamin who learnt the art from Patanjali's commentary. The third important Bhashya was written by Sankara on the Brahma Sutras, in close following with the Sabara-Bhashya. The Bhashyas on the six sets of aphorisms dealing with Indian philosophy were written by Vatsyayana, Prasastapada, Vijnanabhikshu, Vyasa, Sabara and Sankara. On the Vedanta or Brahma Sutras, there are about sixteen Bhashyas, like those of Ramanuja, Madhva, Vallabha, Nimbarka, etc.

Vritti

Sadvrittih sannibandhana

A Vritti is a short gloss explaining the aphorisms in a more elaborate way, but not as extensively as a Bhashya. An example is Bodhayana's Vritti on the Brahma Sutras.

Varttika

Uktānuktaduruktanam
Chinta yatra pravartate
Tam grantham varttikam prahuh
Varttikajnavichakshanah

A Varttika is a work where a critical study is made of that which is said and left unsaid or imperfectly said in a Bhashya, and the ways of making it perfect by supplying the omissions therein, are given. Examples are the Varttikas of Katyayana on Panini's Sutras, of Suresvara on Sankara's Upanishad-Bhashyas, and of Kumarila Bhatta on the Sabara-Bhashya on the Karma-Mimamsa.

Vyakhyana or Tika

A Vyakhyana is a running explanation in an easier language of what is said in the original, with little elucidations here and there. A Vyakhyana, particularly of a Kavya, deals with eight different modes of dissection of the Sloka, like Pada-Chheda, Vigraha, Sandhi, Alankara, Anuvada, etc. This forms an important aspect in the study of Sanskrit Sahitya Sastra. An Anu-Vyakhyana—like the one written by Sri Madhva—is a repetition of what is already written, but in greater detail. An Anuvada is merely a running translation or statement of an abstruse text of the original. Tika is only another name for Vyakhyana. The best Vyakhyanas are of Vachaspati Misra on the Darsanas, especially on Sankara's Brahmasutra-Bhashya.

Tippani

Tippani is just like a Vritti, but is less orthodox than the

Vritti. It is an explanation of difficult words or phrases occurring in the original. Examples are Kaiyata's gloss on the Mahabhashya of Patanjali, Nagojibhatta's gloss on Kaiyata's gloss, or Appayya's gloss on Amalananda's gloss on the Bhamati of Vachaspati Misra.

OTHER SCRIPTURES

The Tevaram and the Tiruvachakam which are the hymns of the Saiva saints of South India, the Divya-Prabandham of the Alvar saints of South India, the songs of Kabir, the Abhangas of Tukaram and the Ramayana of Tulasi Das—all of which are the outpourings of great realised souls—are wonderful scriptures. They contain the essence of the Vedas.

THE SECULAR WRITINGS

THE SUBHASHITAS

The Subhashitas are wise sayings, instructions and stories, either in poetry or in prose. Examples are Bhartrihari's three centuries of verses, the Subhashita-Ratna-Bhandagara and Somadeva Bhatta's Katha-Sarit-Sagara or Kshemendra's Brihat-Katha-Manjari. The Panchatantra and the Hitopadesa also belong to this category.

THE KAVYAS

These are highly scholarly compositions in poetry, prose or both. The greatest of poetical Kavyas are those of Kalidas (*The Raghuvamsa* and *Kumarasambhava*), Bharavi (*The Kiratarjuniya*), Magha (*The Sisupalavadha*), Sri Harsha (*The Naishadha*). The best prose Kavyas in the whole of Sanskrit literature were written by Bhattabana (*The Kadambari* and *Harshacharita*), the great genius in classical Sanskrit. Among those containing both poetry and prose, the Champu-Ramayana and the Champu-Bharata are most famous. These are all wonderful masterpieces which will ever remain to glorify India's literary calibre.

THE NATAKAS

These are marvellously scholastic dramas embodying the

Rasas of Sringara, Vira, Karuna, Adbhuta, Hasya, Bhayanaka, Bibhatsa and Raudra. It is told that none can write on the ninth Rasa, viz., Santi. It is attainable only on final Liberation. The best dramas are written by Kalidasa *(Sakuntala)*, Bhavabhuti *(Uttara-Rama-Charita)*, and Visakha-datta *(Mudrarakshasa)*.

THE ALANKARAS

These are grand rhetorical texts, treating of the science of perfection and beauty of ornamental language and of effective composition with elegance and force, both in poetry and in prose. These are the fundamentals of Sanskrit Sahitya, even superior to the Kavyas and the Natakas. The best Alankara-Granthas are those of Mammata *(Kavyaprakasa)* and Jagannatha *(Rasagangadhara)*.

CONCLUSION

These constitute the entirety of Sanskrit literature—sacred and secular. The Sruti is the root; the Smritis, Itihasas and Puranas are the trunk; the Agamas and Darsanas are the branches; and the Subhashitas, Kavyas, Natakas and Alankaras are the flowers of the tree of India's Culture.

The Smritis, the Itihasas, the Puranas, the Agamas and the Darsanas are only developments of the Veda. Their ultimate source is the Veda. Their one common aim is to enable man to annihilate his ignorance and attain perfection, freedom, immortality and eternal bliss through knowledge of God or the Eternal. Their purpose is to make man like God and one with Him.

CHAPTER 3

HINDU DHARMA

Silent adorations to the Lord, the Embodiment of Dharma, the Controller and Protector of Dharma and the Fountain-head of Dharma.

What is Dharma? Dharma is so called, because it *holds;* Dharma alone holds the people, etc. The word *Dharma* is derived from the root *Dhr*—to hold—and its etymological meaning is 'that which holds' this world, or the people of the world, or the whole creation from the microcosm to the macrocosm. It is the eternal Divine Law of the Lord. The entire creation is held together and sustained by the All-powerful Law of God. Practice of Dharma, therefore, means recognition of this Law and abidance by it.

That which brings well-being to man is Dharma. Dharma supports this world. The people are upheld by Dharma. That which secures preservation of beings is Dharma. Dharma leads to eternal happiness and immortality.

That which is Dharma is verily the Truth. Therefore, whosoever speaks the truth is said to speak Dharma, and whosoever speaks Dharma is said to speak the truth. One and the same thing becomes both.

Dharma includes all external deeds, as well as thoughts and other mental practices which tend to elevate the character of man. Dharma comes from the Divine and leads you to the Divine.

DEFINITION OF DHARMA

No language is perfect. There is no proper equivalent word in English for the Sanskrit term *Dharma*. It is very difficult to define Dharma.

Dharma is generally defined as 'righteousness' or 'duty.' Dharma is the principle of righteousness. It is the principle of holiness. It is also the principle of unity. Bhishma says in his instructions to Yudhishthira that whatever creates conflict is Adharma, and whatever puts an end to conflict and brings about unity and harmony is Dharma. Anything that helps to unite all and develop pure divine love and universal brotherhood, is Dharma. Anything that creates discord, split and disharmony and foments hatred, is Adharma. Dharma is the cementer and sustainer of social life. The rules of Dharma have been laid down for regulating the worldly affairs of men. Dharma brings as its consequence happiness, both in this world and in the next. Dharma is the means of preserving one's self. If you transgress it, it will kill you. If you protect it, it will protect you. It is your sole companion after death. It is the sole refuge of humanity.

That which elevates one is Dharma. This is another definition. Dharma is that which leads you to the path of perfection and glory. Dharma is that which helps you to have direct communion with the Lord. Dharma is that which makes you divine. Dharma is the ascending stairway unto God. Self-realisation is the highest Dharma. Dharma is the heart of Hindu ethics. God is the centre of Dharma.

Dharma means *Achara* or the regulation of daily life. Achara is the supreme Dharma. It is the basis of Tapas or austerity. It leads to wealth, beauty, longevity and continuity of lineage. Evil conduct and immorality will lead to ill-fame, sorrow, disease and premature death. Dharma has its root in morality and the controller of Dharma is God Himself.

Maharshi Jaimini defines Dharma as that which is enjoined by the Vedas and is not ultimately productive of suffering.

Rishi Kanada, founder of the Vaiseshika system of philosophy, has given the best definition of Dharma, in his Vaiseshika Sutras: *"Yato-bhyudayanihsreyasa-siddhih sa dharmah."* "That which leads to the attainment of *Abhyu-*

daya (prosperity in this world) and *Nihsreyasa* (total cessation of pain and attainment of eternal bliss hereafter) is Dharma."

THE SOLE AUTHORITY OF THE VEDAS

The four Vedas, the Smriti texts, the behaviour of those who have entered into their spirit and act according to their injunctions, the conduct of holy men and satisfaction of one's own self—these are the bases of Dharma, according to Manu.

In the matter of Dharma, the Vedas are the ultimate authority. You cannot know the truth about Dharma through any source of knowledge other than the Vedas. Reason cannot be the authority in the matter of Dharma. Among the scriptures of the world, the Vedas are the oldest. This is supported by all leading scholars and antiquarians of the entire civilised world. They all declare with one voice, that of all books so far written in any human language, the Rig-Veda Samhita is undoubtedly the oldest. No antiquarian has been able to fix the date when the Rig-Veda Samhita was composed or came to light.

THE CHANGING DHARMA

Just as a doctor prescribes different medicines for different people according to their constitution and the nature of their disease, so also Hinduism prescribes different duties for different people. Rules for women are different from the rules for men. The rules for different Varnas and Asramas vary. But, non-violence, truth, non-stealing, cleanliness and control of the senses, are the duties common to all men.

Dharma depends upon time, circumstances, age, degree of evolution and the community to which one belongs. The Dharma of this century is different from that of the tenth century.

There are conditions under which Dharma may change its

usual course. Apad-Dharma is such a deviation from the usual practice. This is allowed only in times of extreme distress or calamity.

What is Dharma in one set of circumstances becomes Adharma in another set of circumstances. That is the reason why it is said that the secret of Dharma is extremely profound and subtle. Lord Krishna says in the Gita: "Let the scriptures be the authority in determining what ought to be done and what ought not to be done" (Ch. XVI, 24). The truth of Dharma lies hidden. Srutis and Smritis are many. The way of Dharma open to all is that which a great realised soul has traversed.

DHARMA IN OTHER RELIGIONS

All other religions also lay stress on Dharma. Buddhism, Jainism, Christianity, Sikhism, Zoroastrianism, Islam are all remarkably alive to its value. Plato, Socrates, Aristotle, Kant, Swedenborg and Spinoza are all striking examples in the interesting history of Western philosophy for the high pedestal on which they have placed morality, duty and righteousness, and adored them all as the only means to the attainment of the goal of life. Each religion lays greater stress on certain aspects of Dharma.

BENEFITS OF THE PRACTICE OF DHARMA

Of the four grand objects of human aspiration—*Purushar-thas*—viz., Dharma, Artha, Kama and Moksha, *Dharma* is given the foremost rank in the scriptures. Dharma alone is the gateway to Moksha, to immortality, infinite bliss, supreme peace and highest knowledge. Dharma alone is the primary Purushartha. Dharma is the first and foremost Purushartha. Through the practice of Dharma alone can you ever hope to achieve the crowning glory of all human endeavours, viz., Moksha which is the best and the highest of all desirable things.

Practice of Dharma leads to the perfect realisation of essential unity or the final end, the highest good, namely, Moksha. The practitioner experiences peace, joy, strength and tranquillity within himself. His life becomes thoroughly disciplined. His powers and capacities are exceedingly intensified. He realises that there is one underlying homogeneous essence, a living truth, behind these names and forms. He is transmuted into divinity. His whole nature gets transformed. He becomes one with the Eternal. He beholds Brahman above, Brahman below, Brahman to the right, Brahman to the left, Brahman in front, Brahman at the back, Brahman within, Brahman without and Brahman pervading the whole world.

KINDS OF DHARMA

Dharma can be classified under two heads: (i) *Samanya* or the general, universal Dharma and (ii) *Visesha* or the specific, personal Dharma. Contentment, forgiveness, self-restraint, non-stealing, purity, control of senses, discrimination between right and wrong, between the real and the unreal, spiritual knowledge, truthfulness and absence of anger come under the general or universal Dharma. The rules of the castes and orders of life are specific Dharmas. These are the tenfold characteristics of Dharma according to Manu.

Dharma assumes various kinds: Sanatana Dharma (Eternal Law), Samanya Dharma (general duty), Visesha Dharma (special duty), Varnasrama Dharma (duties of Caste and Order), Svadharma (one's own duty), Yuga Dharma (duty of the Age), Kula Dharma (duty of family), Manava Dharma (duty of man), Purusha Dharma (duty of male), Stri Dharma (duty of female), Raja Dharma (duty of king), Praja Dharma (duty of subjects), Pravritti Dharma (duty in worldly life) and Nivritti Dharma (duty in spiritual life).

SANATANA DHARMA

Sanatana Dharma means the Eternal Religion, the Ancient Law. This is based on the Vedas. This is the oldest of living religions. Hinduism is known by the name Sanatana Dharma. What the Vedas alone declare to be the means of attaining the *summum bonum* or the final emancipation, is the Sanatana Dharma or Hindu Dharma.

The foundation of Sanatana Dharma is Sruti; Smritis are the walls; the Itihasas and Purnas are the buttresses or supports. In ancient times, the Srutis were learnt by heart. The teacher sang them to his pupils and the pupils sang them after him. They were not written in book form. All the sects, all the philosophical systems, appeal to the Sruti as the final authority. The Smriti stands next in authority to the Sruti.

Hinduism stands unrivalled in the depth and grandeur of its philosophy. Its ethical teachings are lofty, unique and sublime. It is highly flexible and adapted to every human need. It is a perfect religion by itself. It is not in need of anything from any other religion. No other religion has produced so many great saints, great patriots, great warriors and great Pativratas. The more you know of it, the more you will honour and love it. The more you study it, the more it will enlighten you and satisfy your heart.

INDIA—THE HOME OF RELIGIONS

The religious history of the world tells us that from time immemorial, India has been the home of great sages, seers and Rishis. All the grand religious ideals that have moulded the character of men, the loftiest of ethics and morality that have raised human beings to magnanimous heights of divine splendour and all the sublime truths of spirituality that have made men divine and have moulded the spiritual ideals of nations and saviours of mankind, first arose in India. The spiritual horizon of India has always been illumined with the glory of the self-effulgent sun of wisdom of the Upanishads.

Whenever there was any upheaval in any part of the world, the origin of this could be traced to the wave of spirituality caused by the birth of a great soul—a special manifestation of Divinity—in some part of India.

Hindus have had a culture, civilisation and religion millennia older than those of any other country or people. God did speak to the world through India's Rishis, Yogins, Mahatmas, Alvars, prophets, Acharyas, Sannyasins and saints. Their teachings and Puranas are really inspired. God is the one Light and Truth from whom emanate the teachings of all faiths.

India is the home and abode of religions. It occupies the proud first place in religious devotion and godliness. It is famous for its Yogins and saints. The goal of India is Self-realisation or attainment of God-consciousness, through renunciation. The history of India is a history of religion. Its social code and regulations are founded upon religion. Minus its Yoga, religion and its regulations, India will not be what it has been for millennia. Some Hindus are still not aware of the distinguishing features of Sanatana Dharma. If every Hindu knew and understood what Hinduism is, the Hindus of today would all be gods on this earth.

May you all be endowed with the knowledge of Sanatana Dharma! May you all endeavour to protect the Eternal Dharma! May the secrets of Sanatana Dharma be revealed unto you all, like a fruit in the palm of your hand, through the Grace of the Lord! May the blessings of Rishis be upon you all! Glory to the Vedas and Sanatana Dharma! Glory to Brahman, the source for all Vedas and Sanatana Dharma!

SAMANYA DHARMA

Every religion has a generic form or *Samanya-Rupa* and a specific form or *Visesha-Rupa*. The general form remains eternally the same. It is never changed by any circumstance whatsoever. It is not affected at all by changes of time, place, surroundings and individual differences. This aspect of religion is called Sanatana or eternal. That which changes according to the change of time, place and surrounding circumstances is the external aspect or ritual, of Dharma.

Samanya Dharma is the general Dharma or law for all men. Varnasrama Dharmas are special Dharmas which are to be practised by particular castes and by men in particular stages of life. The Samanya Dharmas must be practised by all, irrespective of distinctions of Varna and Asrama, creed or colour. Goodness is not the property of any one class, creed, sect or community. Every man should possess this virtue.

FUNDAMENTALS OF DHARMA

THE VISHNU SAMHITA enumerates forgiveness, truthfulness, control of the mind, purity, practice of charity, control of the senses, non-violence, service of the Guru, visiting places of pilgrimage, compassion, simplicity, absence of greed, worship of the gods and the Brahmanas, and absence of malice as the ingredients of Samanya Dharma, the general law for all men.

THE MAHABHARATA enumerates the performance of Sraaddha or offering oblations to the forefathers, religious austerity, truth, restraint of anger, satisfaction with one's own wife, purity, learning, absence of envy, knowledge of the Self and forbearance as the fundamentals of Dharma.

It is said in PADMA PURANA that Dharma proceeds from continence, truthfulness, austerity, charity, self-control, forbearance, purity, non-violence, serenity and non-thieving and that one should recognise Dharma by these ten factors. According to this Purana, bestowing gifts on deserving persons, fixing one's thoughts on Lord Krishna, adoration of one's parents, offering a portion of the daily meal to all creatures and giving a morsel of food to a cow are the characteristics of Dharma.

According to MATSYA PURANA, freedom from malice, absence of covetousness, control of the senses, austerity, celibacy, compassion, truthfulness, forbearance and fortitude constitute the fundamentals of Sanatana Dharma.

PATANJALI MAHARSHI, the exponent of Raja Yoga philosophy, recommends that ten virtues should be practised by all men. The first five are: Ahimsa (non-violence), Satya (truthfulness), Brahmacharya (celibacy in thought, word and deed), Asteya (non-stealing) and Aparigraha (non-covetousness). These constitute Yama or self-restraint. The other five virtues are: Saucha (internal and external purity), Santosha (contentment), Tapas (austerity), Svadhyaya (study of scriptures or recitation of Mantra) and Isvarapranidhana (consecration of the fruits of all works to the Lord). These constitute Niyama or religious observance.

THE GITA enumerates the following virtues as Daivi-Sampat or divine qualities: fearlessness, cleanness of life, steadfastness in the Yoga of Wisdom, alms-giving, self-restraint, sacrifice, study of the scriptures, austerity, straightforwardness, harmlessness, truth, absence of wrath, renunciation, peacefulness, absence of crookedness, compassion to living beings, non-covetousness, mildness, modesty, absence of fickleness, vigour, forgiveness, fortitude, purity and absence of envy and pride. All these virtues are manifestations of the four fundamental virtues: (i) non-violence, (ii) truth, (iii) purity and (iv) self-control. All the above virtues come under the above four cardinal virtues. The virtues that are enumerated under the Noble Eightfold Path of Buddhism and the virtues prescribed by Lord Jesus in his Sermon on the Mount, also come under the above fundamental virtues.

The development of the divine qualities is indispensable for the attainment of Self-realisation. Brahman or the Eternal is purity. The Eternal cannot be attained without the attainment of purity. Brahman is truth. The Eternal cannot be attained without practising truth. Brahman is fearlessness. The

Eternal cannot be attained unless you become absolutely fearless. Attachment to the body causes fear and Dehadhyasa. If only you become fearless, then the identification with the body will vanish.

You have rendered the heart harder than flint, steel or diamond through greed, miserliness, harshness and rudeness. You can soften it only through the practice of mercy, sympathy, charity, generosity, magnanimity, harmlessness, mildness, disinterested action and untiring service of the poor. You have made the heart crooked and narrow through hypocrisy, untruthfulness, backbiting and talebearing. You can expand it through the practice of straightforwardness, truthfulness, cleanness of life, alms-giving and non-covetousness. You have rendered the heart impure through lust. You can purify it through the practice of celibacy in thought, word and deed.

Non-violence

Ahimsa or non-violence is the most important virtue. That is the reason why Patanjali Maharshi has placed it first in Yama. Practice of Ahimsa must be in thought, word and deed. Practice of Ahimsa is not impotence or cowardice or weakness. It is the highest type of heroism. The practice demands immense patience, forbearance and endurance, infinite inner spiritual strength and gigantic will-power.

Ahimsa is a modification or expression of truth only. Satyam and Ahimsa always go together. He who is established in Ahimsa can move the whole world. In his presence, all hostilities vanish; lion and cow, cobra and mongoose, live together peacefully.

Hinduism, Buddhism and Jainism lay great stress on Ahimsa. Lord Jesus also has emphasised much on Ahimsa in his Sermon on the Mount. He says: "If anyone beats you on one cheek, show him the other cheek also."

He who is firmly established in Ahimsa can hope to attain

Self-realisation. He who practises Ahimsa develops cosmic love to a maximum degree. Practice of Ahimsa eventually leads to realisation of oneness or unity of Self. Such a man only can attain self-restraint. Retaliation—tooth for tooth, blow for blow—is the maxim, doctrine or principle of an Asura or a man of diabolic nature. This belongs to the beastly nature. To return good for evil is divine. Constant vigilance and alertness are needed in the practice of Ahimsa. If you are careless even a bit, you will be carried away by the force of previous wrong Samskaras and impulses and will become a victim of Himsa, despite your good intentions.

Truth

Brahman is Sat or Existence-Absolute. Truth must be observed in thought, word and deed. If you are established in truth, all other virtues will cling to you by themselves. Harischandra sacrificed everything for the sake of truth. He lives still in our hearts. Yudhishthira was also devoted to truth. There is no virtue higher than truth. Practice of truth and Ahimsa constitute the crown and glory of ethical life. In the Taittiriya Upanishad, the preceptor says in his convocation address to the students: *"Satyam vada*—Speak the truth." The world is rooted in truth. Dharma is rooted in truth. All religions are rooted in truth. Honesty, justice, straightforwardness and sincerity are only modifications or expressions of truth.

Purity

Purity comprises both external purity and internal purity. Purity implies both purity of body and purity of mind. Purity of body is only the preliminary to purity of mind.

This body is the temple of God. It should be kept clean by daily bathing and clean dress. Cleanliness is a part of godliness.

The restriction in diet is best calculated to make the mind pure. Food exercises a direct influence on the mind. Sattvic food makes the mind pure. Purity of food leads to purity of mind. Mind is only made up of the fine essence of food. As the food is, so is the mind.

You must be pure in thought, word and deed. Your heart must be as pure as crystal or the Himalayan snow. Then only the divine light will descend. Purity comprises such virtues as frankness, innocence, straightforwardness and absence of all evil thoughts. He who is endowed with purity will find it easy to tread the spiritual path.

Self-control

You must have perfect self-control or self-mastery. Self-control implies both control of the body and control of the mind. Self-control does not mean self-torture. You must lead a well-regulated and disciplined life. You must keep all the senses under your perfect control. The senses are like turbulent and wild horses. This body is like a chariot. Mind is the reins. Intellect is the driver. The Atman is the Lord of the chariot. If the senses are not kept under proper control, they will throw this chariot into a deep abyss. You will come to ruin. He who keeps the reins firm and drives this chariot intelligently by controlling the horses (senses), will reach the destination (Moksha or the Abode of Eternal Bliss) safely.

Self-control implies self-sacrifice, annihilation of egoism, patience, endurance, forbearance and humility. Overcome Raga or attachment by Vairagya or dispassion. Dispassion will dawn in your mind if you look into the defects of sensual life such as birth, death, disease, old age, pain, sorrow, etc. (Mithya-Drishti and Dosha-Drishti). Overcome anger and hatred by Kshama or forgiveness, love and selfless service. Overcome evil by good. Return good for evil. Overcome lust by the practice of Brahmacharya and regular Japa and meditation. Conquer greed by charity, generosity and disinterested actions. Conquer pride by humility and delusion by discrimination and enquiry. Overcome jealousy by magnanimity, Atma-bhava and nobility. Conquer egoism by self-sacrifice, self-surrender, self-abnegation and meditation on the non-dual, eternal, self-luminous Brahman, the innermost Self, the Inner Ruler, the Immortal.

May you all attain eternal bliss and immortality through the practice of the cardinal virtues or the fundamental Dharma.

VARNASRAMA DHARMA

The principle of Varnasrama Dharma is one of the basic principles of Hinduism. The Varnasrama system is peculiar to Hindus. It is a characteristic feature of Hinduism. It is also prevalent throughout the world according to Guna-Karma (aptitude and conduct), though there is no such distinct denomination of this kind, elsewhere.

The duties of the castes are Varna Dharma. The four castes are Brahmana, Kshatriya, Vaisya and Sudra. The duties of the stages in life are Asrama Dharma. The four Asramas or orders of life are Brahmacharya, Grihastha, Vanaprastha and Sannyasa.

THE PRINCIPLE

Human society is like a huge machine. The individuals and communities are like its parts. If the parts are weak and broken, the machine will not work. A machine is nothing without its parts. The human body also can work efficiently if its parts and organs are in sound and strong condition. If there is pain in any part of the body, if there is disease in any organ or part of the body, this human machine will go out of order. It will not perform its usual function or work.

So is the case with the human society. Every individual should perform his duties efficiently. The Hindu Rishis and sages formed an ideal scheme of society and an ideal way of individual life, which is known by the name Varnasrama Dharma. Hinduism is built on Varnasrama Dharma. The structure of the Hindu society is based on Varnasrama Dharma. Observance of Varnasrama Dharma helps one's growth and self-evolution. It is very indispensable. If the rules are violated, the society will soon perish.

The aim of Varnasrama Dharma is to promote the development of the universal, eternal Dharma. If you defend Dharma, it will defend you. If you destroy it, it will destroy you. Therefore, never destroy your Dharma. This principle holds true of the individual as much as of the nation. It is Dharma alone which keeps a nation alive. Dharma is the very soul of man. Dharma is the very soul of a nation also.

In the West and in the whole world also, there is Varnasrama, though it is not rigidly observed there. Some Western philosophers have made a division of three classes, viz., philosophers, warriors and masses. The philosophers correspond to the Brahmanas, warriors to Kshatriyas and the masses to Vaisyas and Sudras. This system is indispensable to keep the society in a state of perfect harmony and order.

THE FOUR CASTES

In Purusha-Sukta of the Rig-Veda, there is reference to the division of Hindu society into four classes. It is described there that the Brahmanas came out of the face of the Lord, the Creator, Kshatriyas from His arms, Vaisyas from His thighs, and the Sudras from His feet.

This division is according to the Guna and Karma. Guna (quality) and Karma (kind of work) determine the caste of a man. This is supported by Lord Krishna in the Gita, also. He says in the Gita: "The four castes were emanated by Me, by the different distribution of qualities and actions. Know Me to be the author of them, though the actionless and inexhaustible" (Ch. IV-13).

There are three qualities or Gunas, viz., *Sattva* (purity), *Rajas* (passion) and *Tamas* (inertia). Sattva is white, Rajas is red and Tamas is black. These three qualities are found in man in varying proportions. Sattva preponderates in some persons. They are Brahmanas. They are wise persons or thinkers. They are the priests, ministers or philosophers who guide kings or rulers. In some, Rajas is predominant. They are Kshatriyas. They are warriors or men of action. They fight with the enemies or invaders and defend the country. In some, Tamas is predominant. They are Vaisyas or traders. They do business and agriculture and amass wealth. Sudras are the servants. None of these qualities is highly developed in them. They serve the other three castes.

In a broad sense, a Sattvic man, who is pious and virtuous and leads the divine life, is a Brahmana, a Rajasic man with heroic quality is a Kshatriya, a Rajasic man with business tendencies is a Vaisya and a Tamasic man is a Sudra. Hitler and Mussolini were Kshatriyas. Ford was a Vaisya.

Serenity, self-restraint, austerity, purity, forgiveness, and also, uprightness, knowledge, Realisation and belief in God are the duties of the Brahmanas, born of (their own) nature. Prowess, splendour, firmness, dexterity, and also, not flying from battle, generosity and lordliness are the duties of the Kshatriyas, born of (their own) nature. Agriculture, cattle-rearing and trade are the duties of the Vaisyas, born of (their own) nature. And action consisting of service is the duty of the Sudras, born of (their own) nature.

The Law of Spiritual Economics

The underlying principle in caste system or Varna Dharma, is division of labour. Rishis studied human nature carefully. They came to the conclusion that all men were not equally fit for all kinds of work. Hence, they found it necessary to allocate different kinds of duties to different classes of people, according to their aptitude, capacity or quality. The Brahmanas were in charge of spiritual and intellectual affairs. The work of political administration and defence was given to the Kshatriyas. The Vaisyas were entrusted with the duty of supplying food for the nation and administering its economic welfare. The Sudras did menial work. The Rishis felt all these needs of the Hindu nation and started the system of Varnas and Asramas.

This division of labour began in Vedic times. The Vedas taught that the Brahmana was the brain of the society, the Kshatriya its arms, the Vaisya its stomach, and the Sudra its feet.

There was a quarrel between the senses, the mind and the Prana as to who was superior. There was a quarrel amongst the different organs and the stomach. If the hands quarrel with the stomach, the entire body will suffer. When Prana departed from the body, all the organs suffered. The head or stomach cannot claim its superiority over the feet and hands. The hands and feet are as much important as the stomach or head. If there is quarrel between the different castes as to which is superior, then the entire social fabric will suffer. There will be disharmony, rupture and discord. A scavenger and a barber are as much important as a minister for the running of the society. The social edifice is built on the law of spiritual economics. It has nothing to do with superiority or inferiority. Each class contributes its best to the common weal or world-solidarity. There is no question of higher and lower here.

Character Determines Caste

A Brahmana is no Brahmana if he is not endowed with purity and good character, and if he leads a life of dissipation and immorality. A Sudra is a Brahmana if he leads a virtuous and pious life. What a great soul was Vidura! What a noble, candid, straightforward student was Satyakama Jabala of Chhandogya Upanishad! Caste is a question of character. Varna is no more the colour of the skin, but the colour of one's character or quality. Conduct and character count and not lineage alone. If one is Brahmana by birth and, at the same time, if he possesses the virtues of a Brahmana, it is extremely good, because certain virtuous qualifications only determine the birth of a Brahmana.

Use and Abuse of the Caste System

The Hindus have survived many a foreign conquest on account of their caste system. But they have developed class jealousies and hatred in the name of the caste system. They have not got the spirit of co-operation. That is the reason why they are weak and disunited today. They have become sectarians in the name of the caste system. Hence there is degradation in India.

The caste system is, indeed, a splendid thing. It is quite flawless. But the defect came in from somewhere else. The classes gradually neglected their duties. The test of ability and character slowly vanished. Birth became the chief consideration in determining castes. All castes fell from their ideals and forgot all about their duties. Brahmanas became selfish and claimed superiority over others by mere birth, without possessing due qualifications. The Kshatriyas lost their chivalry and spirit of sacrifice. The Vaisyas became very greedy. They did not earn wealth by honest means. They did not look after the economic welfare of the people. They did not give charity. They also lost the spirit of sacrifice. Sudras gave up service. They became officers. They wished that others should serve them. The greed and pride of man have created discord and disharmony.

There is nothing wrong in Varnasrama. It is arrogance and haughtiness in men that have brought troubles. Man or the little Jiva is imperfect. He is full of defects. He is simply waiting for claiming superiority over others. The Brahmana thinks that the other three castes are inferior to him. The Kshatriya thinks that the Vaisya and Sudra are inferior to him. A rich Sudra thinks that he is superior to a poor Brahmana or a poor Kshatriya or Vaisya.

At the present moment, the Varnasrama system exists in name

only. It has to be rebuilt properly. Brahmanas, Kshatriyas, Vaisyas and Sudras, who have fallen from their ideals and who are not doing their respective duties, must do their respective duties properly. They must be educated on right lines. They must raise themselves to their original lofty level. The sectarian spirit must die. They should develop a new understanding heart of love and devotion, with a spirit of co-operation, sacrifice and service.

THE FOUR ASRAMAS

There are four Asramas or stages in life, *viz.*, Brahmacharya or the period of studentship, Grihastha or the stage of the householder, Vanaprastha or the stage of the forest-dweller or hermit, and Sannyasa or the life of renunciation or asceticism. Each stage has its own duties. These stages help the evolution of man. The four Asramas take man to perfection by successive stages. The practice of the four Asramas regulates the life from the beginning to the end. The first two Asramas pertain to Pravritti Marga or the path of work and the two later stages—the life of Vanaprastha and that of Sannyasa—are the stages of withdrawal from the world. They pertain to Nivritti Marga or the path of renunciation.

Towards Orderly Spiritual Evolution

Life is very systematically and orderly arranged in Sanatana Dharma. There is opportunity for the development of the different sides of human activity. Due occupations and training are assigned to each period of life. Life is a great school in which the powers, capacities and faculties of man are to be evolved gradually.

Every man should pass through the different Asramas regularly. He should not enter any stage of life prematurely. He can enter the next stage, only when each has been completed. In nature, evolution is gradual. It is not revolutionary.

Lord Manu says in his Smriti: "Having studied the Vedas or two Vedas or even one Veda in due order without breaking celibacy, let him dwell in the householder order. When the householder sees wrinkles in his skin and whiteness in his hair and the son of his son, then let him retire to the forest. Having passed the third portion of life in the forests, let him, having abandoned attachments, wander as an ascetic in the fourth portion of life."

In extraordinary cases, however, some of the stages may be omitted. Suka was a born Sannyasin. Sankara took Sannyasa without entering the stage of a householder. In rare and exceptional cases, a student is allowed to become a Sannyasin, his debts to the world having been fully paid in a previous birth. Nowadays, young Sannyasins without qualification are found in abundance. This is contrary to the ancient rules and causes much trouble.

The Brahmacharin or the Celibate Student

The first stage, Brahmacharya, is the period of study and discipline. The student should not indulge in any pleasures. He stays in the house of his preceptor and studies the Vedas and the sciences. This is the period of probation. The teachers in ancient India usually lived in forest hermitages. These hermitages were the Gurukulas or forest universities. The student begged his food. The children of the rich and poor lived together. The student regarded his teacher as his spiritual father and served him with faith, devotion and reverence.

The life of the student begins with the Upanayana ceremony, his second birth. He must be hardy and simple in his habits. He rises early, bathes and does Sandhya and Gayatri Japa. He studies scriptures. He takes simple food in moderation and takes plenty of exercise. He sleeps on a hard mat and does not use soft beds and pillows. He is humble and obedient. He serves and respects elders. He attempts to be chaste in thought, word and deed.

He ever engages himself in doing services to his preceptor.

He refrains from wine, meat, perfumes, garlands, tasty and savoury dishes, women, acids, spices and injury to sentient creatures; from lust, anger, greed; dancing, singing and playing on musical instruments; from dice-playing, gossip, slander and untruth. He sleeps alone.

After the end of his student career, he gives a present to his preceptor according to his ability and returns home to enter the household life. The preceptor gives the final instruction and sends the student home. The teacher delivers a convocation address to the students at the conclusion of their studentship:

"Speak the truth. Do your duty. Never swerve from the study of the Veda. Do not cut off the line of progeny (after giving the preceptor the fee he desires). Never swerve away from truth. Never swerve from duty. Never neglect your welfare. Never neglect your prosperity. Never neglect the study and the teaching of the Vedas.

"Never swerve from the duties to the gods and the forefathers. Regard your mother as a god *(Matridevo Bhava)*. Regard your father as a god *(Pitridevo Bhava)*. Regard your teacher as a god *(Acharyadevo Bhava)*. Regard your guest as god *(Atithidevo Bhava)*. Let only those actions that are free from blemishes be done and not others. Only those that are good acts to us should be performed by you and not others.

"You should remove the fatigue of Brahmanas who are superior to you by serving them with seats, etc. Gift should be given with faith, in plenty, with modesty and sympathy. If there be any doubt regarding rites or conduct, then look up to the lives of great men and follow their examples. This is the injunction. This is the teaching. This is the secret of the Vedas. This is God's word of command. This should be observed. Thus is this to be meditated upon."

The Grihastha or the Householder

The second stage is that of the Grihastha or householder.

The household stage is entered at marriage, when the student has completed his studentship and is ready to take up the duties and responsibilities of householder life. Of all the Asramas, this is the most important, because it supports all the others. As all creatures live supported by the air, so the other Orders exist supported by the householder. As all streams and rivers flow to rest in the ocean, so all the Asramas flow to rest in the householder. The Grihastha is the very heart of Aryan life. Everything depends on him.

Marriage is a sacrament for a Hindu. The wife is his partner in life. She is his Ardhangini. He cannot do any religious ritual without her. She stands by his left side when he performs any religious performance. Husband and wife keep Rama and Sita as their ideal.

A householder should earn money by honest means and distribute it in the proper manner. He should spend one-tenth of his income in charity. He should enjoy sensual pleasures within the limits of the moral law. A householder is permitted to enjoy conjugal happiness on one night in a month.

The householder should perform the Pancha Maha Yajnas. The five Yajnas are:

DEVA-YAJNA—offering oblations unto Devas, with recitation of Vedic Mantras.

RISHI-YAJNA—study of Vedas and teaching of Vedas to students, and offering of oblations to Rishis.

PITRI-YAJNA—Tarpana or ablutions to departed souls and Sraaddha or annual religious rites performed for departed souls.

BHUTA-YAJNA—distribution of food to cows, crows and animals in general.

ATITHI-YAJNA—giving food to guests and honouring them.

Hospitality is one of the householder's chief duties. He must ever feed first his guests, Brahmanas and his relatives, and then he and his wife should eat.

When the householder sees that his sons are able to bear the burden of his duties, when his grandsons are around him, he should know that the time has come for him and his wife to retire from the world and spend their time in study and meditation.

The Vanaprastha or the Recluse

The next stage is that of the Vanaprastha. Brahmacharya is a preparation for the life of the householder. Even so, Vanaprastha is a preparation for the final stage of Sannyasa. After discharging all the duties of a householder, he should retire to the forest or a solitary country place and begin to meditate in solitude on higher spiritual things. He is now free from social bonds and the responsibilities of life. He has ample time for study of scriptures. His wife may go with him or remain with her sons.

The Sannyasin or the Renunciate

The next stage is that of a Sannyasin. When a man becomes a Sannyasin, he renounces all possessions, all distinctions of caste, all rites and ceremonies and all attachments to any particular country, nation, or religion. He lives alone and spends his time in meditation. He lives on alms. When he attains the sublime states of deep meditation he rejoices in his own Self. He is quite indifferent to sensual pleasures. He is free from likes and dislikes, desires, egoism, lust, anger, greed and pride. He has equal vision and balanced mind. He loves all. He roams about happily and disseminates Brahma Jnana or Knowledge of the Self. He is the same in honour and dishonour, praise and censure, success and failure. He is now *Ativarnasrami,* i.e., above Varna and Asrama. He is quite a free man. He is not bound by any social customs and conventions.

Such a Sannyasin is an ideal man. He has attained perfection and freedom. He is Brahman Himself. He is a Jivanmukta or a liberated sage. Glory to such exalted personages who are living Gods on earth!

ASRAMA DHARMA UNDER MODERN CONDITIONS

At the present moment, the Asramas cannot be exactly lived according to the details of the ancient rules, as the conditions have changed very much; but, they may be revived in their spirit, to the great improvement of modern life. In these stages, no one should do the duty of another. The student or Brahmachari should not do the duties of a householder, a recluse or a Sannyasin. The householder must not perform the duties of a Brahmacharin, Vanaprastha or a Sannyasin. A Sannyasin should not seek again the joys of the householder.

Peace and order will prevail in society, only if and when all people do their respective duties efficiently. The abolition of Varnas and Asramas will cut at the very root of social duties. How can the nation hope to live when Varnasrama Dharma is not rigidly practised?

The students of schools and colleges should lead a life of purity and simple living. The householder should lead the life of an ideal Grihastha. He should practise self-restraint, mercy, tolerance, non-injury, truthfulness and moderation in everything. Those who find it difficult to lead the life of the third and the fourth Asramas should, remaining in either of the other two Asramas, gradually withdraw themselves from worldly life and practise selfless service, study and meditation.

THE HIGHEST STATE

Varnasrama pertains to body alone, but not to the pure, all-pervading, immortal soul or Atman. Attain Knowledge of the Self and become an Ativarnasrami like Lord Dattatreya. Hear what he says:—

Mahadadi jagat sarvam
Na kinchit pratibhati me
Brahmaiva kevalam sarvam
Katham varnasramasthitih

"The whole world, from Mahat downwards, does not shine in Me. Everything is Brahman only. Where then is Varnasrama?"

May you all have comprehensive understanding of Varnasrama Dharma! May you all develop universal love and brotherhood! May all barriers which are made by man for his own self-aggrandisement and self-assertion and which create discord and disunion, be broken asunder!

YUGA DHARMA

In Satya-Yuga or the golden age there was a different set of Dharmas or laws; in Treta, they changed into another form; in Dvapara, the Dharmas were different from the Dharmas of other Yugas; and in Kali-Yuga, they assumed still another form. The Dharma changes according to the changes of the cycles. Man is undergoing change. His nature gets transformed through experiences. Hence, his external form of Dharmas also should change.

That which is achieved through contemplation in Satya Yuga, through sacrifices in Treta Yuga, and through the worship of Lord Hari in Dvapara Yuga, may be attained through Kirtana or loud chanting of Lord Vishnu's Name in Kali Yuga or Iron age.

In the Satya Yuga, the mind of men was generally pure. They had no distraction of the mind. There were neither cinemas, nor hotels, nor dancing halls and similar other distractions. Hence, meditation was easy and natural for them. That is the reason why contemplation has been prescribed for men of Satya Yuga. In the Treta Yuga, materials for the performance of Yajnas or sacrifices were easily available. The people had active tendencies. Therefore it was easy for them to perform Agnihotra, Jyotistoma, Darsa-Paurnimas and other Yajnas. That is the reason why Yajna has been described as the external form of Sanatana Dharma in that age. In the Dvapara Yuga, there was the manifestation of Avataras and men could easily have direct worship of God. Hence, worship was prescribed as the principal form of Sadhana in that age. In the Kali Yuga, there are many distractions for the mind. People lack in Brahmacharya, strength of will and power of enquiry or rational investigation. It is very difficult to procure materials for the performance of sacrifices. Therefore, Hari Kirtana or loud chanting of the Divine Name and selfless service of humanity have been recommended as the principal forms of Sadhana.

CONCLUSION

Follow your Dharma with zeal and enthusiasm. Discharge your duties faithfully. Develop all the virtues which constitute Dharma. Never deviate an inch from the path of righteousness. Stick to Dharma with all your heart, with all your mind and with all your soul. Performance of one's duties brings happiness, quick evolution and freedom. You will soon attain immortality, eternal bliss, supreme peace, perennial joy, absolute freedom and perfection. Glory to Dharma, the supreme light that leads you to the kingdom of eternal bliss and everlasting peace.

May the eternal Dharma of Hinduism be preserved for ever! May all Hindus be consolidated by the bond of true love!!

CHAPTER 4

HINDU ETHICS

The mark of *Dharma* is *Achara* or good conduct. Achara is the mark of the good. From Achara is Dharma born. Dharma enhances life. Man attains prosperity and fame, here and hereafter, through the practice of Dharma.

Good conduct is the highest Dharma. It is the root of all Tapas or austerities. Righteousness, truth and good works, power and prosperity—all originate from conduct.

CONDUCT AND CHARACTER

Man wills to obtain his objects of desires. Willing results in action. This is called conduct. Conduct is behaviour. The will that is expressed becomes conduct.

Man has various sorts of desires. Sometimes, there is conflict of desires. That desire which obtains victory is termed 'will'. The inner disposition which makes the will possible is called character. Character is the aggregate of peculiar qualities which constitute personal individuality.

External behaviour is not always a sure guide in judging the character of a man.

ETHICS OR THE SCIENCE OF CONDUCT

Morality or ethics is the science of conduct. Ethics is the study of what is right or good in conduct. Ethical science shows the way in which human beings should behave towards one another, as well as towards other creatures. It contains systematised principles on which a man should act. Ethics is right conduct or Sadachara.

We have human morality, family morality, social morality, national morality, professional morality, etc. A doctor has his professional ethics. He should not divulge to others the secrets of his patients. It is his duty to take all precautionary hygienic measures to stop the spread of an epidemic disease and direct his earnest attention towards public health and hygiene.

Ethics is a relative science. What is good for one man may not be good for another man. What is good at one time and at one place may not be good at another time and at another place. Ethics is relative to the man himself and to his surroundings.

ETHICS, SPIRITUALITY AND RELIGION

Without ethics, you cannot have progress in the spiritual path. Ethics is the foundation of Yoga. Ethics is the cornerstone of Vedanta. Ethics is the strong pillar on which the edifice of Bhakti Yoga rests. Ethics is the gateway to God-realisation.

Without ethical perfection, no spiritual progress or realisation is possible. A Yogic student or aspirant must be strictly ethical. He must be truthful and pure in thought, word and deed. He must possess excellent conduct. He must not injure any living being in thought, word and deed. He must practise rigidly right thought, right speech and right action.

Every religion has its ethics. The Sermon on the Mount of Jesus and the Ten Commandments contain ethical teachings for the uplift of man. The Noble Eightfold Path of the Buddha is the essence of ethics. The Yamas and Niyamas of Patanjali Maharshi constitute the highest ethics. Manu Smriti, Yajnavalkya Smriti and Parasara Smriti contain the code of conduct for man. The three kinds of austerity of the Gita are nothing but ethics in an intensified form.

BENEFITS OF THE PRACTICE OF ETHICS

Morality is the gateway to religion. He who leads a moral or virtuous life attains freedom, perfection or *Moksha*.

Practice of ethics will help you to live in harmony with your neighbours, friends, your own family members, fellow-beings and other people. It will confer on you lasting happiness and Moksha. It will purify your heart. It will keep your conscience ever clean. A moral man who follows strictly the principles of ethics will not deviate even a fraction of an inch from the path of Dharma or righteousness. Yudhishthira had earned an undying reputation for his practice of ethics. He was an embodiment of Dharma. Hence he still lives in our hearts.

Good conduct is the root of material and spiritual prosperity. Conduct increases fame. It is good conduct which prolongs life and destroys all calamities and evils and brings eternal happiness. It is good conduct that begets virtue. Therefore develop good conduct.

ETHICAL CODES IN HINDUISM

Hindu ethics is superb. Hinduism lays great emphasis on ethical discipline. Yama (self-restraint) and Niyama (religious observances or canons) are the foundations of Yoga and Vedanta.

Undeveloped persons cannot think for themselves. Hence rules of conduct have been laid down by great sages or seers like Manu and Sage Yajnavalkya.

Lord Krishna says in the Gita: "Let the scriptures be thy authority in determining what ought to be done or what ought not to be done. Knowing what hath been declared by the ordinances of the scriptures, thou oughtest to work in this world" (Ch. XVI-24). The Smritis written by Yajnavalkya, Manu and other sages distinctly prescribe the rules of conduct. As you have not got the power nor the time to think of the moral principles and rules given in the scriptures, you can get them from the sages and saints and follow them to the very letter.

THE FOUNDATIONAL PRINCIPLES OF HINDU ETHICS

The ethics of the Hindus is subtle, sublime and profound. All religions have taught ethical precepts such as: "Do not kill, do not injure others, love your neighbour as your self," but they have not given the reason. The basis of Hindu ethics is this: "There is one all-pervading Atman. It is the innermost soul of all beings. This is the common, pure consciousness. If you injure your neighbour, you really injure yourself. If you injure any other creature, you really injure yourself, because the whole world is nothing but your own Self." This is Hindu ethics. This is the basic metaphysical truth that underlies all Hindu ethical codes.

The Atman or Self is one. One life vibrates in all beings. Life is common in animals, birds and human beings. Existence is common. This is the emphatic declaration of the Upanishads or Srutis. This primary truth of religion is the foundation of ethics or morality or science of right conduct. Morality has Vedanta as its basis.

The first thing you learn from religion is the unity of all selves. The Upanishads says: "The neighbour is, in truth, the very Self and what separates you from him is mere illusion." One Atman or Self abides in all beings. Universal love is the expression of the unity. Universal brotherhood has its basis in the unity of Self. All human relations exist because of this unity. Yajnavalkya said to his wife Maitreyi: "Behold, my · dear, not indeed for the love of the husband is the husband dear, for the love of the Self is the husband dear." And so with wife, sons, property, friends, worlds and even the Devas themselves. All are dear, because the one Self is in all. If you injure another man, you injure yourself. If you help another person, you help yourself. There is one life, one common consciousness in all beings. This is the foundation of right conduct. This is the foundation of ethics.

SERVICE AS WORSHIP

A philanthropist donates big sums to social institutions. He regards this as some kind of social service only. That is all. He has not got the *Bhava* or mental attitude, that the whole world is a manifestation of the Lord and that he is serving the Lord. He has not got the *Bhava* that the Lord is working through his instruments or senses, that every act is an offering unto the Lord, and that every deed is a Yogic activity.

In India, dinner is prepared for five hundred persons even when two hundred persons are invited. Feeding is worship of Narayana or the Lord, for a Hindu. It is *Atithi-Yajna* or sacred sacrifice. A Hindu regards every creature as the Lord.

The Hindus are very generous, noble, large-hearted, charitable, God-fearing, sympathetic, merciful and hospitable. If they see a hungry man in the street, they will take him to their house, treat him as *Atithi-Narayana* (God in the form of guest), feed him first and then take their food. Nowhere in the world you will hear of such a treatment. You cannot get even a morsel of food free in other countries.

A Hindu believes that if he feeds a single sage or a Mahatma, he is feeding the whole world, because he has realised that a realised sage is identical with the whole Virat or Brahman and is one with all beings of the entire universe. Hindu ethics is based on the sublime philosophy of Vedanta which propounds the doctrine of oneness of life and unity of consciousness. Ethics or morality and doing good to others, is the manifestation of this oneness. A Hindu distributes food to the crows, dogs, cows and fish first before he takes his food. He tries to recognise the one Atman that is hidden in all these forms. He endeavours to become one with the Universal Being. He knows that in loving others he loves himself and in injuring others he injures himself. Through the practice of cosmic love he feels that all bodies are his, all hands are his, all feet are his and that the whole world is his home *(Vasudhaiva*

Kutumbakam). Gradually he becomes one with the soul of the universe and one with the Oversoul also. Hindu ethics leads eventually to Self-realisation. Ethics is a means to Yoga.

ETHICAL CULTURE OR THE PROCESS OF PURIFICATION

The very root and core of all moral discipline is mental purification through refraining from all evil action and the active practice of virtue. Do good at all times. *Ahimsa, Satya* and *Brahmacharya* symbolise the three processes of avoiding sin, sticking to virtue and Self-purification.

All harm arises out of man's egoism. The ego manifests itself as ambition, desire and lust. Under their influence man indulges in hatred, love, flattery, pride, unscrupulousness, hypocrisy and delusion.

To eradicate egoism arising out of *Deha-Abhimana* (body-idea), think constantly on the foulness and perishability of the body and the pains arising out of the senses. Reject them as evil and mentally rise above them. Dwell upon that which is desirable, elevating and divine.

Improper action—thoughtless action without discrimination—gives rise to all misery. To get freedom from misery, the noble path of virtue—*Sadachara*—is to be followed. Rigidly observe truth and purity in your thoughts, speech, actions, inner motive and general conduct. Be loving, tolerant and charitable in your opinion of men and things and in your dealings with others.

In every sphere, the individual should strive to adhere to these qualities and to manifest them. Thus, this ideal is to be practised between parents and children, elders and youngsters, teacher and pupil, friend and friend, Guru and disciple, leader and follower, subject and ruler, and nation and nation.

You must proceed along the path of virtue. Be determined never to swerve even an inch from Dharma. The mind has to be carefully trained and the will should be developed and strengthened. Therefore much importance has been laid by the ancients upon Yama, Niyama and Shat-Sampat (six treasures of virtue). The mind and will must be exercised and disciplined through deliberate acts of self-denial and self-sacrifice in everyday life. Ethical culture, therefore, demands moral vigilance and right exertion. The development of a sensitive conscience and positive admiration for goodness and nobility plays a great part in ethical culture.

PHILOSOPHY OF RIGHT AND WRONG

Everybody speaks: "This is right, that is wrong; you are right, he is wrong;" but he cannot tell you exactly what he means by 'right' and 'wrong'.

What is the criterion by which we judge an action to be right or wrong, and good or bad? "Right and wrong" and "good and bad" are relative terms. Right and wrong refer to the moral standard, as *law*. Good and bad refer to it, as *end*. You will have to adjust your conduct according to this moral standard. That which is in accordance with a rule is right. That which is worthy of achievement is good. Religion gives us the ultimate data upon which ethical science may be built.

RELATIVE NATURE OF RIGHT AND WRONG

Right and wrong—*Dharma* and *Adharma*—are relative terms. It is very difficult to define these terms precisely. Even sages are bewildered sometimes in finding out what is right and what is wrong in some special circumstances. That is the reason why Lord Krishna says in the Gita: "What is action? What is inaction? Even the wise are herein perplexed. Therefore I will declare to thee the action by knowing which thou shalt be liberated from evil. It is needful to discriminate action, to discriminate unlawful action, and to discriminate inaction; mysterious is the path of action. He who seeth inaction in action and action in inaction, he is wise among men; he is harmonious, even while performing all actions" (Ch. IV-16, 17, 18).

ILLUSTRATIONS OF RIGHT AND WRONG

Right and wrong are always relative to the surrounding circumstances. What is right in one situation is not right in another. Right and wrong vary according to time, special circumstances, *Varna* (status or class in society) and *Asrama* (order or stage of life). Morality is a changing and relative term. That passionate man who molests his legally married wife frequently to gratify his passion is more immoral than a man who visits the house of his sister of ill-fame once in six months. That man who dwells constantly on immoral thoughts is the most immoral man. Do you clearly note the subtle difference now? To kill an enemy is right for a Kshatriya king. A Brahmin or Sannyasin should not kill anybody even for protecting himself during times of danger. They should practise strict forbearance and forgiveness. To speak an untruth to save the life of a Mahatma or one's Guru, who has been unjustly charged by the unjust officer of a state, is right. Untruth has become a truth in this particular case. To speak a truth which brings harm to many is untruth only. To kill a dacoit who murders the wayfarers daily is Ahimsa only. Himsa becomes Ahimsa under certain circumstances.

Forgiveness or *Kshama* befits an ascetic or Sannyasin who leads the life of Nivritti Marga or renunciation. It cannot befit a ruler. The ruler may forgive one who has injured him, but he cannot forgive one who has done the greatest harm to the public.

There are special Dharmas during critical, dangerous circumstances. They are called Apad-Dharma. Rishi Visvamitra took forbidden meat from a Chandala or outcaste when there was a severe famine, and offered this in his sacrifice to the Devas. Ushasti, a learned sage, took the polluted beans from the hands of an elephant-driver when the former was suffering from acute hunger and when he was not able to get food from anyone else.

INDICATORS OF RIGHT AND WRONG

Rishi Kanada, author of the Vaiseshika system of philosophy, says in the opening Sutra: "That which elevates you and brings you nearer to God, is right. That which brings you down and takes you away from God, is wrong. That which is done in strict accordance with the injunctions of the scriptures is right and that which is done against their injunctions is wrong." This is one way of defining the terms 'right' and 'wrong'. To work in accordance with the Divine Will is right and to work in opposition to the Divine Will is wrong.

It is very difficult for the man in the street to find out what exactly the Divine Will is, in certain actions. That is the reason why wise sages declare that people should resort to Sastras, learned Pundits and realised persons, for consultation. A pure man who has done Nishkama Karma-Yoga for several years and who is doing worship of Isvara for a long time, can readily find out the Divine Will when he wants to do certain actions. He can hear the inner, shrill, silent voice. Ordinarily people should not attempt to hear this Divine Voice, the Voice of the Silence. They may mistake the voice of the impure mind for the Voice of God. The lower instinctive mind will delude them.

Selfishness clouds understanding. Therefore, if a man has got even a tinge of selfishness, he cannot detect what is right and wrong. A very pure, subtle and sharp intellect is needed for this purpose. The Bhagavad-Gita describes the nature of Sattvic reason, Rajasic reason and Tamasic reason as follows: "That which knoweth energy and abstinence, what ought to be done and what ought not to be done, fear and fearlessness, bondage and liberation, that reason is pure, O Partha. That by which one wrongly understandeth right and wrong, and also what ought to be done and what ought not to be done, that reason, O

ALL ABOUT HINDUISM

Partha, is passionate. That which is enwrapped in darkness, thinketh wrong to be right and seeth all things subverted, that reason, O Partha, is of darkness" (Ch. XVIII-30, 31, 32).

Various other definitions are given by wise men to help the students in the path of righteousness. In the Bible it is said: "Do unto others as you would be done by." This is a very good maxim. The whole gist of Sadachara or right conduct is here. If one practises this very carefully, he will not commit any wrong act. Do not do to another what is not good for yourself. Do not do any act which does not bring good to another or which injures another and makes you feel ashamed for it. Do that act which brings good to others and which is praiseworthy. Do as you would be done by. Do unto others as you wish others should do unto you. This is the secret of Dharma. This is the secret essence of Karma Yoga. This is a brief description of what right conduct is. This will lead you to the attainment of eternal bliss.

"Ahimsa Paramo Dharmah—non-injuring in thought, word and deed is the highest of all virtues." If one is well-established in Ahimsa in thought, word and deed, he can never do any wrong action. That is the reason why Patanjali Maharshi has given Ahimsa great prominence in his Raja Yoga philosophy. Ahimsa comes first in the practice of Yama or self-restraint. To give happiness to others is right; to spread misery and pain to others is wrong. One can follow this in his daily conduct towards others and can evolve in his spiritual path. Do not perform any act that brings to you shame and fear. You will be quite safe if you follow this rule. Stick to any rule that appeals to your reason and conscience and follow it with faith and attention. You will evolve and reach the abode of eternal happiness.

That work which gives elevation, joy and peace to the mind is right and that which brings depression, pain and restlessness to the mind is wrong. This is an easy way to find out right and wrong.

That which helps you in your spiritual evolution is right and that which obstructs and hinders your spiritual evolution is wrong. That which leads to unity of self is right and that which leads to separation is wrong. That which is in accordance with the injunctions of the holy scriptures is right and that which is not in accordance with the sacred lore is wrong. To work in accordance with the Divine Will is right and to work in disharmony with the Divine Will is wrong. To do good to others, to serve and help others, to give joy to others, is right and to give pain to others, to injure others is wrong. All that which is free from any motive of injury to any being is surely morality. Moral precepts have been made to free creatures from all injuries.

Why is charity right? Because it is in conformity with the law: "Do charity." Why is stealing wrong? Because it is against the law: "Thou shalt not steal." Why is it good to help a man when he is in trouble and difficulties? Because it will refine and ennoble your character. It will instil mercy in your heart. The cultivation of virtues will help you to realise the Supreme Self. Why is it bad to kill any being? The end is unworthy. It will corrupt your character. It will reduce you to the level of a brute.

YOGIC GARDENING

By doing wrong actions, you taint your character. By doing virtuous actions, you develop a noble character. Without character, man falls down to the level of a brute. A man of character is honoured, trusted and adored everywhere. Therefore, develop a good character when you are young. Learn how to eradicate vices and how to cultivate virtues in the garden of your heart. Vices and evil habits are the weeds. Virtues are priceless fruits and flowers. Learn the Yogic method of

Pratipaksha Bhavana or cultivation of the opposites. Purity or celibacy, forgiveness, generosity, humility and selflessness are the opposites of lust, anger, greed, pride and selfishness. Become a skilful Yogic gardener. Plant good flowers in the garden of your heart and enthrone the Lord in the centre of the heart-garden and meditate on Him. You will enjoy eternal bliss and immortality.

CONCLUSION

You must obey the laws or rules of conduct. The rules are given for you by the law-givers for your own betterment and spiritual uplift. The law-givers are great sages who had direct God-realisation.

To stick to Sadachara is difficult, no doubt. Mockery, misunderstanding and persecution will have to be faced. Therefore, the cultivation of forbearance, meekness of spirit, calm endurance and spirit of forgiveness are of great importance. Uphold virtue at any cost. For its sake, bear any calumny. Return good for evil.

Do not leave the path of morality even if your life is in danger. Do not leave righteousness for the sake of some material gain. Consult the Sastras and Mahatmas whenever you are in doubt. Build up your character. Grow. Evolve. Keep up your ideal always before your mind. Stick to Sadachara or right conduct. Practise it. You will soon attain eternal bliss and immortality.

CHAPTER 5

HINDU TENETS

THE LAW OF KARMA

WHAT IS KARMA?

Karma means not only action, but also the result of an action. The consequence of an action is really not a separate thing. It is a part of the action, and cannot be divided from it. Breathing, thinking, talking, seeing, hearing, eating, etc., are Karmas. Thinking is mental Karma. Karma is the sum total of our acts both in the present life and in the preceding births.

Any deed, any thought that causes an effect, is called a Karma. The Law of Karma means the law of causation. Wherever there is a cause, there an effect must be produced. A seed is a cause for the tree which is the effect. The tree produces seeds and becomes the cause for the seeds.

HOW KARMA IS FASHIONED

Man is threefold in his nature. He consists of Ichha (desire, feeling), Jnana (knowing) and Kriya (willing). These three fashion his Karma. He knows objects like chair, tree, etc. He feels joy and sorrow. He wills to do this, or not to do that.

Behind the action, there are desire and thought. A desire for an object arises in the mind. Then you think how to get it. Then you exert to possess it. Desire, thought and action always go together. They are the three threads, as it were, that are twisted into the cord of Karma.

Desire produces Karma. You work and exert to acquire the objects of your desire. Karma produces its fruits as pain or pleasure. You will have to take births after births to reap the fruits of your Karmas. This is the Law of Karma.

The Law of Karma is one of the fundamental doctrines not only in Hinduism, but also in Buddhism, and in Jainism. As a man sows, so he shall reap. This is the Law of Karma. If you do an evil action, you must suffer for it. If you do a good action, you must get happiness. There is no power on this earth which can stop the actions from yielding their fruits. Every thought, every word, every deed is, as it were, weighed in the scales of eternal, divine Justice. The Law of Karma is inexorable.

Things do not happen in this universe by accident or chance in a disorderly manner. They happen in regular succession. They follow one another in a regular order. There is a certain definite connection between what is being done now by you, and what will happen in the future.

Every action produces a threefold effect. It gives you an appropriate reward or fruit. It also affects your character. It leaves behind an impression in your mind. This impression will urge you to repeat the act again. The impression will assume the form of a thought-wave in the mind on account of a stimulus, either external or internal. An action produces an effect in the world also.

As You Sow, So You Reap

If you put a seed in the earth, it sends up a little stem. Then leaves come out of the stem. Then come flowers and fruits. There are seeds again in the fruits. Mango seed only produces mango tree. If you sow rice, you cannot expect a crop of wheat. The same sort of seed produces the same kind of plant. A human being alone is born from the womb of a woman, a horse from a horse and a dog from a dog. Similarly, if you sow the seed of an evil action, you will reap a harvest of pain and suffering. If you sow the seed of a virtuous action, you will reap a harvest of pleasure. This is the Law of Karma.

Whatever you sow by your actions come back to you. If

you make others happy through service, charity and kind acts, you sow happiness like a seed; and it will give you the fruit of happiness. If you make others unhappy through harsh words, insult, ill-treatment, cruel acts, oppression, etc., you sow unhappiness like a seed; and it will give you the fruit of pain, suffering, misery and unhappiness. This is the immutable Law of Karma.

Your actions in the past are responsible for your present condition. Your present actions will shape or mould your future. There is nothing chaotic or capricious in this world. You become good by your good actions, and bad by your evil actions.

If you entertain evil thoughts, you must suffer the consequences. You will be in difficulties. You will be surrounded by unfavourable circumstances. You will blame your surroundings and circumstances. Understand the law and live wisely. Entertain noble thoughts. You will be happy always.

Action—Habit—Character—Destiny

Thought moulds your character. If you entertain noble thoughts, you will develop a noble character; and if you entertain evil thoughts, you will develop a base character. This is the immutable Law of Nature. Therefore, you can deliberately shape your character by cultivating sublime thoughts. Thought materialises and becomes an action. If you allow the mind to dwell on good, elevating thoughts, you will do naturally good and laudable actions.

Conduct or behaviour reveals your character. Conduct also moulds your character. Cultivation of good conduct needs rigorous discipline and constant vigilance. You will have to watch every thought, word and action. You must be extremely careful when you conduct yourself with others. With all your good intentions, you will be carried away by the force of your previous wrong impressions, instincts and impulses. Even highly educated people lack in behaviour. Good behaviour indicates that you have a refined or polished, disciplined mind and real, good spiritual culture. The practice of Japa, Pranayama and Mauna (or vow of silence) will help you to control the impulses etc.

You sow an action and reap a habit. You sow a habit and reap a character. You sow a character and reap your destiny. Hence, destiny is your own make-up. You have built it. You can undo it by entertaining noble thoughts, and doing virtuous actions, and changing your mode of thinking. Now you are thinking that you are the body, Mr. So and so. Now, start the anti-current of thought. Think that you are all-pervading, immortal Brahman. Brahman you will become. This is an immutable Law.

THE THREE KINDS OF KARMA

Sanchita, Prarabdha and Agami

Karma is of three kinds, viz., Sanchita (accumulated works), Prarabdha (fructifying works) and Kriyamana or Agami (current works). Sanchita is all the accumulated Karmas of the past. Part of it is seen in the character of man, in his tendencies and aptitudes, capacities, inclinations and desires, etc. Tendencies come from this. Prarabdha is that portion of the past Karma which is responsible for the present body. That portion of the Sanchita Karma which influences human life in the present incarnation is called Prarabdha. It is ripe for reaping. It cannot be avoided or changed. It is only exhausted by being experienced. You pay your past debts. Prarabdha Karma is that which has begun and is actually bearing fruit. It is selected out of the mass of the Sanchita Karma. Kriyamana is that Karma which is now being made for the future. It is also called Agami or Vartamana.

In Vedantic literature, there is a beautiful analogy. The bowman has already sent an arrow and it has left his hands. He cannot recall it. He is about to shoot another arrow. The bundle of arrows in the quiver on his back is the Sanchita; the arrow he has shot is Prarabdha; and the arrow which he is about to shoot from his bow is Agami. Of these, he has perfect control over the Sanchita and the Agami, but he must surely work out his Prarabdha. The past which has begun to take effect he has to experience.

There is another beautiful analogy also. The granary represents the Sanchita Karma; that portion taken from the granary and put in the shop for future daily sale corresponds to Agami; that which is sold daily represents Prarabdha.

The whole lot of Sanchita Karma is destroyed by attaining Knowledge of Brahman or the Eternal. It can be greatly modified by entertaining lofty, divine thoughts, and doing virtuous actions. Agami Karma can be destroyed by expiatory rites or Prayaschitta; and by removing the idea of agency through *Nimitta Bhava* (attitude that one is an instrument in the hands of God) and *Sakshi Bhava* (attitude that one is silent witness of the actions of the senses and of the mind).

THE SUPREMACY OF FREE-WILL

You are the master of your own fate. You are the architect of your own fortune. You are responsible for what you suffer. You are responsible for your present state. If you are happy, it has been your own making. If you are miserable, it has also been your own making. Every action bears a fruit sooner or later. A virtuous action produces pleasure as its effect. An evil deed causes pain.

You have no *Bhoga-Svatantrya* (freedom to determine the result of action), but you have *Karma-Svatantrya* (freedom to determine the course of action). That is the reason why the Lord Krishna says: "*Karmanyeva Adhikaraste Ma Phaleshu Kadachana*—Thy business is with the action only, never with its fruits." Janaka and others attained to perfection by action. You can change your character, your thoughts and desires. Man's will is ever free. Through selfishness his will has become impure. He can render his will pure, strong and dynamic by getting rid of his base desires, and likes and dislikes. Every soul is like a husbandman who has got a plot of land. The acreage, the nature of the soil, the conditions of weather are all predetermined. But the husbandman is quite at liberty to till the earth, manure it and get good crops, or to allow it to remain as a waste land.

What you are now at present is the result of what you thought and did in the past. What you shall be in the future will be the result of what you think and do now. You find an environment which is best suited to the tendencies you acquired in a former life. You can create better conditions for the future. You can make your Karma what you choose. You can rise to a very high state of perfection. You can become an Indra or you may become a perfect Yogin. You can change your character, thoughts and actions. Therefore Bhishma and Vasishtha have placed Purushartha or exertion, above destiny.

A boatman without oars, rudder and sails is carried away helplessly by the winds and currents; but a clever boatman with oars, sails and rudder, ably directs the boat in any direction he likes and reaches the other shore safely. Even so, he who knows the Laws of Nature—the law of thought, the law of Karma, the law of cause and effect—can sail fearlessly in this ocean of Samsara and reach the other shore of fearlessness and immortality quite safely. He will utilise the helping forces to his best advantage and neutralise the opposing forces skilfully, with the help of the knowledge of the Laws. Knowledge is a torch-light. Hence, knowledge is absolutely indispensable. Ignorance is the greatest sin. An ignorant man becomes a victim or a slave of nature.

THE GLORY OF SELFLESS WORK

Selfish Karma leads you to rebirth and rebirth generates new Karma while working off the old. Get rid of Karma if you wish to get rid of the miseries of rebirth. Selfless work will not bind you. It will purify your heart and lead to the descent of the divine light and grace. Understand the Law of Karma and the law of cause and effect. Think rightly. Act nobly. Meditate regularly and attain eternal bliss and immortality.

THE DOCTRINE OF REINCARNATION

The doctrine of reincarnation or transmigration of souls is a fundamental tenet of Hinduism. The word *reincarnation* literally means embodiment again, coming again into a physical body. The individual soul takes again a fleshy covering. The word *transmigration* means passing from one place to another—passing into a new body.

The Sanskrit term *Samsara* is derived from the Sanskrit root *Sr*, which means 'to pass'. The prefix *Sam* means 'intensely'. The individual soul passes repeatedly through this world and other subtle higher worlds. This repeated passing of souls—*Samsriti*—is what is really meant by the term *Samsara*.

Samsara exists in order that the individual soul may learn to realise itself.

Man contains within himself infinite possibilities. The magazine of power and wisdom is within him. He has to unfold the divinity within. This is the object of living and dying.

ENUNCIATION OF THE DOCTRINE IN THE HINDU SCRIPTURES

You will not cease to exist after death. Before this birth, you have passed through countless lives. The Lord Krishna says in the Gita: "O Arjuna, both you and I have had many births before this; only I know them all, while you do not. Birth is inevitably followed by death, and death by rebirth. As a man casting off worn-out garments taketh new ones, so the dweller in the body, casting off worn-out bodies, entereth into others that are new."

The Upanishads also declare: "Just as a caterpillar which has come to the top of a blade of grass, draws itself over to a new blade, so also does the soul draw itself over to a new body, after it has put aside its old body" (Brihadaranyaka Upanishad). "Just as a goldsmith, having taken a piece of gold, makes another form, new and more beautiful, so also, verily the Atman having cast off this body and having put away Avidya or ignorance, makes another new and more beautiful form" (Brihadaranyaka Upanishad). "Like corn, does a mortal ripen; like corn, does he spring to life again" (Kathopanishad).

KARMA AND REBIRTH

The doctrine of rebirth is a corollary to the Law of Karma. The differences of disposition that are found between one individual and another must be due to their respective past actions. Past action implies past birth. Further, all your Karmas cannot certainly bear fruit in this life. Therefore, there must be another birth for enjoying the remaining actions. Each soul has a series of births and deaths. Births and deaths will continue till you attain Knowledge of the Imperishable.

Good Karmas lead to incarnation into higher spheres and bad Karmas into lower. By virtue is obtained ascent to higher planes and by vice, descent to the lower. From wisdom results beatitude, and bondage from the reverse. So long as Karmas— whether good or bad—are not exhausted, men do not attain Moksha or the final emancipation even in hundreds of Kalpas. Both good and bad Karmas bind tight the Jiva in their chains. One is a chain of gold and the other is that of iron. Moksha cannot be attained by man, so long as Knowledge of the Eternal is not attained.

PROOFS FOR THE EXISTENCE OF PREVIOUS BIRTHS

A new-born child manifests marks of joy, fear and grief. This is inexplicable unless we suppose that the child, perceiving certain things in this life, remembers the corresponding things of the past life. The things which used to excite joy, fear and grief in the past life, continue to do so in this life. The memory of the past proves the previous birth, as well as the existence of the soul.

A child, just born, drinks the breast of its mother through the remembrance that it did so in the previous life, as a means of satisfying hunger. The child's desire for milk in this life is caused by the remembrance of its experience in the previous life. This proves that the child's soul, though it has abandoned a previous body and has taken on a new one, remembers the experiences of the previous body.

You do not come into the world in total forgetfulness and in utter darkness. You are born with certain memories and habits acquired in the previous birth. Desires take their origin from previous experiences. We find that none is born without desire. Every being is born with some desires which are associated with the things enjoyed by him in the past life. The desires prove the existence of his soul in previous lives.

PASSAGE OF THE SOUL BETWEEN DEATH AND REBIRTH

The soul migrates with the astral body, or *Sukshma-Sarira* or *Linga-Deha*. This astral body is made up of nineteen *Tattvas* or principles, viz., five organs of action, five organs of knowledge, five Pranas, mind, intellect, *Chitta* (the subconscious), and *Ahankara* or egoism. This subtle body carries with it all sorts of *Samskaras* or impressions, and *Vasanas* or tendencies, of the individual soul. The subtle body moves towards heaven. When the fruits of good Karmas have been exhausted, it gathers for itself a new physical body and reincarnates on this earth plane.

Those whose conduct has been good attain good births and those whose conduct has been evil are thrown into sinful wombs or lower births.

THE DEVAYANA AND THE PITRIYANA

When a man who has practised meditation and worship dies, he first goes to light, then from light to day, from day to the bright half of the moon, from the bright half of the moon

ALL ABOUT HINDUISM

to the six months when the sun goes to the north, from that to the year, from the year to the sun, from the sun to the moon, from the moon to the lightning. When he comes to the sphere of lightning, he meets a person who is not human. That person leads him to the Karya Brahman or Hiranyagarbha. This is the Way of the Devas or Devayana.

He who has done works of public utility and alms, first goes to the smoke when he dies, from smoke to night, from night to the dark half of the moon, from the dark half of the moon to the six months when the sun goes to the south; and from that, he goes to the region of the forefathers, from the world of the forefathers to the ether, from the ether to the moon. He lives there so long as his good works will allow. When the effect of the good works is exhausted, he comes back to this earth by the same route. He first becomes ether, and then air, and then smoke, and then mist, then cloud, and then falls upon the earth as rain-drops. Then he gets into food which is eaten up by man, and finally becomes his child.

He passes through the various existences of the mineral kingdom, of the plant and of the animal realms—the Udbhijja (born of seed), the Svedaja (born of sweat) and the Andaja (born of eggs), before coming into the Jarayuja (viviparous or of placental origin).

HOW TO BREAK THE BOND OF SAMSARA

The chains that tie you to this wheel of *Samsara* or *Bhava-Chakra* or round of births and deaths, are your desires. So long as you desire objects of this world, you must come back to this world in order to possess and enjoy them. But, when all your desires for the mundane objects cease, then the chains are broken and you are free. You need not take any more births. You attain Moksha or the final emancipation.

You wander in this Samsara as you think that you are different from the Lord. If you unite yourself with Him through meditation and Yoga, you will obtain immortality and eternal bliss. Cut the bonds of Karma through Knowledge of the Eternal and enjoy the Supreme Peace of the Atman, thy innermost Self and Inner Ruler. You will be freed from the round of births and deaths. Freed from sin, freed from passion, you will become a Jivanmukta or liberated sage. You will see the Self in the self and see the Self as all.

THE CONCEPT OF AVATARA

Avatara is the decent of God on earth for the ascent of man. The Lord Krishna says: "Though unborn, the Imperishable Self and also the Lord of all beings, yet brooding over nature which is Mine own, I am born through My Own Power. Whenever there is decline of righteousness, then I Myself come forth. For the protection of the good, for the destruction of the evil-doers, for the sake of firmly establishing righteousness, I am born from age to age" (Ch. IV-6, 7, 8).

THE DOCTRINE OF GRACE

The Bhagavatas had their own scriptures called the Pancharatra Agamas which expounded the cult of Vasudeva and which were, therefore, looked upon by them as being equal to the Upanishads. Their religion was based on God's Grace to erring humanity. It, therefore, greatly emphasised the doctrine of Avatara or incarnation and popularised the immortal stories which were afterwards collected together in the Harivamsa, Vishnu Purana and the Bhagavata Purana. If you study these books, you will clearly know about the glory of Lord Krishna.

You can attain God-realisation through worship of Avataras like Krishna and Rama. Many have already attained God-realisation. Tukaram, Ramdas, Surdas, Mira Bai, Tulsidas and several others have seen God face to face. Their powerful writings bespeak of their high spiritual attainments.

DEGREE OF GOD'S MANIFESTATION

There are Purna-Avataras (full incarnations), Amsa-

Avataras (partial incarnations), Avesa-Avataras (inspirational incarnations), etc. The Lord Krishna has sixteen rays. He is a Purna-Avatara. He still exists. There are His Nitya-Lilas in Go-Loka or Celestial Vrindavana.

It is only ignorant, deluded souls who speak against the doctrine of Avatara, who say that the Lord Krishna was a human being only. They have not studied properly the holy scriptures. They are Tamasic persons with little understanding. They cavil and carp. The Lord Krishna says: "The evil-doing, the deluded, the vilest men, they come not to Me, they whose wisdom is destroyed by illusion, who have embraced the nature of demons. Such is their fate."

Friends! Worship Rama or Krishna at all times with all your heart and with all your mind. Glorify Him in your heart. He will soon reveal Himself to you and you will feel His Presence. You will attain immortality and eternal bliss. Glory to Avataras. Glory to the Lords, Krishna and Rama, the Avataras of Lord Vishnu! May their blessings be upon you all.

CHAPTER 6

HINDU RITUALS

SANDHYOPASANA

Sandhyopasana literally means 'worship at the junctions of time.' It is a prayer and worship offered to the Lord at the junction *(Sandhi)* of night and morning, forenoon and afternoon and at the junction of evening and night. The Arghyapradana to the sun and the meditation on and recitation of Gayatri, form the heart of the worship. Properly understood, the whole Sandhya is an earnest prayer addressed to the Lord to forgive all one's sins committed during one's routine, daily activities and to bestow illumination and grace.

Sandhyopasana must be performed at the proper Sandhyas. Then only the performer can derive much merit. There is a special manifestation of force at Sandhyas. This force disappears when the Sandhya is past.

AN OBLIGATORY DUTY

Sandhyopasana is the daily religious practice of the Hindus whose investiture with the holy thread has been performed. Sandhya is a Nitya Karma or an action that is to be done daily. Sandhya is an obligatory duty to be performed daily for self-purification and self-improvement.

Sandhya should be performed by all followers of the Sanatana Dharma. Every Brahmachari and every householder must perform it every day. If he fails to perform it, there is Pratyavaya Dosha or the sin of omission. He loses his Brahma-Tejas.

According to the Hindu Sastras, a Brahmana, a Kshatriya and a Vaisya will get hell, if they do not perform three times Sandhyopasana (Traikalika Sandhya) daily. It is for the purpose of Sandhya only, the law of Yajnopavita-Samskara is laid down in the Yajnavalkya Smriti which says: "The Brahmana in his eighth year, the Kshatriya in his eleventh year and the Vaisya in his twelfth year are fit to be given Yajnopavita." Because, only after this particular Samskara, they are supposed to be worthy to worship Sandhya and take to Vedic rites. They should keep themselves pure internally and externally. They can nicely understand the sacred glory of this divine science.

BENEFITS OF SANDHYOPASANA

Sandhya is a combination of *Japa, Upasana, Svadhyaya,* meditation, concentration, *Asana, Pranayama,* etc. He who does Sandhya daily has *Brahma-Tejas* or spiritual lustre, in his face. A man who performs his daily Sandhya, according to the prescribed rules, at the appointed time as laid down in the scriptures, attains purity and success in his every effort. He becomes powerful as well as calm. Regular Sandhya cuts the chain of old Samskaras and changes everybody's old situation entirely. It brings purity, Atma-Bhava, devotion and sincerity.

THE CEREMONY

The important features of this ceremony are: (i) *Achamana* or sipping of water with recitation of Mantras (viz., Achyutaya Namah, Anantaya Namah, Govindaya Namah, etc.), *Marjana* or sprinkling of water on the body which purifies the mind and the body, *Aghamarshana* or expiation for the sins of many births, and *Surya Arghya* or oblations of water to the Sun-god, (ii) *Pranayama* or control of breath which steadies the wandering mind, and silent recitation of Gayatri, (iii) *Upasthana* or religious obeisance.

Arghya

The first part up to *Arghya* consists of hymns addressed to water and its benefits. The sprinkling of water on the face and the head and the touching of the different organs (the mouth, nose, eyes, ears, chest, shoulders, head, etc.) with wetted fingers, are meant to purify those parts of the body and invoke the respective presiding deities on them. They also stimulate the nerve-centres and wake up the dormant powers of the body.

The Arghya drives the demons who obstruct the path of the rising sun. Esoterically, lust, anger and greed are the demons who obstruct the intellect from rising up. The intellect is the sun.

Pranayama and Japa

The second part of Sandhya consists of Pranayama and Japa of Gayatri.

Suryopasthana

The third part of Sandhya is the Suryopasthana. It is a prayer for forgiveness, mercy and grace. The prayer is: "Let me not go down to the earthly house. Have mercy, O Lord! My strength was very weak, O Lord! I did wrong actions. Have mercy, O Lord!" These are Vedic hymns addressed to the sun in the morning, noon and evening. The sun is the intellect in man. Ignorance is the night. Knowledge is the light. When you rise up from the darkness of ignorance, when the eye of intuition is opened through the grace of Gayatri, the Blessed Mother of the Vedas, you attain eternal bliss, supreme peace and immortality. It is that divine light which dispels delusion and the darkness of ignorance. It is that adorable splendour with which the world is glowing. It is that holy lustre which graciously fills the heart of a devotee with eternal bliss. It is this supreme Light which the aspirant craves from God through the Gayatri Mantra. He begs of God this Knowledge for his Realisation.

SANDHYOPASANA—AN EXACT SCIENCE

Man naturally wants to realise the Truth. He wants to know the secret of Creation. In this connection, scriptures emphatically declare: "Only at the moment when all doubts are cleared, ignorance is destroyed, hypocrisy and cruelty are rent asunder, and when a man sees Him in the abode of his heart, the real and ultimate Truth is revealed."

Sandhya-Vijnana or the Science of Sandhya is an exact science to attain success in the realm of Truth. One need not have any kind of superstition to learn this divine science. One need not prove its greatness. Its greatness, its glory, is open truth. Even the materialistic society of today agrees with the truth of Sandhya-Vijnana. In the scriptures, it is laid: "Brahmanhood is the tree, Sandhya is its root, Vedas are its branches, religious acts are its leaves; therefore take care of its root, i.e., Sandhya." Now the glory of Sandhya is very clear. Sandhya is absolutely necessary for a man who is treading the path of Truth. *Aharahah Sandhyamupasita*, i.e., a Brahmin should perform regularly his daily Sandhya at any cost—is the injunction of the scriptures.

PREREQUISITES FOR THE PRACTICE OF SANDHYA

Diet

If you want to learn this science, you must be careful about your diet. Take regular and light Sattvic food. Man is much influenced by his diet. See the difference between a small lion and a big elephant. You will be able to improve yourself by adjusting your diet. Idleness is due to a variety of rich diet only. Therefore, be strict in your daily diet. You will be ever active and strong.

Sitting Pose

A man who performs Sandhya does not care about his sitting pose. He sits in any posture. This is not much beneficial. He should daily sit in a perfect posture, Padmasana or Sukhasana, facing the particular direction. As far as possible, he must finish his Sandhya in one sitting. He must have perfect mastery over Asana. Then he will have concentration in his Sandhya.

Faith and Devotion

You must do your Sandhya with faith and devotion. Mere repetition will not bring much good. Pray from the core of your heart to the Lord to forgive your sins.

A WORD TO THE YOUNGER GENERATION

Our young college students, who are under the influence of wrong Samskaras and wrong education and evil company, have forgotten all about the glory and high efficacy of Sandhya. They are not doing Sandhya. Sandhya has no meaning for them. They have become Godless men. They want laboratory tests and scientific proofs for the usefulness of Sandhya, before they begin to do Sandhya. It must be supported by the statements of western scientists. The words of ancient Rishis do not appeal to them. What a greatly degraded state!

O young students! Do not ruin yourself by neglecting Sandhya. Regular performance of Sandhya will give you success in life and material and spiritual prosperity, good health and long life, purity of heart, and help you to attain God-realisation. Do it from now at least. Yet there is hope for you. Wake up. Be sincere.

Now take strict resolve from this very moment to be regular in your daily Sandhya, even under many distractions and obstacles. Begin it from this very moment. Do not delay. Reduce your useless activities. Talk little. Do not mix much. You will get plenty of time for your Sandhya.

Be strict in your Sandhya. Let there be rain or wind. Even if the Pralaya comes, do not leave it half-done. Many people say that they have not got time to perform Sandhya. They have to attend several functions. This is due to their weakness and lack of good Samskaras. They do not know the glory of this divine science. If they see one of their friends sitting on the banks of the river and performing Sandhya, they will begin to shout or they will play some sort of mischief. But these poor creatures do not know what secret is hidden behind the Sandhya. The Secret of secrets is hidden in this sacred performance. This is why ancient Rishis say: "One who does not perform daily Sandhya is a real animal."

May God give you the mind to perform daily Sandhya at any cost. May you follow the rules of Sandhya. May you realise the glory of Sandhya-Vijnana and be free from all tribulations and torments. May the divine science named Sandhya-Vijnana bestow purity, immense joy and immortality on you!

THE TEN SCRIPTURAL SAMSKARAS

The rites that pertain to the stages of life of man are called *Samskaras*. The Samskaras are purificatory rites which sanctify the life of the Hindu. They give a spiritual touch to the important events in the life of the individual from conception to cremation. They mark the important stages of a man's life. Just as the outline of a picture is lighted up slowly with the filling in of many colours, so also is Brahmanya with scriptural Samskaras. There are the Samskaras of childhood, of boyhood, of manhood and of old age and death.

There are fiftytwo Samskaras. Among these, ten are important. The ten principal and generally recognised Samskaras are: *Garbhadana, Pumsavana, Simantonnayana, Jatakarma, Namakarana, Annaprasana, Chudakarma, Upanayana, Samavartana* and *Vivaha*. Of these ten, only some are now performed. Some of the Samskaras pertain to infantile life and early childhood. Some are ceremonies which may be performed daily or on special occasions. The whole life of the Hindu is thus consecrated and protected from the cradle to the grave.

GARBHADANA

The Garbhadana sanctifies the creative act. The husband prays fervently from the core of his heart that a child may be conceived. He repeats sacred Mantras during Ritu-Santi ceremony or nuptials. The new child is conceived amidst the vibration of Mantras. Good impressions are impressed in the brain-cells of the embryo. For a real Hindu who is endowed with pure intellect and right understanding, the sexual union is not for the sake of mere enjoyment. He utilises the divine, creative, vital energy for the formation of a human body. Husband and wife should be cheerful and pious when they have intercourse. When their minds are perturbed or agitated, or when there is anger or hatred, they should avoid copulation. They should study holy scriptures. If they have the image of Arjuna, they will have a chivalrous and wise son. If they have the image of Lord Buddha, they will bring forth a son with mercy and other good virtues. If they have the image of Dhanvantari, they will get a son who will turn out to be a reputed Ayurvedic doctor. If they think of Surya or Sun-God, they will bring forth a lustrous son with splendour and effulgence.

PUMSAVANA

In the third month, the Pumsavana is performed with Mantras. The food-sheath and the vital-sheath of the child are formed.

SIMANTONNAYANA

The Simantonnayana is performed at the seventh month with recitation of Veda Mantras. This protects the mother from evil influences and bestows health on the child. The above three Samskaras protect the mother and the child. The body of the child develops nicely. The harmonious vibrations set up by the recitation of Mantras and the performance of the ceremonies help in shaping the body of the child beautifully.

JATAKARMA

The next Samskara, the ceremony performed immediately after the birth of the child, is the Jatakarma. The father welcomes his new-born child. He prays for its long life, intelligence and well-being, and feeds it with honey and butter.

NAMAKARANA

Then comes Namakarana or the naming ceremony. The new-born child is given a name on the tenth, eleventh or twelfth day with recitation of Mantras.

ANNAPRASANA

The Annaprasana comes in the sixth month when the child is given solid food for the first time. Mantras are recited and oblations are offered to the various deities.

CHUDAKARMA

The Chudakarma, the tonsure or shaving of the head, is performed in the first or third year. The Karnavedha or ear-boring ceremony is performed in the fifth or the seventh year or at the end of the first year with the Chudakarma. The body of the child is protected and harmonised by these ceremonies. Any hereditary defect that arises from defect of semen and embryo is removed. Vidyarambha also is another Samskara. Alphabet is taught to the child. This is also known by the name Aksharabhyasa. These Samskaras pertain to the child stage of life.

UPANAYANA

The most important ceremony which marks the beginning of the next stage of life—the stage of youth—is Upanayana. Upanayana is a very important Samskara. It is a landmark in the life of the child. It is his second or spiritual birth. The word *Upanayana* means *bringing near.* The boy is brought near his Guru, spiritual teacher. The preceptor invests him with the sacred thread, Yajnopavita, and initiates him by giving him the Gayatri Mantra, and gives him a staff. This is the beginning of Brahmacharya Asrama, during which Brahmacharya—perfect or entire celibacy—is enjoined. He is to begin the life of study. The initiation makes him a Dvija, twice-born. The father and the mother gave birth to him from mutual desire. This is his physical birth. Initiation into Gayatri Mantra is his another, true birth. According to Yajnavalkya, the Upanayana ceremony is performed at the eighth year for a

Brahmana, eleventh for a Kshatriya and twelfth for a Vaisya. Manu gives the age at the fifth year for a Brahmana, the sixth for a Kshatriya and the eighth for a Vaisya.

Significance of the Sacred Thread and Other Symbols

The sacred thread or Yajnopavita consists of three threads knotted together. He who wears the thread should have a triple control, over his mind, speech and body—thought, word and deed. The holy thread signifies the various triads which exist in the world, viz., Sat, Chit and Ananda; creation, preservation and destruction; the three states of waking, dreaming and deep sleep; the three qualities of Sattva, Rajas and Tamas; the Trimurtis Brahma, Vishnu and Siva; etc.

The staff signifies that the student should have control over his thoughts, words and actions. He who practises control over his thoughts, words and actions, and he who practises Brahmacharya in thought, word and deed, attains perfection.

The boy wears a Kaupina, a small yellow cloth and a girdle of Munja grass. The Acharya puts on him a deer-skin. The new yellow cloth represents the new body. Yellow colour is a symbol of spirituality. Wearing of Kaupina indicates that the boy should lead a pure life of perfect celibacy. The girdle is wound round thrice. This indicates that the boy has to study the Samhitas, the Brahmanas and the Upanishads. The deer-skin represents the ascetic life he should lead.

SAMAVARTANA

Then comes the end of the student stage, the Samavartana. The student, having completed the Vedic studies and the Vratas, presents his preceptor with a gift and obtains permission to take the formal bath which marks the close of his student-career. He returns home and performs the Samavartana, the returning ceremony. He is now ready to marry and enter the second stage or Grihastha Asrama, the life of a householder.

Vivaha is marriage or entry into the second Asrama. The life of the householder begins. Now he takes up his duties as man and pays his spiritual debts by sacrifice, by study and by procreating children. The bridegroom tells the bride: "I take your hand for good fortune." They walk round the sacred fire hand-in-hand. The bride sacrifices grains in the fire and prays: "May my husband live long. May my relations increase."

THE LAST TWO STAGES OF LIFE

There are two more stages, viz., *Vanaprastha* and *Sannyasa,* with their rites.

Man withdraws himself from all worldly activities, retires into the forest and prepares himself for taking Sannyasa. This is the life of a Vanaprastha.

A Sannyasin renounces the world and leads a life of study and meditation by living on alms.

Pretakarma is funeral rite. When a man dies, the funeral ceremonies are performed by his son and heir.

THE PANCHA MAHAYAJNAS

There are five great daily sacrifices that are to be performed by every householder. They are: (i) Brahma Yajna, called also Veda Yajna, sacrifice to Brahman or the Vedas or the sages; (ii) Deva Yajna, sacrifice to the celestials; (iii) Pitri Yajna, sacrifice to the manes; (iv) Bhuta Yajna, sacrifice to all the creatures; and (v) Manushya Yajna, sacrifice to men.

The performance of these five Yajnas is conducive to the spiritual evolution or growth of a man. He gradually learns that he is not a separate entity or isolated creature or isolated unit, but is a part of a great whole. He obtains knowledge by studying the sacred scriptures written by great Rishis. He gets help from his friends, relatives and fellow-beings. He parents gave his physical body. His body is nourished by the milk of cows, grains, vegetables and fruits. The five elements help him. He cannot live without oxygen and water. The Devas and the Pitris bless him. Therefore, he owes a fivefold debt to Nature. He must pay back his debt by performing these five sacrifices daily. Further, numerous insects are killed by him unconsciously during walking, sweeping, grinding, cooking, etc. This sin is removed by performance of these sacrifices.

THE FIVE YAJNAS

The Rishis, the Devas, the Pitris, the Bhutas and the guests expect help from the householders. Hence, they should perform these five sacrifices daily. Teaching and study of scriptures is Brahma Yajna; Tarpana or offering of water to the ancestors, and Sraaddha, form Pitri Yajna: Homa or oblations into the fire is Deva Yajna; Bali or offering of food to all creatures is Bhuta Yajna; and hospitality to guests is Manushya Yajna or Atithi Yajna.

Brahma Yajna or Rishi Yajna

Every man should study daily the sacred scriptures. He should share the knowledge with others. This is Brahma Yajna or Rishi Yajna. By so doing, he pays the debt to Rishis.

Deva Yajna

Lord Krishna says in the Bhagavad-Gita: "Having, in ancient times, emanated mankind together with sacrifice, the Lord of Creation said, 'By this shall ye propagate; be this to you the fulfiller of desires. With this, nourish ye the shining ones; and may the shining ones nourish ye. Thus nourishing one another, ye shall reap the highest good. For, nourished by sacrifice, the shining ones shall bestow on you the enjoyments you desire. A thief verily is he who enjoyeth what is given by them without returning them anything. The righteous, who eat the remains of the sacrifice, are freed from all sins; but the unpious who cook for their own sake, they verily eat sin," (Ch. III-10, 11, 12, 13). Manu says: "Let a man ever engage in the study of the Vedas and in the rites of the Devas; engaging in the rites of the Vedas, he supports the movable and the immovable kingdoms." These sacrifices turn the wheel of life in accordance with the divine will and thus help the evolution of man and the worlds.

Pitri Yajna

Offering libations, etc., to the forefathers, regularly, is Pitri Yajna.

Bhuta-Yajna

Distribution of food to cows, dogs, birds, fish, etc., is Bhuta Yajna.

Manushya Yajna

Feeding the poor is Manushya Yajna. Feeding the hungry, clothing the naked, giving shelter to the homeless, comforting the distressed, etc., are all forms of Manushya Yajna. Any kind of service to the suffering humanity is Manushya Yajna. Feeding a guest is Manushya Yajna.

BENEFITS OF THE PANCHA MAHAYAJNAS

By daily doing such acts of kindness and sympathy, man develops mercy. Hatred vanishes. His hard egoistic heart is gradually softened. He cultivates cosmic love. His heart expands. He has a wider outlook on life. He tries to feel his oneness with all beings. His old feeling of separateness on account of selfishness and egoism is gradually thinned and eventually eradicated. He learns that he can be happy only by making others happy, by serving others, by helping others, by removing the sufferings of others and by sharing what he has with others. The five great daily sacrifices teach man his relations with his superiors, his equals and his inferiors.

Man has no separate individual existence. He is connected with the world. He is like a bead in the rosary. His whole life must be a life of sacrifice and duties. Then only he will have rapid evolution. Then only he will realise the supreme bliss of the Eternal. Then only he will free himself from the round of births and deaths and attain immortality.

SRAADDHA AND TARPANA

Sraaddha is the name of the ceremonies performed by relatives to help the Jiva who has cast off his physical body in death. A Jiva who has cast off his physical sheath is called a Preta. The part of the Sraaddha performed to help him at this stage is called the Preta Kriya.

HOW SRAADDHA AND TARPANA BENEFIT THE DEPARTED SOULS

Gifts to deserving Brahmanas for the benefit of the Pitris, in the proper time and place and with faith, are known as Sraaddha. Sraaddha gives satisfaction to the Pitris. By the offering of the sixteen Sraaddhas, the son helps his father to dwell in joy with the Pitris. The son should perform the Sapindikarana rites for his father. Performance of Sraaddha and Tarpana relieves the hunger and thirst of the departed soul during its journey to the Pitri Loka.

Those who go to hell are extremely oppressed by hunger and thirst. Performance of Sraaddha and offerings of rice and oblations to them, relieve their sufferings. Hence, performance of Sraaddha is indispensable. Those who dwell in heaven also get satisfaction, strength and nourishment.

THE ADVANTAGES OF CREMATION

Cremation is the best way of destroying a dead body. This is highly beneficial for the departed soul. If the body is not burnt, the Jiva is linked to the earth. The soul hovers round or hangs about the dead body on account of Moha or attachment to the physical body. Its journey to the celestial regions is interfered with. The vibrations set up by the recitation of Mantras and the offerings and oblations of water, bring solace and comfort to the departed soul. The Sapindikarana ceremony helps the Jiva to pass from the Preta Loka to the Pitri Loka. He is then enrolled among the Pitris or the ancestors. The son walks three times round the dead body of his father before fire is set to the pyre and sprinkles water once, reciting the Mantra: "Go away. Withdraw and depart from here." The bones are collected on the next day and thrown into a river. Those who can afford take them to Benares or Haridwar and throw them into the Ganga. It is believed that the soul whose mortal remains are consigned to the sacred Ganga attains to the higher regions of spiritual light and splendour and, in the end, salvation.

THE TWO CLASSES OF PITRIS

Immediately after death, the Jiva obtains the Ativahika body which is made up of fire, air and ether. Later on, it may have a Yatana Deha for suffering the tortures of hell if it had done great sins on the earth-plane, or a celestial body for enjoying the pleasures of heaven if it had done virtuous actions while living in the world. In the Yatana Deha, the air-element preponderates; while, in the celestial body, the element of fire is dominant. It takes one year for the Jiva to reach the Pitri Loka.

There are two classes of Pitris, viz., the *celestial Pitris* who are the lords of the Pitri Loka, and the *human Pitris* who go there after death. Brahma is the paternal grandfather of all. Kasyapa and the other Prajapatis are also Pitris, as they are the original progenitors. Pitri Loka or the Abode of the Pitris is also called by the name Bhuvar Loka.

The word *Pitris* primarily means the immediate ancestors, viz., father, mother, etc. Sraaddha proper is performed for three generations of Pitris, or to all Pitris. Three cakes are offered to the father, the grandfather and the great grandfather. Two Brahmins are fed first. Seven generations can mutually influence one another by the giving and receiving of food.

PITRIPAKSHA AND MAHALAYA AMAVASYA

The dark fortnight of the month of Asvayuja is known as the Pitripaksha or the fortnight of the month specially sanctified for offering oblations to the departed ancestors. And the last day, the day of the new moon, is considered as the most important day in the year for performing obsequies and like rites.

Now, ordinarily, the orthodox Hindus offer oblation of water—Tarpana-Arghya—to the departed every new-moon day. The prescribed rites are also performed every year on the anniversary of the day of death. This is the Sraaddha ceremony. What, then, is the special import of these observances particularly during the Asvayuja Krishna Paksha? The reason is that such ceremonies done during this fortnight have a very special effect. The offerings reach the Pitris immediately and directly, due to a boon from Lord Yama. The occasion for the boon arose as follows:

ORIGIN OF THE PITRIPAKSHA

A Story from the Mahabharata

The renowned hero of the Mahabharata, Danavira Karna, when he left the mortal coil, ascended to the higher worlds and reached the region of the heroes. There, the fruit of his extraordinary charity while upon earth came to him multiplied thousandfold, but it came to him in the form of immense piles of gold and silver. Karna had done limitless charity of wealth, but had neglected to do Anna-Dana. Thus he found himself in the midst of wealth and plenty, but with no food to appease him. He prayed to Lord Yama. The Great Ruler responded to Karna's prayer and granted him a respite for fourteen days to return to the earth-plane once again and make up for his former neglect. Karna came down from the Mrityu Loka, and for fourteen days, he fed the Brahmins and the poor, and made offerings of water, etc. He performed the prescribed rites also on the last day. On his return once again to the higher world, the effect of Karna's observances during this fortnight removed all his wants there. The time of this occurrence was the dark fortnight of Asvayuja.

Due to the grace of Lord Yama, it came to be so ordained

that such rites done at this particular period acquired the following unique merits. Offerings made at this time reached all departed souls, whether they were kins directly in the line of the offerer or not. Even those who died without progeny received these oblations given on this Pitripaksha Amavasya day. All those who had failed to do deeds of charity and Anna-Dana and were thus denied these comforts in the Pitri Loka, benefited by these ceremonies. Those deceased whose date of death is not known and whose annual Sraaddha cannot be done, they also get these oblations of Pitripaksha. Souls whose life was cut off by violent, accidental or unnatural death and to whom, therefore, offerings cannot reach in the ordinary course, to them, too, the Pitripaksha offerings reach directly. All these the boon of Lord Yama made possible from the time the great Karna performed the Asvayuja-Paksha rites. The Hindus now observe this Paksha with great faith, with strict regulation, taking bath thrice, with partial fasting, etc. On the newmoon day, Sarvapitri Amavasya, the full rites are done and plenty of charity given.

PROPITIATION OF DEPARTED SPIRITS

The day of Mahalaya Amavasya is a day of great significance and importance to all Hindus. It is the annual festival for propitiating the spirits of our ancestors, with devout prayers for peace. The Hindu Itihasas say, that on the Mahalaya Amavasya, there is a conjunction of the sun and the moon and that the sun enters the sign Virgo (Kanya). On this day, the departed manes, i.e., our ancestors, leave their abode in the world of Yama and come down to the world of mortals and occupy the houses of their descendants.

The fortnight preceding the new moon is specially consecrated for the propitiation of such departed spirits. The ceremonies performed in honour of the manes or ancestors during each day of this fortnight are considered to be equal to those performed at Gaya. The principle in all such rites is the

worship of the departed souls and the satisfaction of their
wishes so that they might be in peace during the rest of the
year.

NAVARATRI OR THE NINE-DAY WORSHIP OF DEVI

Religious observances, traditional worship and Vratas have,
at times, more than one significance. Apart from being the
adoration of the Divine, they are commemorative of stirring
bygone events, allegoric when interpreted from the occult
standpoint, and are significant pointers guiding the Jiva on his
path to Realisation.

Outwardly, the nine days' worship of Devi or the Mother,
known as Navaratri Puja, is in the nature of a Vijaya-Utsava.
The nine days' triumphs are offered to the Mother for Her suc-
cessful struggle with the formidable demons led by Sumbha
and Nisumbha. But, to the spiritual aspirant in his life of Sadhana, the particular division of the Navaratri into sets of three
days to adore different aspects of the Supreme Goddess has
got a very sublime, yet thoroughly practical, truth to reveal. In
its cosmic aspect, it epitomises the stages of the evolution of
man into God, from Jivahood to Sivahood. In its individual
import, it shows the course that his spiritual Sadhana should
take.

Now, the central purpose of existence is to recognise
your eternal identity with the Supreme Spirit. It is to grow
into the image of the Divine. The Supreme One embodies
the highest perfection. It is spotless purity, Niranjana. To
recognise your identity with That, to attain union with That,
is verily to grow into the very likeness of the Divine. The Sadhaka has, therefore, as the initial step, to get rid of the countless impurities and the undivine elements, that have come to
cling to him in his embodied state. Then he has to acquire
lofty virtues and auspicious divine qualities. Thus purified and
rendered full of Sattva, Knowledge flashes upon him like the

brilliant rays of the sun upon the crystal waters of a perfectly calm lake.

WORSHIP OF DURGA
The Eradication of Vices

This process of Sadhana implies resolute will, determined effort and arduous struggle. In other words, strength, infinite Sakti, is the prime necessity. It is the Divine Mother, Supreme Sakti of Brahman, that has to operate through the aspirant. On the first three days, Mother is adored as Power, Force—Durga, the Terrible. You pray to Mother Durga to destroy all your impurities, your vices, your defects. She is to fight with and annihilate the baser animal qualities in the Sadhaka, the lower Asura in his nature. Also, she is the power that protects your Sadhana from its many dangers and pitfalls. Thus, the first three days, marking the first stage of destruction of Mala (impurities) and determined effort and struggle to root out the evil Vasanas in your mind, are set apart for the worship of the Destructive Aspect of the Mother.

WORSHIP OF LAKSHMI
The Cultivation of Virtues

Once you have accomplished your task on overcoming the negative side, that of breaking down the impure Vasanas, propensities and old habits, the next step is to build up a sublime spiritual personality, to acquire positive qualities in place of the eliminated Asuric qualities. The divine qualities—Daivi Sampat—that Lord Krishna enumerates in the Bhagavad-Gita have to be acquired. The Sadhaka must cultivate and develop all the auspicious qualities. He has to pile up immense spiritual wealth to enable him to pay the price for the rare gem of divine wisdom (Jnana Ratna). If this development of the opposite qualities (Pratipaksha Bhavana) is not undertaken in right earnest, the old Asuric nature will raise its head again and again. Hence, this stage is as important in an aspirant's career as the previous one. The essential difference is that while the former is a ruthless, determined annihilation of the filthy, egoistic, lower self, the latter is an orderly, steady, calm and serene effort to develop purity. This pleasanter side of the aspirant's Sadhana is depicted by the worship of Mother Lakshmi. She bestows on Her devotees the inexhaustible wealth or Daivi Sampat. Lakshmi is the Sampat-Dayini aspect of Brahman. She is Purity Itself. Thus, worship of Goddess Lakshmi is performed during the second set of three days.

WORSHIP OF SARASVATI

The Dawn of Supreme Wisdom

Once the aspirant succeeds in routing out the evil propensities and in developing Sattvic, pure, divine qualities, he becomes an Adhikari. He is ready now to receive the Light of Supreme Wisdom. He is fit to obtain Divine Knowledge. At this stage comes the devout worship of Sri Sarasvati, who is Divine Knowledge personified, the embodiment of Brahma Jnana. The sound of Her celestial Vina awakens the notes of the sublime Mahavakyas and the Pranava. She bestows the knowledge of the Supreme Nada and then gives full Atma-Jnana as represented by Her pure dazzling snow-white apparel. To propitiate Sri Sarasvati, the giver of Jnana, is therefore, the third stage.

The tenth day—Vijaya Dasami—marks the triumphant ovation of the Jiva at having attained Jivanmukti through the descent of Knowledge by the grace of Goddess Sarasvati. The Jiva rests in its own supreme Self of Sat-Chit-Ananda (Existence-Knowledge-Bliss Absolute). This day celebrates the victory, the achievement of the Goal. The banner of victory flies aloft. Lo! I am He! I am He! Chidananda Rupah Sivoham, Sivoham; Chidananda Rupah Sivoham, Sivoham.

AN ARRANGEMENT THAT ENSURES SPIRITUAL SUCCESS

This arrangement has also a special significance in the

aspirant's spiritual evolution. It marks the stages of evolution which are indispensable for every Sadhaka, through which every one should pass. One naturally leads to the other, and to short-circuit this would inevitably result in a miserable failure. Nowadays, many ignorant Sadhakas aim straight at the appropriation of Knowledge without the preliminaries of purification and acquisition of Daivi Sampat, and complain that they are not progressing in the path. How can they? Knowledge will not descend till the impurities are washed out and purity is developed. The Sattvic plant can grow on no impure soil.

Follow this arrangement and your efforts will be attended with sure success. This is your path. No other path is known for salvation. Destroy all evil qualities and develop their opposite virtues. By this process you would soon bring yourself up to that perfection which would culminate in the identity with Brahman, which is your Goal. Then all knowledge will be yours, you will be omniscient and omnipotent, and you will feel your omnipresence. You will see yourself in all. You will be a Jivanmukta. You shall achieve eternal victory over the wheel of birth and death, over the demon of Samsara. No more of pain, no more of misery, no more of birth, no more of death for you. Victory, victory be yours!

Glory unto the Divine Mother! Let Her take you, step by step, to the top of the spiritual ladder and unite you with the Lord!!

CHAPTER 7

HINDU WORSHIP

WORSHIP OR UPASANA

Worship is the expression of devotion, reverence and love to the Lord, of keen yearning to be united with Him and of spiritual thirsting to hold conscious communion with Him. The devotee prays to the Lord for granting him intense devotion and removing the veil of ignorance. He pines for His benign grace. He constantly remembers His Name. He repeats His Mantra. He sings His praise. He does Kirtana. He hears and recites His Lilas. He lives in His Dhama in the company of His devotees. He meditates on His form, His nature, His attributes and His Lilas. He visualises the form of the Lord with closed eyes and enjoys supreme peace and bliss.

Worship is the effort on the part of the Upasaka, i.e., he who does Upasana or worship, to reach the proximity or presence of God or the Supreme Self. *Upasana* literally means *sitting near God.* Upasana is approaching the chosen ideal or object of worship by meditating on it in accordance with the teachings of the Sastras and the Guru and dwelling steadily in the current of that one thought, like a thread of oil poured from one vessel to another (Tailadharavat). It consists of all those observances and practices, physical and mental, by which the aspirant or Jijnasu makes a steady progress in the realm of spirituality and eventually realises in himself—in his own heart—the presence of Godhead.

BENEFITS OF WORSHIP

Worship of the Lord purifies the heart, generates harmonious vibrations, steadies the mind, purifies and ennobles the emotions, harmonises the five sheaths, and eventually leads to communion, fellowship or God-realisation.

Upasana helps the devotee to sit near the Lord or to commune with Him. It fills the mind with Suddha Bhava and Prema or pure love for the Lord. It gradually transmutes man into a divine being.

Upasana changes the mental substance, destroys Rajas and Tamas and fills the mind with Sattva or purity. Upasana destroys Vasanas, Trishnas, egoism, lust, hatred, anger, etc. Upasana turns the mind inward and induces Antarmukha Vritti. It eventually brings the devotee face to face with the Lord, frees the devotee from the wheel of births and deaths, and confers on him immortality and freedom.

The mind becomes that on which it meditates in accordance with the analogy of the wasp and the caterpillar (Bhramara-Kitaka Nyaya). Just as you think, so you become. This is the immutable psychological law. There is a mysterious or inscrutable power (Achintya Sakti) in Upasana which makes the meditator and the meditated identical.

You will find in the Bhagavad-Gita: "But by devotion to Me alone, I may thus be perceived, O Arjuna; and known and seen in essence and entered, O Parantapa" (Ch. XI, 54).

Patanjali Maharshi emphasises in various places, in his Raja Yoga Sutras, on the importance of Upasana. For even a Raja Yogi, Upasana is necessary. He has his own Ishta Devata or guiding Deity—Yogesvara Krishna or Lord Siva. Self-surrender to God is an Anga (limb) of Raja Yoga and Kriya Yoga. Patanjali says: "One can enter into Samadhi through Upasana."

Of all those things which are conducive to spiritual advancement, Adhyatmic uplift and the acquisition of Dharma, Upasana is one which is not only indispensably requisite, but eminently beneficial to all classes and grades of people. It is easy too.

Eating, drinking, sleeping, fear, copulation, etc., are common in brutes and human beings, but that which makes one a real man or a God-man is the religious consciousness. He who leads a mere outward sensual life without doing any Upasana is an animal only, though he wears outwardly the form of a human being.

SAGUNA-UPASANA AND NIRGUNA-UPASANA

Upasana is of two kinds, viz., Pratika-Upasana and Ahamgraha-Upasana. *Pratika* means *a symbol.* Pratika-Upasana is Saguna-Upasana. Ahamgraha-Upasana is Nirguna-Upasana or meditation on the formless and attributeless Akshara or transcendental Brahman. Meditation on idols, Saligrama, pictures of Lord Rama, Lord Krishna, Lord Siva, Gayatri Devi, etc., is Pratika-Upasana. The blue expansive sky, all-pervading ether, all-pervading light of the sun, etc., are also *Pratikas* for abstract meditation. Saguna-Upasana is concrete meditation. Nirguna-Upasana is abstract meditation.

Hearing of the Lilas of the Lord, Kirtana or singing His Names, constant remembrance of the Lord (Smarana), service of His feet, offering flowers, prostration, prayer, chanting of Mantra, self-surrender, service of Bhagavatas, service of humanity and country with Narayana-Bhava, etc., constitute Saguna-Upasana.

Chanting of Om with Atma-Bhava, service of humanity and country with Atma-Bhava, mental Japa of Om with Atma or Brahma Bhava, meditation on Soham or Sivoham or on the Mahavakyas such as *Aham Brahma Asmi* or *Tat Tvam Asi* after sublating the illusory vehicles through 'Neti, Neti' doctrine, constitute Ahamgraha-Upasana or Nirguna-Upasana.

Saguna-Upasana is Bhakti Yoga or the Yoga of Devotion. Nirguna-Upasana is Jnana Yoga or the Yoga of Knowledge.

Worshippers of Saguna (the qualified) Brahman and of Nirguna (the unqualified) Brahman reach the same goal. But, the latter path is very hard, because the aspirant has to give up attachment to the body (Dehabhimana) from the very beginning of his spiritual practice. The Akshara or the Imperishable is very hard to reach for those who are attached to their bodies. Further, it is extremely difficult to fix the mind on the formless and attributeless Brahman. Contemplation on the Akshara or Nirguna Brahman demands a very sharp, one-pointed and subtle intellect.

THE BHAVAS IN BHAKTI YOGA

The Yoga of Bhakti or Devotion is much easier than Jnana Yoga or philosophical meditations. In Bhakti Yoga, the devotee establishes a near and dear relationship with the Lord. He cultivates slowly any one of the six Bhavas according to his temperament, taste and capacity.

Santa Bhava, Dasya Bhava, Sakhya Bhava, Vatsalya Bhava, Kanta Bhava and Madhurya Bhava are the six kinds of attributes of devotees or Bhavas towards God. The Bhavas differ in type and intensity of feeling. The different Bhavas are arranged in order of their intensity. Dhruva and Prahlada had the feeling of a child to its parents. This is Santa Bhava. In Dasya Bhava, the devotee behaves like a servant. His Lord is his master. Hanuman is an ideal servant of God. In Sakhya Bhava, there is a sense of equality. Arjuna and Kuchela had this Bhava. In Vatsalya Bhava, the devotee looks upon the Lord as his own child. Yasoda had this Bhava for Sri Krishna. Kausalya had this Bhava for Sri Rama. Kanta Bhava is the love of the wife towards the husband. Sita and Rukmini had this Bhava. The culmination is reached in Madhurya Bhava. The lover and the Beloved become one through the intensity of love. Radha and Mira had this type of love.

The last Bhava is the highest culmination of Bhakti. It is merging or absorption in the Lord. The devotee adores the Lord. He constantly remembers Him. He sings His Name (Kirtana). He speaks of His glories. He repeats His Name. He chants His Mantra. He prays and prostrates. He hears His Lilas. He does total, ungrudging, unconditional surrender, obtains His grace, holds communion with Him and gets absorbed in Him eventually.

In Madhurya Bhava, there is the closest relationship between the devotee and the Lord. There is no sensuality in Kanta and Madhurya Bhavas. There is no tinge of carnality in them. Passionate people cannot understand these two Bhavas as their minds are saturated with passion and lower sexual appetite. Sufistic saints also have the Bhava of lover and the Beloved, Madhurya Bhava. The Gita Govinda written by Jaya Deva is full of Madhurya Rasa. The language of love which the mystic uses cannot be comprehended by worldly persons. Only Gopis, Radha, Mira, Tukaram, Narada, Hafiz and similar other great devotees of the Lord can understand this language.

PUJA AND ISHTA-DEVATA

Puja is the common term for *ritual worship,* of which there are numerous synonyms such as Archana, Vandana, Bhajana, etc., though some of these stress certain aspects of it. The object of worship is the Ishta Devata or guiding Deity or the particular form of the Deity whom the devotee worships—Narayana or Vishnu as such, or His forms as Rama and Krishna in the case of Vaishnavas, Siva in His eight forms in the case of Saivas and Devi in the case of Saktas.

The devotee selects sometimes his Kuladeva or Kuladevi, family Deva or Devi, for his worship. Sometimes, the Devata is chosen for him by his Guru or spiritual preceptor. Sometimes, he himself chooses that Devata which most appeals to him. This form is his Ishta Devata.

An object is used in the outer Puja such as an image (Pratima), a picture, or an emblem such as Saligrama in the case of Vishnu worship or Linga in the case of worship of Siva.

Whilst all things may be the objects of worship, choice is naturally made of those objects which, by reason of their effect on the mind, are more fitted for it. An image or one of the useful emblems, is likely to raise in the mind of the worshipper the thought of a Devata. Saligrama stone induces easily concentration of mind. Everybody has got predilection for a symbol, emblem or image. Idol or Murti (Vigraha), sun, fire, water, Ganga, Saligrama and Linga are all symbols or Pratikas of God which help the aspirants to attain one-pointedness of mind and purity of heart. These are all personal inclinations in the worshipper due to his belief in their special efficacy for him. Psychologically, all this means that a particular mind finds that it works best in the direction desired by means of particular instruments or emblems or images.

The vast bulk of humanity are either of impure or of weak mind. Therefore, the object of worship must be pure for these people. The objects that are capable of exciting lust and dislike must be avoided. But, a higher, advanced Sadhaka who has a pure mind and who sees the divine presence everywhere and in everything, can worship any kind of object.

In Puja, an image or picture representing some divine form is used as the object of worship. The image is adored. An image, a Sila or Vigraha or Murti, represents the particular Lord who is invoked in it. A Linga represents Siva. It represents the secondless, formless Brahman. The Sruti says: *"Ekamevadvitiyam Brahma*—The Brahman is one alone, without a second."* There is no duality here. A Linga is shining and attractive to the eyes. It helps concentration. Ravana propitiated Siva and obtained boons by worshipping the Linga.

A Saligrama is an idol of Vishnu. Saligrama is the symbol of Vishnu. There are images of Sri Rama, Sri Krishna, Karttikeya, Ganesa, Hanuman, Dattatreya, Sita, Lakshmi, Parvati, Durga, Kali, Sarasvati, etc., according to the taste of the particular devotee.

The images of Vishnu and of His Avataras, and the images of Sakti and Siva, are the popular idols that are worshipped both in temples and in the houses. The idols in the temples of Tirupati, Pandarpur, Palani, Katirgama, etc., are powerful Deities. They are Pratyaksha Devatas. They grant boons to the devotees, cure their ailments and give Darsana. Wonderful Lilas are associated with these Deities. There is no polytheism in Hinduism. Siva, Vishnu, Brahma and Sakti are different aspects of one Lord.

God reveals Himself to His devotees in a variety of ways. He assumes the very form which the devotee has chosen for his worship. If you worship Him as Lord Hari with four hands, He will come to you as Hari. If you adore Him as Siva, He will give you Darsana as Siva. If you worship Him as Mother Durga or Kali, He will come to you as Durga or Kali. If you worship Him as Lord Rama, Lord Krishna or Lord Dattatreya, He will come to you as Rama, Krishna or Dattatreya. If you worship Him as Christ or Allah, He will come to you as Christ or Allah.

You may worship Lord Siva or Lord Hari, Lord Ganesa or Lord Subrahmanya or Lord Dattatreya, or anyone of the Avataras, Lord Rama or Lord Krishna, Sarasvati or Lakshmi, Gayatri or Kali, Durga or Chandi. All are aspects of one Isvara or Lord. Under whatever name and form, it is Isvara who is adored. Worship goes to the Indweller, the Lord in the form. It is ignorance to think that one form is superior to another. All forms are one and the same. Siva, Vishnu, Gayatri, Rama, Krishna, Devi and Brahman are one. All are adoring the same Isvara. The differences are only differences of names due to differences in the worshippers, but not in the object of adoration. It is only out of ignorance that different religionists and different sects fight and quarrel amongst themselves.

THE PHILOSOPHY AND SIGNIFICANCE OF IDOL-WORSHIP

THE IDOL—A PROP FOR THE SPIRITUAL NEOPHYTE

Idol is a support for the neophyte. It is a prop of his spiritual childhood. A form or image is necessary for worship in the beginning. It is an external symbol of God for worship. It is a reminder of God. The material image calls up the mental idea. Steadiness of mind is obtained by image-worship. The worshipper will have to associate the ideas of infinity, omnipotence, omniscience, purity, perfection, freedom, holiness, truth and omnipresence. It is not possible for all to fix the mind on the Absolute or the Infinite. A concrete form is necessary for the vast majority for practising concentration. To behold God everywhere and to practise the presence of God is not possible for the ordinary man. Idol-worship is the easiest form of worship for the modern man.

A symbol is absolutely indispensable for fixing the mind. The mind wants a prop to lean upon. It cannot have a conception of the Absolute in the initial stages. Without the help of some external aid, in the initial stages, the mind cannot be centralised. In the beginning, concentration or meditation is not possible without a symbol.

EVERYONE AN IDOL-WORSHIPPER

There is no reference to worship of idols in the Vedas. The Puranas and the Agamas give descriptions of idol-worship both in the houses and in the temples. Idol-worship is not peculiar to Hinduism. Christians worship the Cross. They have the image of the Cross in their mind. The Mohammedans keep the image of the Kaba stone when they kneel and do prayers. The people of the whole world, save a few Yogis and

Vedantins, are all worshippers of idols. They keep some image or the other in the mind.

The mental image also is a form of idol. The difference is not one of kind, but only one of degree. All worshippers, however intellectual they may be, generate a form in the mind and make the mind dwell on that image.

Everyone is an idol-worshipper. Pictures, drawings, etc., are only forms of Pratima or the idol. A gross mind needs a concrete symbol as a prop or Alambana and a subtle mind requires an abstract symbol. Even a Vedantin has the symbol OM for fixing the wandering mind. It is not only the pictures or images in stone and in wood, that are idols but dialectics and leaders also become idols. So, why condemn idolatry?

A MEDIUM FOR ESTABLISHING COMMUNION WITH GOD

Idols are not the idle fancies of sculptors, but shining channels through which the heart of the devotee is attracted to and flows towards God. Though the image is worshipped, the devotee feels the presence of the Lord in it and pours out his devotion unto it. It is the appalling ignorance of the modern sensual man that clouds his vision and prevents him from seeing Divinity in lovely and enchanting idols of His form. The very scientific advances of this century ought to convince you of the glory of idol-worship. How are the songsters and orators confined to a small box-like thing to be called a radio? It is a mere piece of a mechanical lifeless structure which breaks into a thousand pieces if you throw it away violently; and yet, if you know how to handle it, you can hear through it, the music that is being played several thousands of miles away and the discourse that is being delivered in the remotest part of the globe. Even as you can catch the sound-waves of people all over the world through the radio receiving set, it is possible to commune with the all-pervading Lord through the medium of an idol. The divinity of the all-pervading God is vibrant in every atom of creation. There is not a speck of space where He is not. Why do you then say that He is not in the idols?

There are others who would glibly say: "Oh, God is all-pervading formless Being. How can He be confined to this idol?" Are these people ever conscious of His omnipresence? Do they always see Him and Him alone in everything? No. It is their ego that prevents them from bowing to the idols of God and, with that motive, put this lame excuse forward!

Empty vessels only make much sound. A practical man who does meditation and worship, who is full of knowledge and real devotion, keeps always silence. He influences and teaches others through silence. He only knows whether a Murti is necessary in the beginning for concentration or not.

However intellectual one may be, he cannot concentrate without the help of some symbol in the beginning. An intellectual and learned person, on account of his pride and vanity only says: "I do not like a Murti. I do not wish to concentrate on a form." He cannot concentrate on the formless one. He thinks that people will laugh at him when they come to know that he is meditating on a form. He never does any meditation on the formless one. He simply talks and argues and poses. He wastes his life in unnecessary discussions only. An ounce of practice is better than tons of theories. Intellect is a hindrance in the vast majority of intellectual persons. They say that the existence of Brahman is a guess-work, Samadhi is a bluff of the mind and Self-realisation is an imagination of the Vedantins. Deluded souls! They are steeped in ignorance. They are carried away by their secular knowledge which is mere husk when compared to the Knowledge of the Self. There is no hope of salvation for such people. First, their wrong Samskaras should be flushed by good Samskaras through Satsanga. Then only they will realise their mistakes. May the Lord bestow on them clear understanding and thirsting for real knowledge!

Pratima, the idol, is a substitute or symbol. The image in a temple, though it is made of stone, wood or metal, is precious for a devotee as it bears the mark of his Lord, as it stands for something which he holds holy and eternal. A flag is only a small piece of painted cloth, but it stands for a soldier for something that he holds very dear. He is prepared to give up his life in defending his flag. Similarly, the image is very dear to a devotee. It speaks to him in its own language of devotion. Just as the flag arouses martial valour in the soldier, so also the image arouses devotion in the devotee. The Lord is super-imposed on the image and the image generates divine thoughts in the worshipper.

A piece of ordinary white paper or coloured paper has no value. You throw it away. But, if there is the stamp of the Government on the paper (currency note), you keep it safe in your money-purse or trunk. Even so, an ordinary piece of stone has no value for you. You throw it away. But, if you be-hold the stone Murti of Lord Krishna at Pandarpur or any other Murti in shrines, you bow your head with folded hands, because there is the stamp of the Lord on the stone. The devotee superimposes on the stone Murti his own Beloved Lord and all His attributes.

When you worship an image, you do not say: "This image has come from Jaipur. It was brought by Prabhu Singh. Its weight is 50 lbs. It is made of white marble. It has cost me Rs. 500/-." You superimpose all the attributes of the Lord on the image and pray: "O Antaryamin (Inner Ruler)! You are all-pervading. You are omnipotent, omniscient, all-merciful. You are the source for everything. You are self-existent. You are Sat-Chit-Ananda. You are eternal, unchanging. You are the Life of my life, Soul of my soul! Give me light and knowledge! Let me dwell in Thee for ever." When your devo-tion and meditation become intense and deep, you do not see the stone image. You behold the Lord only who is Chaitanya. Image-worship is very necessary for beginners.

AN INTEGRAL PART OF VIRAT

For a beginner, Pratima is an absolute necessity. By worshipping an idol, Isvara is pleased. The Pratima is made up of five elements. Five elements constitute the body of the Lord. The idol remains an idol, but the worship goes to the Lord.

If you shake hands with a man, he is highly pleased. You have touched only a small part of his body and yet he is happy. He smiles and welcomes you. Even so, the Lord is highly pleased when a small portion of His Virat (cosmic) body is worshipped. An idol is a part of the body of the Lord. The whole world is His body, Virat form. The devotion goes to the Lord. The worshipper superimposes on the image the Lord and all His attributes. He does Shodasopachara for the idol, the sixteen kinds of paying respects or service to the Lord. The presence of the Deity is invoked (Avahana). Then a seat (Asana) is offered. Then the feet are washed (Padya). Then offering of water is given (Arghya). Arghya is offering hospitality. Then comes bathing (Snana). Then the image is dressed (Vastra). Then comes the investiture with the sacred thread (Yajnopavita). Then sandal paste (Chandana) is offered. Then comes offering of flowers (Pushpa). They are the symbols of the heart-flowers of devotion, love and reverence. Then incense is burnt (Dhupa). Then a lamp is lit and waved before the Deity (Dipa). Then food is offered (Naivedya). Then betel is offered (Tambula). Then camphor is burnt (Nirajana). Then Svarnapushpa (gift of gold) is offered. In the end, the Deity is bidden farewell to (Visarjana). In these external forms of worship, the inner love finds expression. The wandering mind is fixed now in this form of worship. The aspirant gradually feels the nearness of the Lord. He attains purity of heart and slowly annihilates his egoism.

To the worshipper who believes the symbol, any kind of image is the body of the Lord under the form of stone, clay, brass, picture, Saligrama, etc. Such worship can never be idolatry. All matter is a manifestation of God. God is present in everything which exists. Everything is an object of worship, for all is a manifestation of God who is therein worshipped. The very act of worship implies that the object of worship is superior and conscious. This way of looking at things must be attained by the devotee. The untutored mind must be trained to view things in the above manner.

IDOL-WORSHIP DEVELOPS DEVOTION

Idol-worship makes concentration of man simpler and easier. You can bring before your mind's eye the great Lilas the Lord has played in His particular Avatara in which you view Him. This is one of the easiest modes of Self-realisation.

Just as the picture of a famous warrior evokes heroism in your heart, so also a look at the picture of God will elevate your mind to divine heights. Just as the child develops the maternal Bhava (mother-feeling) of the future caressing, nursing, protecting mother by playing with its imaginary toy-child made up of rags and suckling the child in an imaginary manner, so also the devotee develops the feeling of devotion by worshipping the Pratima and concentrating on it.

REGULAR WORSHIP UNVEILS THE DIVINITY IN THE IDOL

Regular worship (Puja) and other modes of demonstrating our inner feeling of recognition of Divinity in the idol unveil the Divinity latent in it. This is truly a wonder and a miracle. The picture comes to life. The idol speaks. It will answer your questions and solve your problems. The God in you has the power to awaken the latent Divinity in the idol. It is like a powerful lens that focuses the sun's rays on to a bundle of cotton. The lens is not fire and the cotton is not fire either nor can the sun's rays, by themselves, burn the cotton. When the three are brought together in a particular manner, fire is generated

120

and the cotton is burnt. Similar is the case with the idol, the Sadhaka and the all-pervading Divinity. Puja makes the idol shine with the divine resplendence. God is then enshrined in the idol. From here, He will protect you in a special manner. The idol will perform miracles. The place where it is installed is at once transformed into a temple, nay, a Vaikuntha or Kailasa in reality. Those who live in such a place are freed from miseries, from diseases, from failures and from Samsara itself. The awakened Divinity in the idol acts as a guardian angel blessing all, conferring the highest good on those who bow to it.

THE IMAGE, A MASS OF CHAITANYA

The idol is only a symbol of the Divine. A devotee does not behold therein a block of stone or a mass of metal. It is an emblem of God for him. He visualises the Indwelling Presence in the Murti or image. All the Saiva Nayanars, saints of South India, attained God-realisation through worship of the Linga, the image of Lord Siva. For a devotee, the image is a mass of Chaitanya or consciousness. He draws inspiration from the image. The image guides him. It talks to him. It assumes human form to help him in a variety of ways. The image of Lord Siva in the temple at Madurai in South India helped the fuel-cutter and the old woman. The image in the temple at Tirupati assumed human form and gave witness in the court to help His devotees. There are marvels and mysteries. Only the devotees understand these.

WHEN IDOLS BECAME ALIVE

For a Bhakta or a sage, there is no such thing as *Jada* or insentient matter. Everything is Vasudeva or Chaitanya—*Vasudevah Sarvam Iti.* The devotee beholds actually the Lord in the idol. Narsi Mehta was put to the test by a king. The king said: "O Narsi, if you are a sincere devotee of Lord Krishna, if as you say the idol is Lord Krishna Himself, let this idol move." According to the prayer of Narsi Mehta, the idol moved. The sacred bull Nandi before Siva's idol took the food offered by Tulsidas. The Murti played with Mira Bai. It was full of life and Chaitanya for her.

When Appayya Dikshitar went to the Tirupati temple in South India, the Vaishnavas refused him admission. The next morning they found the Vishnu Murti in the temple changed into Siva Murti. The Mahant was much astonished and startled, asked pardon and prayed to Appayya Dikshitar to change the Murti again into Vishnu Murti.

Kanaka Dasa was a great devotee of Lord Krishna in Udipi, in the district of South Kanara, in South India. He was not allowed to enter the temple on account of his low birth. Kanaka Dasa went round the temple and saw a small window at the back of the temple. He seated himself in front of the window. He was soon lost in singing songs in praise of Lord Krishna. Many people gathered round him. They were very much attracted by the sweet melody of his music and the depth of his devotion. Lord Krishna turned round to enable Kanaka Dasa to get His Darsana. The priests were struck with wonder. Even today, pilgrims are shown the window and the place where Kanaka Dasa sat and sang.

The Murti is the same as the Lord, for it is the vehicle of the expression of the Mantra-Chaitanya which is the Devata. The same attitude should the devotee have in regard to the Murti in the temple, which he would evince if the Lord would appear before him in person and speak to him in articulate sound.

VEDANTA AND IDOL-WORSHIP

A pseudo-Vedantin feels himself ashamed to bow or prostrate himself before an idol in the temple. He feels that his Advaita will evaporate if he prostrates himself. Study the lives of the reputed Tamil saints, Appar, Sundarar, Sambandhar, etc. They had the highest Advaitic realisation. They saw Lord Siva everywhere and yet they visited all temples of Siva, prostrated before the idol and sang hymns which are on record now. The sixty-three Nayanar saints practised *Charya* and *Kriya* only and attained God-realisation thereby. They swept the floor of the temple, collected flowers, made garlands for the Lord and put on lights in the temple. They were illiterate, but attained the highest realisation. They were practical Yogis and their hearts were saturated with pure devotion. They were embodiments of Karma Yoga. All practised the Yoga of Synthesis. The idol in the temple was all Chaitanya or Consciousness for them. It was not a mere block of stone.

Madhusudana Swami, who had Advaitic realisation, who beheld oneness of the Self and who had Advaitic Bhava, was intensely attached to the form of Lord Krishna with flute in His hands.

Tulasidas realised the all-pervading essence. He had cosmic consciousness. He communed with the all-pervading, formless Lord. And yet, his passion for Lord Rama with bow in His hand did not vanish. When he had been to Vrindavana and saw the Murti of Lord Krishna with flute in His hands, he said: "I will not bow my head to this form." At once Lord Krishna's form assumed the form of Lord Rama. Then only he bowed his head. Tukaram also had the same cosmic experience as that of Tulasidas. He sings in his Abhanga: "I see my Lord all-pervading, just as sweetness pervades the sugarcane;" and yet, he always speaks of his Lord Vitthala of Pandarpur with His hands on the hips. Mira also realised her identity with the all-pervading Krishna, and yet she was not tired of repeating again and again: "My Giridhara Nagar."

From the above facts, we can clearly infer that one can realise God through worship of Murti or idol; that the worship of the Lord in Saguna form is a great aid for the realisation of the Lord in His all-pervading, formless aspect also; that the worship of the Murti is very essential for the purpose of concentration and meditation in the beginning and that such a worship is not in anyway a hindrance to the attainment of

God-consciousness. Those who vehemently attack Murti Puja are groping in extreme darkness and ignorance, and they have no real knowledge of Puja and worship. They enter into unnecessary vain debates and discussion against Murti Puja to show that they are learned persons. They have not done any real Sadhana at all. They are persons who have made idle talking and tall talk their habit and profession. They have ruined themselves. They have unsettled the minds of countless persons and ruined them also. The whole world worships symbols and Murtis only in some form or the other. The mind is disciplined in the beginning by fixing it on a concrete object or symbol. When it is rendered steady and subtle, it can be fixed later on, on an abstract idea such as *'Aham Brahma Asmi.'* When one advances in meditation, the form melts in the formless and he becomes one with the formless essence. Image worship is not contrary to the view of Vedanta. It is rather a help.

Those who have not understood the philosophy and significance of idol-worship will have, now at least, a clear understanding of them. Their eyes will be opened now. Ignorant persons only, who have not studied Sastras and who have not associated with Yogis, sages and Bhaktas, raise unnecessary arguments against idol-worship.

FROM RITUALISTIC BHAKTI TO PARA-BHAKTI

Bhakti is of two kinds, viz., higher Bhakti or Para-Bhakti, and lower Bhakti or ritualistic Bhakti. Ritualistic worship is Vaidhi or Gauni Bhakti. It is formal Bhakti. Vaidhi Bhakti is the lower type of devotion depending on external aids. The mind becomes purer and purer. The aspirant gradually develops love for God through ritualistic worship. He who does ritualistic worship rings bells, adores a Pratika (symbol) or Pratima (image), does Puja with flowers and sandal paste, burns incense, waves light before the image, offers Naivedya or food for God, etc.

Mukhya Bhakti or Para Bhakti is advanced type of devotion. It is higher Bhakti. It transcends all convention. A devotee of this type knows no rule. He does not perform any external worship. He beholds his Lord everywhere, in every object. His heart is saturated with love for God. The whole world is Vrindavana for him. His state is ineffable. He attains the acme of bliss. He radiates love, purity and joy wherever he goes and inspires all who come in contact with him.

The aspirant who worships the idol in the beginning beholds the Lord everywhere and develops Para Bhakti. From Vaidhi Bhakti, he passes on to Ragatmika Bhakti or Prema Bhakti. He beholds the whole world as the Lord. The ideas of good and bad, right and wrong, etc., vanish. He sees the Lord in a rogue, dacoit, cobra, scorpion, ant, dog, tree, log of wood, block of stone, sun, moon, stars, fire, water, earth, etc. His vision or experience baffles description. Glory to such exalted Bhaktas who are veritable Gods on earth, who live to lift others from the quagmire of Samsara and save them from the clutches of death!

Hinduism leads the aspirants gradually from material images to mental images, from the diverse mental images to the one Personal God, and from the Personal God to the Impersonal Absolute or the Transcendental Nirguna Brahman.

THE GLORY OF HINDU PHILOSOPHY AND HINDU MODE OF WORSHIP

How sublime is Hindu philosophy and Hindu mode of worship! It does not stop or end with worship of idol alone. The Sadhaka is taken, step by step, to higher stages of devotion and Samadhi or communion, through the worship of the idol. Though he worships the idol, he has to keep before his mental eye the all-pervading Lord. He has to feel His presence in his heart and in all objects also. Even in worshipping a small idol, he has to repeat the Purusha-Sukta and to think of the Virat Purusha with countless heads, countless eyes, countless hands, etc., who extends beyond the universe, the Lord or the Atman who dwells in the hearts of all beings. The same man who burns incense, scented sticks and camphor before the idol says: "The sun does not shine there nor the moon nor the stars nor the lightning. How then could the little fire shine there? All shine after Him. His effulgence alone illumines the whole world." The ways and rules of worship—Puja Vidhi—and the secrets of worship that are described in the Hindu scriptures, are scientifically accurate and highly rational. It is only ignorant people who have not studied the scriptures and who have not associated with the devotees and great souls, who vilify worship of idols or Murtis.

Every other religion lays certain fixed dogmas and attempts to force people to follow them. It has only one kind of drug to treat several diseases. It gives only one kind of food for all and for all conditions. It places before the followers only one coat. It must fit Albert, Atkinson, Ahluwalia, Antony and Abdul Rehman. The Hindus know that the images, crosses and crescents are simply so many symbols to fix the mind in the beginning for developing concentration, so many concrete pegs to hang their spiritual ideas and convictions on. The symbol is not necessary for everyone. It is not compulsory in Hinduism. It is not needed for an advanced Yogi or sage. Symbol is like the slate which is useful for a boy of the first standard. Those who are not in need of it have no right to say that it is wrong. If they say that it is wrong, they only betray their ignorance.

CONCLUSION

There is nothing wrong in worshipping an idol in the beginning. You must superimpose God and His attributes on the idol. You must think of the Antar-Atman hidden in the idol. The aspirant gradually begins to feel that the Lord he worships is in the idol, in the hearts of all creatures and in all the names and forms of this universe. He begins to feel His presence everywhere.

Idol-worship is only the beginning of religion. Certainly it is not its end. The same Hindu scriptures, which prescribe idol-worship for beginners, speak of meditation on the Infinite or the Absolute and contemplation of the significance of *Tat Tvam Asi* Mahavakya, for advanced aspirants.

There are different stages of worship. The first is the worship of idols. The next is recitation of Mantras and offering of prayers. Mental worship is superior to worship with flowers. Meditation on the Absolute or the attributeless Nirguna Brahman is the best of all.

The supreme state is Self-realisation or Brahmasakshatkara. The second in rank is meditation. The Yogi practises Sadhana or unceasing meditation on the Supreme Self. The third is the worship of symbols. The fourth is the performance of rituals and pilgrimages to holy places. The Sastras and Gurus are like kind mothers. They take hold of the hands of the aspirants, take them step by step, stage by stage, till they are established in Nirvikalpa Samadhi or superconscious state. They prescribe gross forms of Sadhana or spiritual practices for the neophytes or beginners with gross mind and give lessons on abstract meditation for the advanced aspirants who are endowed with pure, subtle and sharp intellect.

Each marks a stage of progress. The human soul makes different kinds of attempts to grasp and realise the Infinite or the Absolute according to his strength or degree of evolution. He soars higher and higher, gathers more and more strength, and eventually merges himself in the Supreme and attains oneness or identity.

Glory to the Hindu Rishis and the Hindu scriptures who take the aspirants from the lower to the higher form of worship, stage by stage, step by step, and ultimately help them to rest in the attributeless, all-pervading, formless, timeless, spaceless Brahman or the infinite and unconditioned Brahman of the Upanishads.

Beloved children of the Lord! Shed your ignorant disbelief this moment. Enshrine supreme, unshakable, living faith in your heart this very moment. Recall to your mind the glorious examples of Sri Mira, Sri Ramakrishna Paramahamsa and the South Indian Alvars and Nayanars. They believed and they reaped the rich spiritual harvests. You too can enjoy great peace, happiness and prosperity here, and attain Him here and now, if you have this faith in idol-worship.

Though you may perform external worship at regular intervals, let the internal worship of the Lord in your heart be constant and unbroken. Here worship attains completeness. Life is divine worship. May you realise the significance of the universal worship of the *Virat* in daily life, and performing it, attain the *summum bonum* of life. May the Lord bless you all.

ALL ABOUT HINDUISM

CHAPTER 8

HINDU YOGA

THE FOUR PATHS

The four main spiritual paths for God-realisation are Karma Yoga, Bhakti Yoga, Raja Yoga and Jnana Yoga. Karma Yoga is suitable for a man of active temperament, Bhakti Yoga for a man of devotional temperament, Raja Yoga for a man of mystic temperament, and Jnana Yoga for a man of rational and philosophical temperament, or a man of enquiry.

Mantra Yoga, Laya Yoga or Kundalini Yoga, Lambika Yoga and Hatha Yoga, are other Yogas. *Yoga, really, means union with God.* The practice of Yoga leads to communion with the Lord. Whatever may be the starting point, the end reached is the same.

Karma Yoga is the way of selfless service. The selfless worker is called the Karma-Yogin. Bhakti Yoga is the path of exclusive devotion to the Lord. He who seeks union through love or devotion is called the Bhakti-Yogin. Raja Yoga is the way of self-restraint. He who seeks to have union with the Lord through mysticism is called the Raja-Yogin. Jnana Yoga is the path of wisdom. He who seeks to unite himself with the Supreme Self through philosophy and enquiry is called the Jnana-Yogin.

KARMA YOGA
(Duty for Duty's Sake)

Karma Yoga is the path of action. It is the path of disinterested service. It is the way that leads to the attainment of God through selfless work. It is the Yoga of renunciation of the fruits of actions.

Karma Yoga teaches us how to work for work's sake—unattached—and how to utilise to the best advantage the greater part of our energies. *'Duty for Duty's Sake'* is the motto of a Karma-Yogin. Work is worship for the practitioners of Karma Yoga. Every work is turned into an offering unto the Lord. The Karma Yogin is not bound by the Karmas, as he consecrates the fruits of his actions to the Lord. *Yogah Karmasu Kausalam*—Yoga is skill in action.

Generally, a work brings as its effect or fruit either pleasure or pain. Each work adds a link to our bondage of Samsara and brings repeated births. This is the inexorable Law of Karma. But, through the practice of Karma Yoga, the effects of Karmas can be wiped out. Karma becomes barren. The same work, when done with the right mental attitude, right spirit and right will through Yoga, without attachment and expectation of fruits, without the idea of agency or doership, with a mind balanced in success and failure *(Samatvam Yoga Uchyate),* does not add a link to our bondage. On the contrary, it purifies our heart and helps us to attain salvation through the descent of divine light or dawn of wisdom.

A rigid moral discipline and control of senses are indispensable for the practice of Karma Yoga.

Brahmacharya is, indeed, essential. Cultivation of virtues such as tolerance, adaptability, sympathy, mercy, equal vision, balance of mind, cosmic love, patience, perseverance, humility, generosity, nobility, self-restraint, control of anger, non-violence, truthfulness, moderation in eating, drinking and sleeping, simple living and endurance, is very necessary.

Every man should do his duties in accordance with his own Varna and Asrama, caste and station as well as stage in life. There is no benefit in abandoning one's own work in preference to another's work.

Some people think that Karma Yoga is an inferior type of Yoga. They think that carrying water, cleansing plates, serving food to the poor and sweeping the floor are menial works. This is a sad mistake. They have not understood the technique and glory of Karma Yoga. Lord Krishna, the Lord of the three worlds, acted the part of charioteer of Arjuna. He also acted the part of a cowherd.

BHAKTI YOGA
(Love for Love's Sake)

Bhakti is intense love of God. Bhakti Yoga is the path of devotion. It appeals to the majority of mankind. *'Love for Love's Sake'* is the motto or formula of a Bhakti-Yogin. God is an embodiment of love. You will have to attain Him by loving Him. God can be realised only by means of a love as ardent and all-absorbing as the conjugal passion. Love for God must be gradually cultivated.

He who loves God has neither wants nor sorrows. He does not hate any being or object. He never takes delight in sensual objects. He includes everyone in the warm embrace of his love.

Kama (worldly desires) and *Trishna* (cravings) are enemies of devotion. So long as there is any trace of desire in your mind for sensual objects, you cannot have an intense longing for God.

Atma-Nivedana is total, ungrudging, absolute self-surrender to the Lord. Atma-Nivedana is the highest rung in the ladder of Nava-vidha Bhakti, or nine modes of devotion. Atma-Nivedana is Prapatti or Saranagati. The devotee becomes one with the Lord through Prapatti. He obtains the divine grace or Prasada.

Love of God and the rapturous ecstasy enjoyed by fellowship with God, cannot be adequately described in words. It is as if a dumb man, who had tasted some palatable food, could not speak about it. It could be revealed only to the chosen few. He who has once experienced love will see that alone, hear that alone and speak of that alone, because he constantly thinks of that alone.

Bhakti is one of the chief spiritual sciences. He is wealthy indeed, who has love for the Lord. There is no sorrow other than lack of devotion to the Lord. There is no right course except love of the devotee for the Lord. The Name, qualities and Lilas of the Lord are the chief things to be remembered. The lotus-feet of the Lord are the chief objects of meditation. The devotee drinks the nectar of Prema or divine love.

There are no distinctions of caste, creed, family, colour or race among the devotees. God does not look into these things. He looks to the purity of heart of the devotees. Anyone can become a devotee of the Lord. Nanda, an untouchable; Rai Das, a cobbler; Kannappa, a hunter; Sena, a barber; Kabir, a Moslem weaver; and Sabari, a Bhilini were all devotees of the Lord, and were great saints. Kannappa, an illiterate barbarian who poured water from his mouth on the Linga and who offered swine's flesh, became the best among the Bhaktas. The Vaishnava Alvars and the Saiva Nayanars, of South India, were from different classes of society.

RAJA YOGA

(Discipline of the Mind)

Raja Yoga is the path that leads to union with the Lord through self-restraint and control of mind. Raja Yoga teaches how to control the senses and the mental Vrittis or thought-waves that arise from the mind, how to develop concentration and how to commune with God. There is physical discipline in Hatha Yoga, whereas in Raja Yoga, there is discipline of the mind.

THE YOGA OF EIGHT LIMBS

Yama, Niyama, Asana, Pranayama, Pratyahara, Dharana, Dhyana and Samadhi are the eight limbs of Raja Yoga.

Yama and Niyama constitute the ethical discipline which purifies the heart. Yama consists of Ahimsa (non-injury), Satya (truthfulness), Brahmacharya (continence), Asteya (non-stealing) and Aparigraha (non-receiving of gifts conducive to luxury). All virtues are rooted in Ahimsa.

Niyama is observance. It comprises Saucha (internal and external purity), Santosha (contentment), Tapas (austerity), Svadhyaya (study of scriptures and repetition of Mantra) and Isvara-pranidhana (self-surrender to God). He who is established in Yama and Niyama will have quick progress in the practice of Yoga.

Asana, Pranayama and Pratyahara are preliminary accessories to Yoga. Asana is steady pose. Pranayama is regulation of breath. This produces serenity and steadiness of mind and good health. Pratyahara is abstraction or withdrawal of the senses from their objects. You must practise Pratyahara. Then only you can look within and can have introversion.

Dharana is concentration of the mind on any object, or internal Chakra, or Ishta-Devata or tutelary Deity. Then comes Dhyana, meditation or an unceasing flow of ideas connected with one object. This leads to Samadhi, where the meditator and the meditated become one. All the Vrittis or waves of the mind subside. The mind ceases functioning. All the Samskaras, impressions and Vasanas (tendencies and subtle desires) are burnt *in toto*. The Yogi is freed from births and deaths. He attains Kaivalya or final Liberation (Absolute Independence).

CONCENTRATION—THE KEY TO SUCCESS

How powerful is the searchlight! When the sun's rays are concentrated through a lens, they can burn cotton. Even so, when the dissipated rays of the mind are collected, you can work wonders. You can know all the secrets of nature through the powerful searchlight of mind.

A scientist sits in his laboratory, concentrates all the powers of his mind and brings them into one focus and throws them on the objects of his research and investigation. He gets all knowledge about the elements, etc. The whole hidden knowledge of nature is revealed unto him like the Amalaka fruit in the palm of his hand. The astronomer does the same thing. He concentrates on the stars and planets through his telescope and attains knowledge of the stars. Radio, wireless telegraphy, television, gramophone, telephone, steam engine, etc., are all things invented through deep concentration.

Without concentration, you cannot have success in any walk of life or spiritual pursuit. A cook can prepare things efficiently if he has concentration. If there is no concentration, he spoils the preparations. A surgeon in the operation theatre needs perfect concentration. The captain of a steamer must possess a great deal of concentration. A tailor, a professor, a barrister, a student—all must possess concentration. Then only they can have success in their profession. All great souls, all master-minds who have done great work in this world, had perfect concentration.

In a worldly man, the rays of the mind are scattered in various directions. His mind is jumping like a monkey. It is ever restless He thinks of money, wife, children, property, houses, etc. His mind is ever engaged in earning money and possessing objects of his desires. He has not a bit of concentration. He cannot look within and introspect. His mind is full of outgoing tendencies.

The Yogi concentrates on the Chakras, mind, sun, stars, elements, etc., and attain superhuman knowledge. He obtains mastery over the elements. The power of concentration is the only key to open the treasure-house of knowledge.

Concentration cannot come within a week or a month. It takes some time. Regularity in the practice of concentration is of paramount importance. Brahmacharya, a cool and congenial place, company of saints and Sattvic diet are auxiliaries in concentration.

Concentration and meditation lead to Samadhi or Superconscious Experience, which has several stages of ascent, as attended or not attended with deliberation (Vitarka), analysis (Vichara), joy (Ananda) and self-awareness (Asmita). Kaivalya, or Supreme Independence, is, thus, attained.

THE OBSTACLE OF SIDDHIS OR SUPERNATURAL POWERS

Siddhis or supernatural powers manifest themselves when the Yogi advances in his Yogic practices. These Siddhis such as clairvoyance, clairaudience, etc., are all obstacles in his path. He should shun them ruthlessly and march forward direct to his goal, viz., Asamprajnata or Nirvikalpa Samadhi. Real spirituality has nothing to do with these powers, which are by-products of concentration. He who runs after these Siddhis is a big worldly man or big householder. He may have a downfall, if he is not cautious.

JNANA YOGA

(The Path of Spiritual Insight)

Jnana Yoga is the path of knowledge. Moksha is attained through Knowledge of Brahman. Release is achieved through realisation of the identity of the individual soul with the Supreme Soul or Brahman. The cause for bondage and suffering is Avidya or ignorance. The little Jiva foolishly imagines, on account of ignorance, that he is separate from Brahman. Avidya acts as a veil or screen and prevents the Jiva from knowing his real, divine nature. Knowledge of Brahman or Brahma-Jnana removes this veil and makes the Jiva rest in his own Sat-Chit-Ananda Svarupa (Essential Nature as Existence-Consciousness-Bliss Absolute).

SPIRITUAL INSIGHT AND INTELLECTUAL KNOWLEDGE

The Jnana-Yogin realises that Brahman is the Life of his life, the Soul of his soul. He feels and knows that God is his own Self. He realises that he is one with the Eternal through spiritual insight or intuition, Aparoksha Anubhuti or divine perception, but not through mere study of books or dogmas or theories. Religion is realisation for him now. It is not mere talk. He plunges himself in the deep recesses of his heart through constant and intense meditation—Nididhyasana—and gets the wonderful pearl of Atman, a wonderful treasure much more valuable than all the wealth of the world.

Jnana is not mere intellectual knowledge. It is not hearing or acknowledging. It is not mere intellectual assent. It is direct realisation of oneness or unity with the Supreme Being. It is Para Vidya. Intellectual conviction alone will not lead you to Brahma-Jnana (Knowledge of the Absolute).

The student of Jnana Yoga first equips himself with four means, viz., discrimination (Viveka), dispassion (Vairagya), the sixfold virtues (Shat-Sampat)—viz., tranquillity (Sama), restraint (Dama), satiety or renunciation (Uparati), endurance (Titiksha), faith (Sraddha) and concentration (Samadhana)—and strong yearning for liberation (Mumukshutva). Then he hears the scriptures by sitting at the lotus-feet of a Guru, who is not only learned in the sacred scriptures (Srotriya), but is also one who is himself well-established in Brahman (Brahma-Nishtha). Afterwards, the student practises reflection, which completely dispels all doubts. Then he practises deep meditation on Brahman and attains Brahma-Sakshatkara. He becomes a Jivanmukta or liberated sage. He is released even while he is in this body.

There are seven stages of Jnana or Knowledge: viz., Aspiration for the Right (Subhechha), Philosophical enquiry (Vicharana), Subtlety of mind (Tanumanasi), Attainment of Light (Sattvapatti), Inner Detachment (Asamsakti), Spiritual Vision (Padarthabhavana) and Supreme Freedom (Turiya).

THE ANALOGY OF THE TWO BIRDS

There are two birds on the same tree. One is perched at

the top and the other below. The bird which is sitting on the top is perfectly serene, silent and majestic at all times. It is ever blissful. The other bird, which is perching on the lower branches, eats the sweet and bitter fruits by turns. It dances in joy sometimes. It is miserable at other times. It rejoices now and weeps after some time. Sometimes it tastes an extremely bitter fruit and gets disgusted. It looks up and beholds the other wonderful bird with golden plumage which is ever blissful. It also wishes to become like the bird with golden plumage, but soon forgets everything. Again it begins to eat the sweet and bitter fruits. It eats another fruit that is exceedingly bitter and feels very miserable. It again tries to become like the upper bird. Gradually, it abandons eating the fruits, and becomes serene and blissful like the upper bird. The upper bird is God or Brahman. The lower bird is Jiva or the individual soul who reaps the fruits of his Karmas, viz., pleasure and pain. He gets knocks and blows in the battle of life. He rises up and again falls down as the senses drag him down. Gradually he develops Vairagya (dispassion) and discrimination, turns his mind towards God, practises meditation, attains Self-realisation and enjoys the eternal bliss of Brahman.

THE YOGA OF SYNTHESIS

Some maintain that the practice of Karma Yoga alone is the only means for salvation. Some others hold that devotion to the Lord is the only way to release. Some believe that the path of wisdom is the sole way to attain the final beatitude. There are still others who hold that all the three paths are equally efficacious to bring about perfection and freedom.

Man is a strange, complex mixture of will, feeling and thought. He wills to possess the objects of his desires. He has emotion and so he feels. He has reason and so he thinks and ratiocinates. In some, the emotional element may preponderate, while in some others, the rational element may dominate. Just as will, feeling and thought are not distinct and separate, so also work, devotion and knowledge are not exclusive of one another.

The Yoga of Synthesis is the most suitable and potent form of Sadhana. In the mind there are three defects, viz., *Mala* or impurity, *Vikshepa* or tossing and *Avarana* or veil. The impurity should be removed by the practice of Karma Yoga. The tossing should be removed by worship or *Upasana*. The veil should be torn down by the practice of Jnana Yoga. Then only is Self-realisation possible. If you want to see your face clearly in a mirror, you must remove the dirt in the mirror, keep it steady and remove the covering also. You can see your face clearly in the bottom of the lake only if the turbidity is removed, if the water that is agitated by the wind is rendered still, and if the moss that is lying on the surface is removed. So too is the case with Self-realisation.

The Yoga of Synthesis alone will bring about integral development. The Yoga of Synthesis alone will develop the head, heart and hand and lead one to perfection. To become harmoniously balanced in all directions is the ideal of religion. This can be achieved by the practice of the Yoga of Synthesis.

To behold the one Universal Self in all beings is Jnana, wisdom; to love this Self is Bhakti, devotion; and to serve this Self is Karma, action. When the Jnana-Yogin attains wisdom, he is endowed with devotion and selfless activity. Karma Yoga is for him a spontaneous expression of his spiritual nature, as he sees the one Self in all. When the devotee attains perfection in devotion, he is possessed of wisdom and activity. For him also, Karma Yoga is a spontaneous expression of his divine nature, as he beholds the one Lord everywhere. The Karma-Yogin attains wisdom and devotion when his actions are wholly selfless. The three paths are in fact one in which the three different temperaments emphasise one or the other of its inseparable constituents. Yoga supplies the method by which the Self can be seen, loved and served.

CHAPTER 9

HINDU THEOLOGY

THEOLOGICAL CLASSIFICATIONS

HINDUISM—A FELLOWSHIP OF FAITHS AND A FEDERATION OF PHILOSOPHIES

Hindu theology is mainly the study and doctrine of the worship and adoration of six forms of the Godhead as Ganesa, Devi (Durga, Lakshmi, Sarasvati), Siva, Vishnu, Surya and Skanda. These aspects of divine worship are known as *Shanmatas,* or the sixfold religious practice of the Hindus.

Hinduism is extremely catholic, liberal, tolerant and elastic. This is the wonderful feature of Hinduism. A foreigner is struck with astonishment when he hears about the diverse sects and creeds of Hinduism. But these varieties are really an ornament to Hinduism. They are not certainly its defects. There are various types of minds and temperaments. So there should be various faiths also. This is but natural. This is the cardinal tenet of Hinduism. There is room in Hinduism for all types of souls—from the highest to the lowest—for their growth and evolution.

The term *Hinduism* is most elastic. It includes a number of sects and cults, allied, but different in many important points. Hinduism has, within its fold, various schools of Vedanta; Vaishnavism, Saivism, Saktism, etc. It has various cults and creeds. It is more a League of Religions than a single religion with a definite creed. It accommodates all types of men. It prescribes spiritual food for everybody, according to his qualification and growth. This is the beauty of this magnanimous religion. This is the glory of Hinduism. Hence there is no conflict among the various cults and creeds. The Rig-Veda declares: "Truth is one; sages call it by various names—

Ekam Sat Viprah Bahudha Vadanti." The Upanishads declare that all the paths lead to the same goal, just as cows of variegated colours yield the same white milk. The Lord Krishna says in the Gita: "Howsoever men approach Me, even so do I welcome them, for the path men take from every side is Mine." All diversities are organised and united in the body of Hinduism.

It is rather difficult to answer the question: "What is Hinduism?" It is a fellowship of faiths. It is also a federation of philosophies. It provides food for reflection for the different types of thinkers and philosophers all over the world. All sorts of philosophy are necessary. What appeals to one may not appeal to another, and what is easy for one may be difficult for another. Hence the need for different standpoints. All philosophies of Hinduism are points of view. They are true in their own way. They take the aspirant step by step, stage by stage, till he reaches the acme or the pinnacle of spiritual glory.

Sanatana-Dharmists, Arya-Samajists, Deva-Samajists, Jainas, Bauddhas, Sikhs and Brahma-Samajists are all Hindus only, for they rose from Hinduism, and emphasised one or more of its aspects.

The Hindus are divided into three great classes, viz., Vaishnavas who worship the Lord as Vishnu; Saivas who worship the Lord as Siva; and Saktas who adore Devi or the Mother aspect of the Lord. In addition, there are the Sauras, who worship the Sun-God; Ganapatyas who worship Ganesa as supreme; and Kaumaras who worship Skanda as the Godhead.

THE VAISHNAVAS

SRI SAMPRADAYINS

The Vaishnavas are usually distinguished into four principal Sampradayas or sects. Of these, the most ancient is the Sri Sampradaya founded by Ramanujā Acharya. The followers of

Ramanuja adore Vishnu and Lakshmi, and their incarnations. They are called Ramanujas or Sri Sampradayins or Sri Vaishnavas. They all repeat the Ashtakshara Mantra: *'Om Namo Narayanaya.'* They put on two white vertical lines and a central red line on the forehead.

Vedanta Desika, a follower of Ramanuja, introduced some reform in the Vaishnava faith. This gave rise to the formation of two parties of Ramanujas, one called the Northern School (Vadagalai) and the other the Southern School (Tengalai). The Tengalais regard Prapatti or self-surrender as the only way to salvation. The Vadagalais think that it is only one of the ways. According to them, the Bhakta or devotee is like the young one of a monkey which has to exert itself and cling to its mother (Markata-Nyaya or Monkey Theory); whereas, according to the Southern School, the Bhakta or devotee is like the kitten which is carried about by the cat without any effort on its own part (Marjala-Nyaya or Cat-hold Theory). The Northern School accept the Sanskrit texts, the Vedas. The Southerners have compiled a Veda of their own called *'Nalayira Prabandha'* or 'Four Thousand Sacred Verses', in Tamil, and hold it to be older than the Sanskrit Vedas. Really, their four thousand verses are based on the Upanishad portion of the Vedas. In all their worship, they repeat sections from their Tamil verses.

The Vadagalais regard Lakshmi as the consort of Vishnu, Herself infinite, uncreated and equally to be adored as a means (Upaya) for release. The Tengalais regard Lakshmi as a created female being, though divine. According to them, she acts as a mediator or minister (Purushakara), and not as an equal channel of release.

The two sects have different frontal marks. The Vadagalais make a simple white line curved like the letter U to represent the sole of the right foot of Lord Vishnu, the source of the Ganga. They add a central red mark as a symbol of Lakshmi.

The Tengalais make a white mark like the letter Y which represents both the feet of Lord Vishnu. They draw a white line half down the nose.

Both the sects brand the emblems of Vishnu—the discus and the conch—on their breasts, shoulders and arms.

The Tengalais prohibit their widows from shaving the head.

The usual surnames of the Ramanuja Brahmins are Aiyangar, Acharya, Charlu and Acharlu.

RAMANANDIS

The followers of Ramananda are the Ramanandis. They are well-known in upper Hindusthan. They are a branch of the Ramanuja sect. They offer their worship to Lord Rama, Sita, Lakshmana and Hanuman. Ramananda was a disciple of Ramanuja. He flourished at Varanasi about the beginning of the fourteenth century. His followers are numerous in the Ganga valley of India. Their favourite work is the *'Bhakti-Mala'*. Their sectarian marks are like those of the Ramanujas. The Vairagis are the ascetics among the Ramanandis.

VALLABHACHARINS OR KRISHNA SAMPRADAYINS

The Vallabhacharins form a very important sect in Bombay, Gujarat and the Central India. Their founder was born in the forest Champaranya in 1479. He is regarded as an incarnation of Krishna. The Vallabhacharins worship Krishna, as Bala-Gopala. Their idol is one representing Krishna in his childhood till his twelfth year. The Gosains or teachers are family men. The eight daily ceremonials for God in the temples are Mangala, Sringara, Gvala, Raja Bhoga, Utthapana, Bhoga, Sandhya and Sayana. All these represent various forms of adoration of God.

The mark on the forehead consists of two red perpendicular lines meeting in a semicircle at the root of the nose and having a round spot of red between them. The necklace and rosary are made of the stalk of the Tulasi (holy Basil).

The great authority of the sect is the Srimad-Bhagavata as explained in the Subodhini, the commentary thereon of Vallabhacharya. The members of the sect should visit Sri Nathdvara, a holy shrine, at least once in their lives.

THE CHAITANYAS

This sect is prominent in Bengal and Orissa. The founder, Chaitanya Mahaprabhu or Lord Gouranga, was born in 1485. He was regarded as an incarnation of Lord Krishna. He took Sannyasa at the age of twenty-four. He went to Jagannath where he taught Vaishnava doctrines.

The Chaitanyas worship Lord Krishna as the Supreme Being. All castes are admissible into the sect. The devotees constantly repeat the Name of Lord Krishna.

Chaitanya's Charitamirita by Krishna Das is a voluminous work. It contains anecdotes of Chaitanya and his principal disciples and the expositions of the doctrines of this sect. It is written in Bengali.

The Vaishnavas of this sect wear two white perpendicular streaks of sandal or Gopichandana (a kind of sacred earth) down the forehead uniting at the root of the nose and continuing to near the tip. They wear a close necklace of small Tulasi beads of three strings.

THE NIMBARKAS

The founder of this sect is Nimbarka or Nimbaditya. He was originally named Bhaskara Acharya. He is regarded as an incarnation of the Sun-God (Surya). The followers worship Krishna and Radha conjointly. Their chief scripture is the Srimad-Bhagavata Purana.

The followers have two perpendicular yellowish lines made by Gopichandana earth drawn from the root of the hair to the commencement of each eyebrow and there meeting in a curve. This represents the footprint of the Lord Vishnu.

The Nimbarkas or Nimavats are scattered throughout the

whole of upper India. They are very numerous around Mathura. They are also the most numerous of the Vaishnava sects in Bengal.

THE MADHVAS

The Madhvas are Vaishnavas. They are known as Brahma Sampradayins. The founder of the sect is Madhvacharya, otherwise called Ananda Tirtha and Purna-Prajna. He was born in 1200. He was a great opponent of Sankaracharya's Advaita system of philosophy. He is regarded as an incarnation of Vayu or the Wind-God. He erected and consecrated at Udipi the image of the Lord Krishna.

The Gurus of the Madhva sect are Brahmins and Sannyasins. The followers bear the impress of the symbols of Vishnu upon their breasts and shoulders. They are stamped with a hot iron. Their frontal mark consists of two perpendicular lines made with Gopichandana and joined at the root of the nose. They make straight black line, with a charcoal from incense offered to Krishna, which terminates in a round mark made with turmeric.

The Madhvas are divided into two classes called the Vyasakutas and the Dasakutas. They are found in Karnataka.

Truthfulness, study of scriptures, generosity, kindness, faith and freedom from envy form the moral code of Madhvas. They give the Lord's Names to their children (Namakarana), and mark the body with His symbols (Ankana). They practise virtue in thought, word and deed (Bhajana).

RADHA VALLABHIS

Radha Vallabhis worship Krishna as Radha-Vallabha, the Lord or Lover of Radha. Harivans was the founder of this sect. Seva Sakhi Vani gives a detailed description of the notion of this sect and more of their traditions and observances.

Charana Dasis, Dadu Panthis, Hari Chandis, Kabir Panthis,

Khakis, Maluk Dasis, Mira Bais, Madhavis, Rayi Dasis, Senais, Sakhi Bhavas, Sadma Panthis, are all Vaishnava sects.

THE SAIVAS

SMARTA BRAHMINS OF THE SOUTH

The Saiva Brahmins of the Tamil Nadu have their title *Aiyer.* They are called Smartas. They all wear three horizontal lines of Bhasma or Vibhuti (holy ash) on their forehead. They all worship Lord Siva. The different sects are:

1. *Vadamas:* Vada Desa Vadamas, Chola Desa Vadamas and Inji Vadamas; 2. *Brihatcharanam:* Mazhainattu Brihatcharanam, Pazhamaneri Brihatcharanam, Milaghu Brihatcharanam and Kandramanikka Brihatcharanam; 3. *Vathimars;* 4. *Ashtasahasram;* 5. *Choliyas:* Otherwise called Pandimars and inhabitants of Tiruchendur; and 6. *Gurukkal:* A sub-sect of Vadamas not recognised as one amongst them and whose duties are to worship at temples. They are also known by the name of Pattar in southern districts of Madras. These are different from Archaks. Archaks belong to any of the above sub-sects and inter-marry with persons of other professions, but not Gurukkal or Pattar. While Gurukkal is used only for Saivites, Pattar and Archak are used for Vaishnavites also.

SAIVA BRAHMINS OF MALABAR

1. Nambudiri, 2. Muse and 3. Embrantiri.

SAIVA BRAHMINS OF BENGAL

1. Chakravarti, 2. Chunder, 3. Roy, 4. Ganguli, 5. Choudhury, 6. Bisvas, 7. Bagchi, 8. Majumdar and 9. Bhattacharji.

SAIVA BRAHMINS OF KARNATAKA

1. Smarta, 2. Haviga, 3. Kota, 4. Shivalli, 5. Tantri, 6. Kardi and 7. Padya.

TELUGU SMARTAS

1. Murukinadu, 2. Velanadu, 3. Karanakammalu, 4. Puduru

Dravidis, 5. Telahanyam, 6. Konasimadravidi and 7. Aruvela Niyogis.

LINGAYATS

They are called Vira Saivas. They are found in Mysore and Karnataka. They wear on their neck a Linga of the Lord Siva put in a small silver box.

OTHER SAIVA SECTS

Akas Mukhis, Gudaras, Jangamas, Karalingis, Nakhis, Rukharas, Sukharas, Urdhabahus, Ukkaras are all Saiva sects.

THE SAKTAS

The Saktas are worshippers of Devi, the Universal Mother. Dakshinis, Vamis, Kancheliyas, Kararis are all Sakta sects.

MISCELLANEOUS

The Sauras adore the Sun, the Ganapatyas adore Ganesa, and the Kaumaras adore Skanda.

The non-Brahmins of South India are Naidu, Kamma Naidu, Chetty, Mudaliar, Gounder, Pillai, Nair, Nayanar and Reddy.

Nanak Shahis of seven classes (viz., Udasis, Ganjbakshis, Ramrayis, Sutra Shahis, Govinda Sinhis, Nirmalas, Nagas), Baba Lalis, Prana Nathis, Sadhus, Satnamis, Siva Narayanis are other miscellaneous sects.

THE ARYA SAMAJISTS AND THE BRAHMA SAMAJISTS

The founder of the Arya Samaj was Swami Dayananda Saras-vati, who was born in Kathiawar in 1824. This Samaj is more of a social institution, with a religious background. It has Gurukulas, schools and Pathasalas. The Suddhi Sabha is a proselytising branch of the Arya Samaj.

The Brahma Samaj was founded originally by Raja Ram Mohan Roy, early in the nineteenth century. The Brahma Samajists do not perform idol-worship. Keshab Chandra Sen introduced some changes in the year 1860. There are now two branches within the Samaj, viz., Adi Brahma Samaj which holds to the tenets laid down by Raja Ram Mohan Roy and the Sadharana Brahma Samaj which is a little modern and which follows Keshab Chandra Sen more closely. The Samaj has followers in Bengal.

SADHUS AND SANNYASINS

Salutations unto the ancient Rishis, seers, saints, Paramahamsa Sannyasins and Sadhus, who are the repositories of divine knowledge and wisdom and who guide the destiny of the world in the past, present and future.

Every religion has a band of anchorites who lead the life of seclusion and meditation. There are Bhikkus in Buddhism, Fakirs in Mohammendanism, Sufistic Fakirs in Sufism, and Fathers and Reverends in Christianity. The glory of a religion will be lost absolutely if you remove these hermits or Sannyasins or those who lead a life of renunciation and divine contemplation. It is these people who maintain or preserve the religions of the world. It is these people who give solace to the householders when they are in trouble and distress. They are the messengers of the Atman-knowledge and heavenly peace. They are the harbingers of divine wisdom and peace. They are the disseminators of Adhyatmic science and Upanishadic revelations. They heal the sick, comfort the forlorn and nurse the bedridden. They bring hope to the hopeless, joy to the depressed, strength to the weak and courage to the timid, by imparting the knowledge of the Vedanta and the significance of the *'Tat Tvam Asi'* Mahavakya.

DASANAMA SANNYASINS

Sanaka, Sanandana, Sanat-Kumara and Sanat-Sujata were the four mind-born sons of Lord Brahma. They refused to enter the Pravritti Marga or worldly life and entered the Nivritti Marga or the path of renunciation. The four Kumaras were the pioneers in the path of Sannyasa. Sri Dattatreya also is among the original Sannyasins. The Sannyasins of the present day all descendants of the four Kumaras, Dattatreya and Sankaracharya.

Sri Sankaracharya, regarded as an Avatara of Lord Siva and the eminent exponent of Kevala Advaita philosophy, established four Mutts—one at Sringeri, another at Dvaraka, a third at Puri and a fourth at Joshi-Mutt in the Himalayas, on the way to the Badarinarayana shrine.

Sri Sankara had four Sannyasin disciples, viz., Suresvara, Padmapada, Hastamalaka and Totaka. Suresvara was in charge of Sringeri Mutt, Padmapada was in charge of Puri Mutt, Hastamalaka was in charge of Dvaraka Mutt and Totaka was in charge of Joshi-Mutt.

The Sannyasins of Sringeri Mutt, the spiritual descendants of Sri Sankara and Suresvaracharya, have three names, viz., Sarasvati, Puri and Bharati. The Sannyasins of the Dvaraka Mutt have two names, viz., Tirtha and Asrama. The Sannyasins of the Puri Mutt have two names, viz., Vana and Aranya. The Sannyasins of the Joshi-Mutt have three names, viz., Giri, Parvata and Sagara.

The Dasanamis worship Lord Siva or Lord Vishnu, and meditate on Nirguna Brahman. The Dandi Sannyasins, who hold staff in their hands, belong to the order of Sri Sankara. Paramahamsa Sannyasins do not hold staff. They freely move about as itinerant monks. Avadhutas are naked Sannyasins. They do not keep any property with them.

The Sannyasins of the Ramakrishna Mission belong to the order of Sri Sankara. They have the name Puri.

Then, there are Akhada Sannyasins, viz., Niranjani Akhada and Jhuna Akhada. They belong to the order of Sri Sankara.

They are Dasanamis. They are found in the Uttar Pradesh State only.

Rishikesh and Haridwar are colonies for Sannyasins. Varanasi also is among the chief abodes of Sannyasins.

SAIVAS

In South India, there are Tamil Sannyasins who belong to the Kovilur Mutt, Thiruvavaduthurai and Dharmapuram Adhinams. They do not belong to the Sri Sankara order. They are Saivas.

NAGAS

Nagas are Saiva Sannyasins. They are in a naked state. They smear their bodies with ashes. They have beard and matted locks.

UDASIS

Guru Nanak's order of ascetics are called Udasis. They correspond to Sannyasins and Vairagis. They are indifferent to the sensual pleasures of this world (Udasina). Hence they are called Udasis.

VAIRAGIS

A Vairagi is one who is devoid of passion. Vairagis are Vaishnavas. They worship Lord Rama, Sita and Hanuman. They read the Ramayana of Tulasidas. The mendicant Vaishnavas of the Ramanandi class are the Vairagis. This ascetic order was instituted by Sri Ananda, the twelfth disciple of Ramananda.

RAMA SANEHIS

The founder of this order was Ramcharan who was born in the year 1718 in a village near Jaipur in Rajasthan. The Rama Sanehi mendicants are of two classes, viz., the Videhis who are naked and the Mohinis who wear two pieces of cotton cloth dyed red in ochre. Their monastery is in Shahapur in Rajasthan. The Rama Sanehi sect has the largest following in

Mewar and Alwar. They are found also in Bombay, Gujarat, Surat, Poona, Ahmedabad, Hyderabad and Varanasi.

KABIR PANTHIS

Kabir Panthis are the followers of saint Kabir. They are numerous in all the provinces of Upper and Central India. There are twelve branches. Kabir Chaura is at Varanasi. It is a big monastery of Kabir Panthis. Dharamdas was the chief disciple of Kabir. The followers are expected to have implicit devotion to the Gurus, in thought, word and deed. They should practise truthfulness, mercy, non-injury and seclusion. The followers of Kamal, son of Kabir, practise Yoga.

DADU PANTHIS

The Dadu Panthis form one of the Vaishnava cults. Dadu, the founder of this sect, was a disciple of one of the Kabir Panthi teachers. The followers worship the Lord Rama.

Dadu was a cotton cleaner. He was born at Ahmedabad. He flourished about the year 1600. The Dadu Panthis are of three classes, viz., the Viraktas who are bareheaded and have one cloth and one water-pot, the Nagas who carry arms and who are regarded as soldiers and the Vistar Dharis who do the avocations of ordinary life.

The Dadu Panthis are numerous in Marwar and Ajmer. Their chief place of worship is at Naraina, which is near Sambhur and Jaipur. Passages from the Kabir writings are inserted in their religious scriptures.

GORAKHNATH PANTHIS

Gorakhnath was a contemporary of Kabir. He is regarded as the incarnation of Lord Siva. He calls himself as the son of Matsyendranath and grandson of Adinath. There is a temple of Gorakhnath at Gorakhpur in Uttar Pradesh. Bhartrihari was a disciple of Gorakhnath.

Goraksha-Sataka, Goraksha-Kalpa and Goraksha-Nama were written by Gorakhnath. They are in Sanskrit.

The followers of Gorakhnath are usually called Kanphatas, because their ears are bored and rings are inserted in them, at the time of their initiation. They worship the Lord Siva.

NIMBARKA SAMPRADAYIS AND RAMANUJA SAMPRADAYIS

There are Sadhus of the Nimbarka Sampradaya. There are Vaishnavas. The Sannyasins of the Ramanuja Sampradaya wear orange-coloured cloth, a holy thread and tuft and Tridanda or three-staff. At present, they are very few in number.

PARINAMI SECT

Sri Pirannath is the founder of this sect. He was born in 1675 at Jamnagar, district Rajkot, in Kathiawar. He was the Divan of Raja Jam Jasa. The followers are to practise Ahimsa, Satya and Daya—non-violence, truthfulness and compassion. They study the sacred book, Kul Jam Svarup, or Atma-Bodha, in Hindi, which contains the teachings of Sri Pirannath. It contains 18,000 Chaupais. They worship Bala-Krishna, i.e., Krishna as a small lad.

The followers are found mostly in the Punjab, Gujarat, Assam, Nepal and Bombay. There are two Mutts or monasteries—one at Jamnagar and the other at Pamna.

CHAPTER 10
HINDU MYTHOLOGY AND SYMBOLS
HINDU MYTHOLOGY

Mythology is a part of every religion. Mythology is concretised philosophy. Mythology is the science which investigates myths or fables or legends founded on remote events, especially those made in the early period of a people's existence. Mythology inspires the readers through precepts and laudable examples and goads them to attain perfection or the highest ideal. The abstract teachings and high subtle ideas are made highly interesting and impressive to the masses through the garb of stories, parables, legends, allegories and narratives. The sublime and abstract philosophical ideas and ideals of Hinduism are taken straight to the heart of the masses through impressive stories.

MYTHOLOGY AND HISTORY

All religions have their own mythology. Mythology is slightly mixed up with a little history. It is difficult to make a fine distinction between history and mythology. If a Christian stands up and says: "My prophet did such and such a marvellous thing," others will say: "This is only a myth. Our prophets did still more marvellous things which are really historical." It is not easy to differentiate the two into watertight compartments.

The doctrine of Avatara of the Hindus is a myth for the people of other religions. To worship a cow is superstition for the followers of other religions. The beautiful image or idol of Lord Krishna, which captivates the hearts of the sincere devotees and inspires them to enter into Bhava Samadhi, is horrible to look at for some other religionists. A Christian, a Jew and all others have their own various superstitions and myths. But these myths are really historical for each of them, severally. Mythology has no reference to anything 'unreal', but presents truths as clothed in conceptual categories.

PHILOSOPHY, MYTHOLOGY AND RITUAL

In every religion there are three parts, viz., philosophy, mythology and ritual. Philosophy is the essence of religion. It sets forth its basic principles or fundamental doctrines or tenets, the goal and the means of attaining it. Mythology explains and illustrates philosophy by means of legendary lives of great men or of supernatural beings. Ritual gives a still more concrete form to philosophy so that everyone may understand it. Ritual consists of forms, ceremonies, etc.

Puranas contain various myths. The cosmogonic myths of the Puranas are very interesting. A certain portion of Hindu mythology is even now presented to the public in the form of dramas during days of Hindu festivals. Thus the minds of the people are saturated with sublime ideas and ideals and lifted to great spiritual heights.

STUDY OF MYTHOLOGY AND ITS ADVANTAGES

There are great truths behind the ancient mythology of Hinduism. You cannot ignore a thing simply because it has a garb of mythology. Do not argue. Shut up your mouth. Keep your intellect at a respectable distance when you study mythology. Intellect is a hindrance. It will delude you. Give up arrogance and vanity. Cultivate love for imagery. Sit like a child and open your heart freely. You will comprehend the great truths revealed by mythology. You will penetrate into the hearts of the Rishis and sages who wrote the mythology. You will really enjoy mythology now.

You study geography through maps. There is no real country or town in a map, but it helps you to know a great deal about the different countries. Similar is the case with myths. You can grasp the subtle philosophical truths through myths.

By studying mythology, you will get several object lessons for moulding your character and leading an ideal divine life. The lives of Sri Rama, Sri Krishna, Bhishma, Nala, Harischandra, Lakshmana, Bharata, Hanuman, Yudhishthira, Arjuna, Sita, Savitri, Damayanti, Radha, etc., are sources of great spiritual inspiration for moulding your life, conduct and character. When you are in a dilemma as to what to do in puzzling situations and when there is conflict of duties, you will get the exact solutions through study of mythology.

Thus, mythology has its own benefits and advantages. It stamps on the minds the subtle and abstract teachings of the Vedas through instructive stories and illuminating discourses and paves the way for men to lead a divine life and attain perfection, freedom and immortality.

HINDU SYMBOLS

Outward symbols are necessary and beneficial. When viewed from the right angle of vision, you will find that they play a very important part in your material as well as spiritual life. Though they may look very simple and unimportant, they are very scientific and effective.

TILAKA—A MARK OF AUSPICIOUSNESS

Tilaka is a mark of auspiciousness. It is put on the forehead with sandal paste, sacred ashes or Kumkuma. The devotees of Siva apply sacred ashes (Bhasma) on the forehead, the devotees of Vishnu apply sandal paste (Chandana), and the worshippers of Devi or Sakti apply Kumkuma, a red turmeric powder. The scriptures say: "A forehead without a Tilaka, a woman without a husband, a Mantra the meaning of which is not known while doing Japa, the head that does not bend before holy personages, a heart without mercy, a house without a well, a village without a temple, a country without a river, a society without a leader, wealth that is not given away in charity, a preceptor without a disciple, a country without justice, a king without an able minister, a woman not obedient to her husband, a well without water, a flower without smell, a soul devoid of holiness, a field without rains, an intellect without clearness, a disciple who does not consider his preceptor as a form of God, a body devoid of health, a custom (Achara) without purity, austerity devoid of fellow-feeling, speech in which truth is not the basis, a country without good people, work without wages, Sannyasa without renunciation, legs which have not performed pilgrimages, a determination unaided by Viveka or discrimination, a knife which is blunt, a cow which does not give milk, a spear without a point—all these are worthy of condemnation. They exist for name's sake only." From this you can imagine the importance of Tilaka or the sacred mark.

Tilaka is applied at the Ajna Chakra, the space between the two eyebrows. It has a very cooling effect. Application of sandal paste has great medicinal value, apart from the spiritual influence. Application of sandal paste will nullify the heating effect when you concentrate and meditate at the Bhrumadhya. Tilaka indicates the point at which the spiritual eye opens. Lord Siva has a third eye at the Bhrumadhya. When He opens the third eye, the three worlds are destroyed. So also, when the third eye of the Jiva is opened, the three kinds of afflictions—Adhyatmika, Adhidaivika and Adhibhautika—are burnt to ashes. The three Karmas—Sanchita, Prarabdha and Agami—and also all the sins committed in the countless previous births, are burnt. When you apply the Tilaka, you mentally imagine: "I am the one non-dual Brahman free from all duality. May my eye of intuition open soon." You should remember this every time you apply a Tilaka.

There are various methods of applying Tilaka. Saivas apply three horizontal lines with the sacred ashes. The Vaishnavas apply three vertical lines (Tripundra) on the forehead. When they apply Tilaka, they say: "O Lord, protect me from the evil effects of the Trigunatmika Maya which has Sattva, Rajas and Tamas as its binding cords." Some Vaishnavas apply only one vertical line. Only the method of application differs, but the significance is the same in both the Vaishnavas and the Saivas.

THE TUFT—ITS UTILITY AND SIGNIFICANCE

Brahmins (Brahmanas) as well as the other castes grow Choti or Sikha, a tuft of hair. This tuft of hair was not so small in olden days, as seen in the present day. It covered the whole brain. They allowed the hair to grow. They never cut the tuft. It protects the brain from any sudden stroke and keeps it cool. The heat of the sun does not affect the head directly. Lack of this tuft has necessitated the use of umbrellas, etc.

The tuft is most scientific as well as religious. Any religious act should be performed after tying the tuft. Only the funeral and death anniversaries are performed with tuft untied or with dishevelled hair. It is very inauspicious to remain with dishevelled hair. It is done only in times of great sorrow or calamity. Draupadi took an oath in the assembly of the Kurus when she was molested by Dussasana that she would remain with dishevelled hair until the enemies were properly revenged. Kaikeyi remained with dishevelled hair in her apartment with the object of getting two boons from Dasaratha which were detrimental to the interests of Rama, the favourite of Dasaratha. Auspicious acts are never undertaken with tuft untied. Nowadays, very few people wear tuft, and even women are neglecting this vital point in their feverish anxiety to copy the West. The tuft of hair has a salutary effect on the essential parts of the brain and the central nervous system.

SIGNIFICANCE OF THE SACRED THREAD

Yajnopavita or the sacred thread is worn by the Brahmins, Kshatriyas and the Vaisyas. Wearing the sacred thread is a very holy and sacred ceremony amongst the Hindus. Brahmin boys between the ages of five and eight are invested with the sacred thread on a very auspicious day. By this ceremony, they become fit for the repetition of Gayatri. A Brahmin becomes a true Brahmin only after this ceremony. It is said: *"Janmana Jayate Sudrah Karmana Jayate Dvijah*—By birth one is a Sudra; by Karma (i.e., the investiture with the sacred thread) he becomes a Dvija or Brahmin."* Upanayana or thread ceremony is the second birth; hence, the Brahmins are called Dvijas (Dvi-ja means 'born twice').

The sacred thread or Yajnopavita consists of three threads. It denotes that one should be a Brahmachari in thought, word and deed. Each thread represents a Veda, viz., the Rik, Yajus and Sama. It represents also Brahma, Vishnu and Siva. The knot in the middle represents the formless Brahman, the Supreme Principle. The three threads represent also Sattva, Rajas and Tamas of the Trigunatmika Maya, and the knot represents the Isvara who controls Maya. Those who worship God at the three Sandhyas and repeat the Gayatri holding the Brahma knot of the sacred thread, derive immense strength and power. In days of yore, a Brahmana meditating upon the Gayatri holding the Brahma knot, had the power to bless and curse others. The educated intelligentsia of the present day are quite ignorant of the power of the sacred thread and the performance of Sandhya. That is the reason why they have ignored it. The sacred thread is a great power for the Brahmin who leads a regulated life devoted to the worship of God. Kshatriyas and Vaisyas, too, acquire power, fame and wealth by the power of the sacred thread.

A householder wears, at the time of marriage, an additional sacred thread. A Brahmachari has only one. The additional thread at the time of marriage is intended for the well-being of the partner. The sacred thread should be on the body always. The custom of washing it after removing it from the body or sending it to the washerman, is a wrong procedure. Some people are ashamed to wear the thread when they go to the office and they leave it at home. How ignorant they are!

Yajnopavita, the Choti, caste-mark, etc., are the external symbols to show that one is a Hindu. Purity, self-restraint, non-violence, patience, love for one's fellow-beings—these are the internal marks of a Hindu.

ACHAMANA AND PROKSHANA

Achamana is sipping water three times, repeating the Names of the Lord. Prokshana is sprinkling water over one's body for the sake of purity, when a bath is not possible. This is for internal as well as external purity. While sipping water, the following Mantras are repeated: *"Achyutaya Namah*—prostrations to the immutable Lord; *Anantaya Namah*—prostrations to the unlimited Lord; *Govindaya Namah*—prostrations to the Lord who is known by the Name of Govinda."* Then the various Names of the Lord—Kesava, Narayana, Madhava, Govinda, Vishnu, Madhusudana, Trivikrama, Vamana, Sridhara, Hrishikesa, Padmanabha and Damodara—are repeated, touching the various parts of the body, viz., the eyes, the ears, the face, the navel, the head, etc. One becomes pure by doing Achamana after he answers calls of nature, after walking in the streets, just before taking food and after food, and after a bath. This reminds you of the Lord now and then. Every act, every ritual, every symbol has a deep philosophical importance. They help you in changing the mental substance from Rajas and Tamas to Sattva. They give you an opportunity to think of God frequently.

OFFERING FOOD TO GOD, GUESTS AND THE PANCHA-PRANAS

Before sitting for food, the place is purified, a seat is put and in a leaf the articles of food are served. Before taking the food, a little water is sprinkled making a line all round the leaf repeating some Vedic Mantras. This repetition purifies the food. Then a little water is sipped. According to science as well as medicine, a little water, if drunk before the food is taken, is highly beneficial. Then the food is offered to the five Pranas and Brahman seated in the heart, by repeating *Om*

Pranaya Svaha, Apanaya Svaha, Vyanaya Svaha, Udanaya Svaha, Samanaya Svaha, and lastly, *Brahmane Svaha.* Just mark the importance of this offering. The person who takes the food offers it to the deities who dwell in the body in the form of Prana, Apana, etc. He does not eat for himself. The physical body is not the eater. It is the Pancha Prana that takes the food. Thus, taking food also can be converted into an act of Yoga or sacrifice.

One should daily offer to the Lord the food that he has prepared, before he partakes of it. He should say: *"Tvadiyam Vastu Govinda Tubhyameva Samarpaye—*I offer to Thee, O Govinda, this (food) which belongs to Thee only." The custom of the Hindus is that they should feed the guest who comes to their house before they take food. The guest is a representative of the Lord. The Srutis say: *"Atithi Devo Bhava."*

BELLS, LIGHTS, DHUPA, CAMPHOR AND SANDAL PASTE

Bells are rung in temples while doing Puja, to shut out the external sounds and to make the mind inward and concentrated.

Lights are waved before the Deity. This denotes that the Lord is Jyotis-Svarupa. He is all-light. The devotee says: "O Lord! Thou art the self-effulgent Light of the universe. Thou art the light in the sun, moon and fire. Remove the darkness in me by bestowing your divine light. May my intellect be illumined." This is the significance of waving lights.

Dhupa or scented sticks are burnt before the Deity. The smoke spreads the whole room. It acts as a disinfectant. Burning of Dhupa denotes that the Lord is all-pervading and that He fills the whole universe by His living presence. It is to remind this fact that Dhupa is burnt. The devotee prays: "O Lord! Let the Vasanas and Samskaras dormant in me vanish like the smoke of this Dhupa and become ashes. Let me become stainless."

Burning of camphor denotes that the individual ego melts

like the camphor and the Jivatman becomes one with the supreme Light of lights.

The sandal paste reminds the devotee that he should, in his difficulties, be as patient as the sandal. Sandal emanates sweet odour when it is rubbed on a hard surface and made into a paste. So also the devotee should not murmur when difficulties arise, but on the other hand, remain cheerful and happy and emanate sweetness and gentleness like the sandal. He should not hate even his enemy. This is another precept we learn from this. Though the sandalwood is crushed and made into a paste, it silently wears out emanating only very sweet odour. One should not wish evil even to his enemy.

PRASADA—ITS SACREDNESS AND GLORY

Prasada is that which gives peace. Prasada is the sacred food offering of the Lord. During Kirtana, worship, Puja, Havan and Arati, the devotee offers sweet rice, fruits, jaggery, milk, coconut, plantain and such other articles to the Lord, according to his ability. After offering them to the Lord, they are shared between the members of the house or the Bhaktas in a temple.

Water, flowers, rice, etc., are offered to the Lord in worship. This denotes that the Lord is pleased with even the smallest offering. What is wanted is the heart of the devotee. The Lord says in the Gita: *"Patram Pushpam Phalam Toyam Yo Me Bhaktya Prayacchati; Tadaham Bhaktyupahritamasnami Prayatatmanah*—Whoever offers a leaf, a flower, a fruit or even water, with devotion, that I accept, offered as it is with a loving heart."* It is not necessary that one should offer gold, silver and costly dress to the Lord. The devotee offers these according to his ability and position in life, thereby denoting that the whole wealth of the world belongs to the Lord. A rich man offers costly things to the Lord. He feeds the poor and serves the sick, seeing the Lord in his fellow-beings.

Puja is done with Bael leaves, flowers, Tulasi, Vibhuti and

these are given as Prasada from the Lord. Vibhuti is the Prasada of Lord Siva. It is to be applied on the forehead. A small portion can be taken in. Kumkuma is the Prasada of Sri Devi or Sakti. It is to be applied at the space between the eyebrows (Ajna or Bhrumadhya). Tulasi is the Prasada of Lord Vishnu, Rama or Krishna. It is to be taken in. They are charged with mysterious powers by the chanting of Mantras during Puja and Havan.

The mental Bhava of the devotee offering Bhog to the Lord has a very great effect. If an ardent devotee of the Lord offers anything to the Lord, that Prasada, if taken, would bring very great change even in the minds of atheists. The Grace of the Lord descends through Prasada. Go through the life of Narada. You will realise the greatness of the sacred leavings of the Lord as well as those of advanced Sadhakas and saints.

Namadeva offered rice, etc., to Panduranga Vitthala and He ate the food and shared it with Namadeva as well. If the food is offered with an yearning heart, sometimes, the Lord takes that food assuming a physical form. In other cases, the Lord enjoys the subtle essence of the food offered, and the food remains as it is in the shape of Prasada. While feeding Mahatmas and the poor people, that which is left behind is taken as Prasada. When a sacrifice is performed, the participants share the Prasada which bestows the blessings of the gods. When Dasaratha performed Putrakameshti (a sacrifice performed wishing for son), he got a vessel full of sweetened rice which he gave to his queens, by taking which they became pregnant. Prasada is the most sacred object for a devotee. One should consider himself lucky to take the Prasada, and there is no restriction of any kind in taking Prasada. Time and place, and the condition in which one is placed—all these do not affect him in any way. Prasada is all-purifying.

The benefits of Prasada and Charanamrita are beyond description. They have the power to change entirely the outlook of a man's life. Prasada and Charanamrita have the power to cure diseases and even bring back to life dead persons. There had been ever so many instances in the past in this holy land of ours which bear witness to the potency and efficacy of Prasada. Prasada destroys all pains and sins. It is an antidote for misery, pain and anxiety. Faith is the important factor in testing the accuracy of this statement. For faithless persons, it brings very little effect.

Those who are brought up in modern education and culture have forgotten all about the glory of Prasada. Many English-educated persons do not attach any importance to Prasada when they get it from Mahatmas. This is a serious mistake. Prasada is a great purifier. As they are brought up in the western style of living, they have imbibed the spirit of westerners and forgotten the spirit of the true children of Indian Rishis of yore. Live for a week in Vrindavana or Ayodhya or Varanasi or Pandharpur. You will realise the glory and the miraculous effects of Prasada. Many incurable diseases are cured. Many sincere devotional aspirants get wonderful spiritual experiences from mere Prasada alone. Prasada is a panacea. Prasada is a spiritual elixir. Prasada is the Grace of the Lord. Prasada is a cure-all and an ideal pick-me-up. Prasada is an embodiment of Sakti. Prasada is Divinity in manifestation. Prasada energises, vivifies, invigorates and infuses devotion. It should be taken with great faith.

THE JAPA MAALA

Significance of the Number of Beads

Generally, the rosary or Maala used for Japa contains 108 beads. A man breathes 21,600 times every day. If one does 200 Malas of Japa, it becomes 21,600; thereby, he does one Japa for every breath. If he does 200 Maalas of Japa every day, that amounts to remembrance of God throughout the day. Maalas may contain beads which form divisions of 108 also, so that the same calculation can be maintained. The Meru (the central bead in the Maala) denotes that you have done your Japa 108 times. This also denotes that every time you come to the Meru bead, you have gone one step further on the spiritual path and crossed over one obstacle. A portion of your ignorance is removed. A rosary or Maala is a whip to goad you to do Japa. Mohammedans also have a rosary (Tasbi) in their hands when they repeat their prayers. They roll the beads and repeat the name of Allah. Christians have their paternoster.

THE RAKSHA STOTRA

Before sitting for Japa and meditation, the Raksha Stotra is generally repeated. It means: "May the Lord protect me, staying in every part of my body." Each part is separately named and a particular Name of the Lord is repeated for the protection of that part. Anganyasa and Karanyasa also have the same effect. They drive away the evil effects of evil spirits, if any. The obstacles that stand in the way of concentration and meditation are removed. Evil thoughts will not enter the mind. This is a prayer to remove obstacles in Japa and meditation.

THE OCHRE CLOTH AND THE SHAVEN HEAD

Symbols of Renunciation

The ochre colour (Gerua) of the dress of a Sannyasin indicates that he is as pure as fire itself. He shines like the burnt gold, free from all impurities of desires and Vasanas. It denotes purity. It stands for purity. For an aspirant who has taken to the path of Nivritti Marga, it is a help. He will swerve and shrink from evil actions. This cloth will remind him that he is not entitled to worldly enjoyments. Gradually his nature will be moulded. This coloured cloth serves as an external symptom to show that one is a Sannyasin.

A Sannyasin shaves his head completely. This removes from him all beauty. He will not have to take care about dressing his hair with scented oils, etc. This shows that he has renounced all external beauties and that he dwells in the Self which is Beauty of beauties. This Mundana (shaving of head) indicates that he is no more of the world. He should not desire any sensual object. It is only an external symbol of the mental state of complete dispassion and turning away from the pleasures of the world. He removes his Choti also at the time of Sannyasa to indicate that he is no more bound by the various Nitya and Naimittika Karmas and that they have been burnt in the fire of Vairagya. Further, this shaving of the head is suitable for a wandering life. The existence of long hairs will prevent him from taking bath whenever he likes. Shaving will relieve him of much worry, and the time he would have otherwise spent in drying, combing and dressing his hair he may spend in prayers and meditation.

CONCLUSION

The Vedas and the Upanishads state that the ultimate truth in its pure and naked form, very unceremoniously. The Itihasas, Puranas and Agamas give this truth a homely, personal and symbolic touch through narration of history, legend and mythology.

Do not neglect outward symbols. Make a research study of our Vedic customs and injunctions. You will find wonderful and precious gems in every one of them. Their utility and efficacy will be revealed in following them.

May you all tread the path of Dharma and attain Kaivalya Moksha in this very birth.

CHAPTER 11

HINDU PHILOSOPHY—I

(THE SHAD-DARSANAS)

PHILOSOPHY—ITS ORIGIN AND ITS LIMITATIONS

Philosophy is the rational aspect of religion. It is an integral part of religion in India. It is a rational enquiry into the nature of Truth or Reality. It gives clear solutions for the profound, subtle problems of life. It shows the way to get rid of pain and death and attain immortality and eternal bliss.

Philosophy has its root in the practical needs of man. Man wants to know about transcendental matters when he is in a reflective state. There is an urge within him to know about the secret of death, the secret of immortality, the nature of the soul, the Creator and the world. Philosophy helps him to know all these things. Philosophy is the self-expression of the growing spirit of man. The philosophers are its voice. Great creative thinkers and philosophers appear in all ages. They elevate and inspire the people.

Certain philosophical questions arise in the mind of man. What is this Samsara? Has it any purpose? Is the world real or mere appearance? Is there any Creator or Governor of this universe? If there is a Creator, what is His nature? What is the relation between man and the Creator? Is there any way to escape from the round of births and deaths? Is there any such thing as the Impersonal Absolute? If so, what is Its essential nature? How did man come into bondage? What is his essential nature? Is he a *part* of the Supreme Soul, or is he *identical* with It? What is the difference between Personal God and the Impersonal Absolute? What is the source for this world? What is matter? What is mind? What is individual soul? What is the goal of life? The search for a solution of these problems is philosophy. Philosophy solves beautifully all these problems.

DEATH—THE STARTING POINT OF PHILOSOPHY

The idea of death has ever been the strongest motive-power of religion and religious life. Man is afraid of death. Man does not want to die. He wants to live for ever. This is the starting point of philosophy. Philosophy enquires and investigates. It boldly proclaims: "O man! Do not be afraid of death. There is an immortal abode. That is Brahman. That is your own Atman which dwells in the chamber of your heart. Purify your heart and meditate on this pure, immortal, changeless Self. You will attain immortality." Death is the ultimate pointer to the transiency of all things and the existence of an ultimate Reality.

VARIOUS SCHOOLS OF PHILOSOPHY

A clear understanding of man's relation to God is a matter of momentous importance to students of philosophy and to all aspirants. Philosophers, prophets, saints, sages, thinkers, Acharyas and great religious leaders of the world have tried to explain the relation of man to God and the universe. Various schools of philosophy and different kinds of religious beliefs have come into existence, on account of various explanations given by different philosophers.

PHILOSOPHY AND INTUITION

Philosophy will take you to the gates of the realm of eternal bliss, but it cannot allow you to enter that realm. Intuition or realisation is necessary for entering into that holy land of everlasting joy and ineffable glory.

Hindu philosophy is not mere speculation or guesswork. It is lofty, sublime, unique and systematic. It is based on mystic spiritual experience, or Aparoksha Anubhuti. The seers, sages and Rishis who had direct, intuitive perception of the Truth are the founders of the different philosophical systems in India. The different schools of philosophy are all based on the

Srutis or the Vedas, directly or indirectly. Those who have studied carefully the Upanishads will find that the revelations of the Srutis are in harmony with the conclusions of philosophy.

THE ORTHODOX AND THE HETERODOX SYSTEMS OF INDIAN PHILOSOPHY

The six systems of Indian philosophy or the Shad-Darsanas are the six orthodox systems of philosophy. They are the six ways of looking at the Truth. They are (1) The Nyaya; (2) The Vaiseshika; (3) The Sankhya; (4) The Yoga; (5) The Purva-Mimamsa; and (6) The Uttara-Mimamsa, or the Vedanta.

The orthodox systems of philosophy believe in the authority of the Vedas. The heterodox systems of philosophy do not believe in the authority of the Vedas. The six heterodox systems of philosophy are:

1. The Materialistic School of Charvaka;
2. The System of the Jainas;
3. The School of Presentationists or Vaibhashikas (Buddhistic);
4. The School of Representationists or Sautrantikas (Buddhistic);
5. The School of Idealism or Yogacharas (Buddhistic); and
6. The School of Nihilism of the Madhyamikas (Buddhistic).

THE SHAD-DARSANAS OR THE SIX ORTHODOX SCHOOLS

The Shad-Darsanas or the six orthodox systems grew directly out of the Vedas. *Darsana* means literally *sight* or *vision*. Darsana means a system of philosophy. The Darsana literature is philosophical. Each Darsana is a way of looking into the Truth; is a standpoint in respect of the Truth.

Gautama Rishi systematised the principles of Nyaya or the

Indian logical system. Kanada composed the Vaiseshika Sutras. Kapila Muni founded the Sankhya system. Patanjali Maharshi is the first systematiser of the Yoga school. He composed his Yoga Sutras. The Yoga-Darsana of Patanjali is a celebrated text-book on Raja Yoga. Jaimini, a disciple of Vyasa, composed the Sutras of the Mimamsa school, which is based on the ritual-sections of the Vedas. Badarayana composed his famous Vedanta-Sutras or Brahma-Sutras which expound the teachings of the Upanishads. The different schools of the Vedanta have built their philosophy on the foundation of these Sutras.

DIFFERENT WAYS OF APPROACH TO THE SAME GOAL

The six schools of thought are like the six different roads which lead to one city. You may go to Bombay by train or aeroplane or motor bus or any other vehicle. Even so, you can reach the goal of life through Yoga, or Vedanta, or any other path. The methods or ways of approach to the Goal are different to suit people of different temperaments, capacities and mental calibre. But they all have one aim, viz., removal of ignorance and its effects of pain and sufferings and the attainment of freedom, perfection, immortality and eternal bliss by union of the individual soul (Jivatman) with the Supreme Soul (Paramatman).

No student of Hinduism ought to be satisfied without acquiring a clear and accurate knowledge of the principal distinguishing characteristics of the six philosophical schools. The more advanced scholar should study the original Sutras in which the doctrines of each school are enunciated. Study of the six schools of philosophy will sharpen the intellect and give you vast knowledge. You will have a clear and comprehensive understanding of the Truth. Each system is a step or rung in the spiritual ladder.

INTERRELATION BETWEEN THE SIX SYSTEMS

The six schools are divided into three groups: (i) The

Nyaya and the Vaiseshika, (ii) The Sankhya and the Yoga, and (iii) The Mimamsa and the Vedanta. The Vaiseshika is a supplement of the Nyaya. The Yoga is a supplement of the Sankhya. The Vedanta is an amplification and fulfilment of the Sankhya. Study of Vyakarana (grammar), Mimamsa, Nyaya and Sankhya is necessary to understand the Vedanta. The Nyaya sharpens the intellect and enables the aspirants to grasp the Vedanta. The Nyaya is considered as a prerequisite for all philosophical enquiry.

The Vaiseshika is not very much in honour now. The Nyaya is popular. The Sankhya is not a living faith. The Yoga is practised by a few in its practical form. The Vedanta is the most popular of all the schools today.

The Nyaya and the Vaiseshika will give you an analysis of the world of experience. They arrange all the things of the world into certain kinds or categories (Padarthas). They explain how God has made all this material world out of atoms and molecules. They show the way to attain knowledge of God. The Sankhya will provide you with deep knowledge of Hindu psychology. Kapila Muni was the father of psychology. The Yoga deals with the control of Vrittis, or thought-waves, and with meditation. The Yoga system shows the ways to discipline the mind and the senses. The Yoga will help you to cultivate concentration and one-pointedness of mind and enter into Nirvikalpa Samadhi or the Superconscious State. The Purva-Mimamsa deals with the Karma-Kanda of the Vedas, and the Uttara-Mimamsa with the Jnana-Kanda. The Uttara-Mimamsa is also known as the Vedanta-Darsana. This is the corner-stone of Hinduism. The Vedanta philosophy explains in detail the nature of Brahman or the Eternal Being, and shows that the individual soul is, in essence, identical with the Supreme Self. It gives methods to remove Avidya or the veil of ignorance and to merge oneself in the ocean of bliss or Brahman.

The Nyaya calls ignorance Mithya Jnana, false knowledge. The Sankhya styles it Aviveka, non-discrimination between the real and the unreal. The Vedanta names it Avidya, nescience. Each philosophy aims at its eradication by Knowledge or Jnana. Then one attains eternal bliss or immortality.

By study of Nyaya and Vaiseshika, one learns to utilise his intellect to find out fallacies and to know the material constitution of the world. By study of Sankhya, one understands the course of evolution. By study and practice of Yoga, one gains self-restraint and obtains mastery over mind and senses. By practice of Vedanta, one reaches the highest rung of the ladder of spirituality or the pinnacle of divine glory, oneness with the Supreme Being, by the destruction of ignorance (Avidya).

VEDANTA—THE MOST SATISFACTORY SYSTEM OF PHILOSOPHY

Some of the doctrines of the Nyaya, the Vaiseshika, the Sankhya and the Yoga are opposed to the teachings of the Vedas. These systems are only superficially based on the Vedas. The Nyaya and the Vaiseshika schools rely too much on human reason, though they accept the Vedas as the supreme authority. Human intellect is frail and finite. It has got its limitations. It functions within time, space and causation. Its findings cannot be infallible. It cannot solve transcendental matters. Vedas only are infallible and authoritative. They contain the revelations or direct intuitional experiences of seers and Rishis. These experiences will tally with the experiences of those who have attained Knowledge of the Self (Brahma-Jnana).

The Vedanta is the most satisfactory system of philosophy. It has been evolved out of the Upanishads. It has superseded all other schools. The Mimamsa school had laid great stress on rituals, or Karma-Kanda. According to the Mimamsa school, Karma or ritual is all-in-all in the Veda. Upasana (worship) and Jnana (knowledge) are only accessories to Karma. This view is refuted by the Vedanta school. According to the vedanta, Self-realisation (Jnana) is the foremost thing, and ritual and worship are accessories. Karma will take one to heaven which is only an impermanent place of refined sensual enjoyment. Karma cannot destroy the cycle of births and deaths, and cannot give eternal bliss and immortality.

During the time of Sankaracharya, all the six schools of philosophy flourished. Therefore, he had to refute the other systems in order to establish his absolute monism (Kevala Advaita). But, nowadays, Sankhya, Vaiseshika, etc., are in name only. Even now, some Hindu preachers, Sannyasins and Mandalesvars try to establish Advaita Vedanta by refuting these old systems. This is a mistake. They will have to refute at the present moment materialism, agnosticism, atheism and science, and then establish Advaita Vedanta.

THE NYAYA

INTRODUCTION

Salutations to Rishi Gautama, the founder of the Nyaya system of philosophy.

The Nyaya or Hindu logic was founded by Gautama Rishi, who is also known by the names Akshapada and Dirghatapas. The Nyaya and the Vaiseshika are analytic types of philosophy. The word *Nyaya* signifies *going into a subject,* i.e., investigating it analytically. In this sense of analysis, the word Nyaya is exactly opposed to Sankhya, synthesis. The Nyaya is sometimes called Tarka-Vidya or the Science of Debate, Vada-Vidya or the Science of Discussion. Tarka is the special feature of the Nyaya.

The Nyaya is not merely formal logic, but a complete epistemology. Ordinary people think that the Nyaya is chiefly concerned with logic. Logic is merely a part or a single topic. The purpose of the Nyaya is a critical examination of the objects of knowledge by means of the canons of logical proof. The

Nyaya system deals critically with metaphysical problems. It contains discussions on psychology, logic, metaphysics and theology.

The Nyaya—A Method of Philosophical Enquiry

The Nyaya is intended to furnish a correct method of philosophical enquiry into all the objects and subjects of human knowledge, including the process of reasoning and laws of thought. The evidence of the senses is submitted to a critical enquiry. The Nyaya gives a description of the mechanism of knowledge in detail. The Nyaya and the Vaiseshika explore the significance of time, space, cause, matter, mind, soul and knowledge for experience, and give the results in the form of a theory of the universe. The Nyaya and the Vaiseshika are regarded as parts of one whole. The Vaiseshika is a supplement to the Nyaya. They are allied systems. They both believe in a Personal God, a plurality of souls and an atomic universe. Further, they use many arguments in common.

The Nyaya is the basis of all Sanskrit philosophical studies. It is an introduction to all systematic philosophy. It is the preliminary course for a student of philosophy. You cannot understand the Brahma-Sutras of Sri Vyasa without a knowledge of the Nyaya. A study of the Nyaya develops the power of reasoning or arguing. It renders the intellect sharp and subtle. You cannot make Vedantic enquiry without a sharp and subtle intellect. The Kathopanishad says: *"Drisyate Tvagryaya Buddhya Sukshmaya Sukshma-Darsibhih—It* (the Atman) is beheld by subtle seers through their sharp and subtle intellect."

The 'Nyaya Sutra' by Gautama is the first work on Nyaya philosophy. This is the most famous book of the school. Numerous commentaries have been written on this book by various authors, viz., Nyaya-Bhashya by Vatsyayana, Nyayalankara by Srikantha, Nyaya-Manjari by

Jayanta, Nyaya-Bodhini by Govardhana, Nyaya-Varttika-Tatparya-Tika by Vachaspati Misra, etc.

KNOWLEDGE

All knowledge implies four conditions: (i) the subject or the Pramata, the cogniser, (ii) the object or the Prameya, (iii) the resulting state of cognition or the Pramiti and (iv) the means of knowledge or the Pramana.

Prameya, or the objects of which right knowledge is to be obtained, are twelve, viz., (i) Soul (Atman), (ii) Body (Sarira), (iii) Senses (Indriyas), (iv) Objects of senses (Artha), (v) Intellect (Buddhi), (vi) Mind (Manas), (vii) Activity (Pravritti), (viii) Fault (Dosha), (ix) Transmigration (Pretyabhava), (x) Fruit (Phala), (xi) Pain (Duhkha), and (xii) Salvation (Apavarga).

Perception (Pratyaksha), inference (Anumana), comparison (Upamana), and word, or verbal testimony (Sabda) are the Pramanas or the means of right knowledge. Sabda, or verbal testimony, includes Vedic revelation. Pratyaksha is perception by the senses.

GOD, SOUL AND UNIVERSE

God

The Nyaya says that the actions of man produce their fruits, called Adrishta, under the control of God. God supervises the work of Adrishta. The intelligent principle of Adrishta, which governs the fate of man, acts under the direction of God. God does not alter the course of Adrishta, but renders possible its operation. God is the bestower of the fruits of actions of human beings. God is a Special Soul endowed with omnipotence and omniscience, by which He guides and regulates the world.

God is a Personal Being. He is free from Mithya-Jnana (false knowledge), Adharma (demerit), and Pramada (carelessness). He has Jnana (knowledge), Ichha (desire) and Prayatna (volitional effort). God is ONE, Creator, who is endowed with Nitya Jnana (eternal knowledge) and Ichha-Kriya (desire-action) as His Gunas (attributes). He is Vibhu (all-pervading).

The Soul

The soul is a real being. It is an eternal entity. Desire, aversion, volition, pleasure, pain, intelligence and cognition are its qualities or marks. The object of the notion of 'I' is the soul. No cognition or recollection is possible without a soul. The eye cannot see objects and the ear cannot hear sounds without a soul. There should be an agent to use the instruments (senses). That agent is the soul. After an object is seen, even if the eyes are both destroyed, the knowledge that *I have seen* remains. This knowledge is not a quality of either the objects or the senses. The mind is not the soul. It is only an instrument of the soul, by means of which it thinks. The self is the subject. The soul exists even when the body perishes, the senses are cut off and the mind is controlled. There are infinite numbers of souls.

The Universe

The universe is a composite of eternal, unalterable, causeless atoms, which exists independently of our thoughts. The universe is the modification of the atoms (Paramanus) of the physical elements: Earth (Prithvi), Water (Apas), Fire (Tejas) and Air (Vayu). The Nyaya admits nine objects (Dravyas), viz., Earth, Water, Fire, Air, Ether, Time, Space (Quarters), Mind and the Self (Atman).

THE CAUSE OF BONDAGE AND THE MEANS TO EMANCIPATION

Misapprehension (Mithya-Jnana), faults (Dosha), activity (Pravritti), birth (Janma) and pain (Duhkha) constitute the world. False notion or false knowledge is at the root of all misery and pain. From Mithya-Jnana or false notion comes the fault of like and dislike (Raga-Dvesha); from Raga-Dvesha proceeds Karma or action—virtuous or vicious—which forces a man to pass through repeated births for the sake of its reward or punishment. From these births proceed misery and pain. It is the aim of philosophy to eradicate the false notion or Mithya-Jnana which is at the root of all miseries and pains. On the successive annihilation of misapprehension, faults, activity, birth and pain, there follows release (Apavarga).

The Sixteen Categories

One can remove misapprehension or false knowledge and attain supreme felicity by the true knowledge of the sixteen categories. The sixteen categories are: means of right knowledge (Pramana), object of right knowledge (Prameya), doubt (Samsaya), purpose (Prayojana), familiar instance (Drishtanta), established tenet (Siddhanta), members (Avayava), argumentation (Tarka), ascertainment (Nirnaya), discussion (Vada), wrangling (Jalpa), cavil (Vitanda), fallacy (Hetvabhasa), quibble (Chala), futility (Jati), and occasion for rebuke (Nigraha-sthana).

There is, first, the state of Samsaya or doubt about the point to be discussed. Next comes the Prayojana or motive for discussing it. Next follows a Drishtanta or example which leads to the Siddhanta or established conclusion. Then comes the objector with his Avayava or argument, split up into five members. Next follows the Tarka or refutation, and the Nirnaya or ascertainment of the true state of the case. A further Vada or controversy takes place, which leads to Jalpa or mere wrangling. This is followed by Vitanda or cavilling, Hetvabhasa or fallacious reasoning, and Nigraha-sthana, the putting an end to all discussion by a demonstration of the objector's incapacity for argument.

When one attains the true knowledge, his faults, viz., affection (Raga), aversion (Dvesha) and stupidity (Moha) vanish. Aversion includes anger, envy, malice and hatred. Attachment includes lust, greed, avidity and covetousness. Stupidity includes suspicion, conceit, carelessness and misapprehension.

Stupidity generates dislike and attachment. You must put an end to the chain, which begins with misapprehension or false knowledge and ends with pain, if you wish to attain release. If false knowledge vanishes, faults will disappear. If faults vanish, one is freed from activity and the consequent transmigration and pains.

Transmigration, which consists in the soul's leaving one body and taking another, is the cause of its undergoing pleasure and pain. A soul which is no longer subject to transmigration is freed from all pains. The soul attains release as soon as there is an end to the body, and consequently to pleasure and pain.

The State of Apavarga or Release

Apavarga, or release, is absolute deliverance from pain. It is freedom from pain. It is cessation of pain. It is not the enjoyment of positive pleasure. It is not annihilation of the self. It is destruction of bondage. Release from the twenty-one kinds of pain or Duhkha is liberation (Moksha). In the state of release, there is no connection of mind with the Atman. The Atman is destitute of desire, effort, merit, demerit, hatred, mental impressions, etc., in the state of liberation, as, then, there is no mind. The liberation (Moksha) of the Naiyayikas is a word without meaning. It is a state of painless, passionless existence, like that of a stone without sensation and interest.

TO SUM UP

This world has begun by a combination of atoms. It has Samyoga (conjunction) and Viyoga (disassociation). The cause of the world is the Paramanus (atoms) and the nine Dravyas (materials), including Isvara (God). Isvara has Nitya-Jnana (eternal knowledge) who has also Ichha-Kriya (desire-action) as Gunas (qualities). He is Vibhu (all-pervading). Jiva is doer and enjoyer. He has several attributes. Jivas are endless. The cause for bondage is ignorance (Ajnana). Twenty-one kinds of pain constitute bondage. Moksha is destruction of all kinds of pain. Knowledge of the Atman, as is distinct from others, is Moksha-Sadhana. Gautama advocates Arambhavada and Anyathakhyati (theory of the production of a new effect from every cause and of realistic epistemology).

THE VAISESHIKA

INTRODUCTION

Silent adorations to Kanada Rishi, the founder of the Vaiseshika system of philosophy.

Rishi Kanada is also known by the names, Aulukya and Kasyapa.

The Vaiseshika system takes its name from *Visesha* or particularity which is the characteristic differentia of things. The aphorisms of Kanada contain the essence of the Vaiseshika philosophy. The principal subject treated therein is Visesha, one of the six Padarthas or categories enumerated by the founder.

The Nyaya and the Vaiseshika

The Vaiseshika and the Nyaya agree in their essential principles, such as the nature and qualities of the Self and the atomic theory of the universe. The Vaiseshika is a supplement to the Nyaya. The Vaiseshika has, for its chief objective, the analysis of experience. It begins by arranging its enquiries under categories (Padarthas), i.e., enumeration of certain general properties or attributes that may be predicated of existing things. It formulates general conceptions, which apply to things known, whether by the senses or by inference, or by authority.

THE APHORISMS OF KANADA

There are ten chapters in Kanada's book. The first chapter deals with the entire group of Padarthas or predicables. In the second chapter, Kanada has ascertained substance. In the third chapter, he has given a description of the soul and the inner sense. In the fourth chapter, he has discussed the body and its constituents. In the fifth chapter, he has established Karma or action. In the sixth chapter, he has considered Dharma or virtue according to scriptures. In the seventh chapter, he has established attribute and Samavaya (co-inherence or combination). In the eighth chapter, he has ascertained the manifestation of knowledge, its source, and so on. In the ninth chapter, he has established the particular or concrete understanding. And, in the tenth chapter, he has established the differences in the attributes of the soul.

There is enumeration of Padarthas (substances) in the beginning. Then there is definition. Then comes examination or demonstration.

This system is chiefly concerned with the determination of the Padarthas and yet, Kanada opens the subject with an enquiry into Dharma, because Dharma is at the root of the knowledge of the essence of the Padarthas. The first Sutra is: *Yatobhyudayanihsreyasa-siddhih sa dharmah*—Dharma is that which exalts and bestows the Supreme Good or Moksha (cessation of pain).

THE SEVEN PADARTHAS OR CATEGORIES

Padartha means literally *the meaning of a word.* But here it denotes a substance discussed in philosophy. A Padartha is an object which can be thought (Artha) and named (Pada). All things which exist, which can be perceived and named, all objects of experience, are Padarthas. Compound substances are dependent and transitory. Simple substances are eternal and independent.

The Padarthas of the Vaiseshika are the following: (i) Substance (Dravya), (ii) Quality or property (Guna), (iii) Action (Karma), (iv) Generality of properties (Samanya), (v) Particularity (Visesha), (vi) Co-inherence or perpetual intimate relation (Samavaya), and (vii) Non-existence or negation of existence (Abhava). The first three categories of substance, quality and action have a real objective existence. The next three, viz., generality, particularity and inherence are logical categories. They are products of intellectual discrimination. Kanada enumerated only six categories, the seventh was added by later writers.

Earth, water, fire, air, ether, time, space, soul and mind are the nine Dravyas or substances. The first four of these and the last are held to be atomic. The first four are both eternal and non-eternal, non-eternal in their various compounds and eternal in their ultimate atoms to which they must be traced back.

Mind is an eternal substance. It does not pervade everywhere like the soul. It is atomic. It can admit only one thought at a time.

There are seventeen qualities inherent in the nine substances, viz., colour (Rupa), taste (Rasa), smell (Gandha), touch (Sparsa), numbers (Sankhya), measures (Parimanani), separateness or individuality (Prithaktvam), conjunction and disconjunction (Samyoga-vibhagam), priority and posterity (Paratva-aparatva), intellection or understanding (Buddhayah), pleasure and pain (Sukha-duhkha), desire and aversion (Ichha-dvesha), and volitions (Prayatnah). Seven others are said to be implied, viz., gravity, fluidity, viscidity, faculty, merit, demerit and sound—making twenty-four in all. Sixteen of these qualities belong to material substances. The other eight, viz., understanding, volition, desire, aversion, pleasure, pain, merit and demerit are the properties of the soul.

The third category, Karma or action, consists of five kinds of acts, viz., elevation or throwing upwards, depression or throwing downwards, contraction, expansion and motion.

The fourth category, Samanya or generality of properties, is twofold, viz., (i) higher and lower generality and (ii) that of genus and species.

The fifth category, Visesha or particularity, belongs to the nine eternal substances of the first category, all of which have an eternal ultimate difference distinguishing each from the others. Therefore, the system is called Vaiseshika.

The sixth category, Samavaya or co-inherence, is of only one kind. It is the co-inherence between a substance and its qualities, between a genus or species and its individuals, between any object and the general idea connected with it and is thought to be a real entity.

There are four kinds of Abhava, the seventh category, viz., antecedent non-existence, cessation of existence, mutual non-existence and absolute non-existence.

Knowledge of the Padarthas Secures Supreme Good

Knowledge of the Padarthas is the means of attaining the Supreme Good. The Supreme Good results from the knowledge produced—by a particular Dharma—of the essence of the Padarthas, by means of their resemblances and differences.

THE PRINCIPLE OF ADRISHTA AND ITS INADEQUACIES

Kanada does not openly refer to God in his Sutras. His belief was that the formation of the world was the result of Adrishta, the *unseen* force of Karmas or acts. He traces the primal activities of the atoms and souls to the principle of Adrishta.

The followers of Kanada introduce God as the efficient cause of the world. The atoms are the material cause of the universe.

The unthinking atoms have not the power and the intelligence to run this universe in an orderly manner. Surely, the activities of the atoms are regulated by an omniscient and omnipotent God. Inference and scriptures compel us to admit God. What is that intelligence which makes the Adrishta to operate? That intelligence is God. The five elements are effects. They must be preceded by someone who has a knowledge of them. That 'someone' is God. There must be an author for the Vedas. The contents of the Vedas are destitute of error. The author is free from deceit. He must be an omniscient Being.

The souls are destitute of intelligence in the state of dissolution. Hence they cannot control the activities of the atoms. There is no source of motion within the atoms. Therefore, there must be a first mover of the atom. That First Mover is the Creator or God.

ATOMIC THEORY OF THE UNIVERSE

In the Vaiseshika system, the formation of the world is supposed to be effected by the aggregation of atoms. These atoms are countless and eternal. They are eternally aggregated, disintegrated and redisintegrated by the power of Adrishta. An atom is defined as 'something existing, having no cause, and eternal'. It is less than the least, invisible, indivisible, intangible and imperceptible by the senses. Each atom has a Visesha or eternal essence of its own. The combination of these atoms is first into an aggregate of two (Dvyanu, dyad). Three of them, again combine into a particle, called Trasarenu (Triad), which like a mote in a sunbeam has just sufficient magnitude to be perceptible.

There are four classes of Paramanus, viz., Paramanus of earth, water, fire and air. The individual atoms combine with others, and again disintegrate after some time.

The Vaiseshika cosmogony is dualistic in the sense of assuming the existence of eternal atoms side by side with eternal souls. It has not decided positively the exact relation between soul and matter.

BODY AND SOUL

The body is subtle in Pralaya and gross in creation. The time, place and circumstances of birth, family and the span of life are all determined by the Adrishta.

The individual souls are eternal, manifold, eternally separate from one another, and distinct from the body, senses and mind; and yet capable of apprehension, volition, desire, aversion, pleasure, pain, merit and demerit. They are infinite, ubiquitous or omnipresent and diffused everywhere throughout space. A man's soul is as much in New York as in Bombay, although it can only apprehend and feel and act where the body is. The soul and the mind are not objects of perception.

The soul is absolutely free from all connections with qualities in the state of Moksha or release. It regains its independence.

BIRTH, DEATH AND SALVATION

Conjunction of soul with body, sense and life, produced by Dharma and Adharma, is called birth, and disjunction of body and mind produced by them is called death.

Moksha consists in the non-existence of conjunction with the body, when there is, at the same time, no potential body existing and consequently rebirth cannot take place.

BONDAGE AND RELEASE

Pleasure and pain result from the contact of soul, sense, mind and object.

From pleasure arises desire. From pleasure derived from the enjoyment of garlands, sandal paste, women and other objects, Raga or desire is produced successively for pleasure of a similar kind or for the means of attaining it. From pain caused by snakes, scorpions, thorns and the like, aversion arises with regard to such pain or with regard to its source.

A very powerful impression is produced by constant or habitual experience of objects, through the influence of which, a sad lover who does not win his mistress sees his beloved in every object. He who has been bitten by a snake beholds snakes everywhere, on account of a strong impression regarding that.

The Faults That Lead to Bondage

Desire (Raga), aversion (Dvesha) and infatuation (Moha) are called faults (Doshas), as they are incentives to activity which serves to bind the doer to this world. Gautama also says: "Faults have for their characteristic, incitement to activity or worldly occupation" (Nyaya Sutras, I-1-xviii).

The Knowledge That Results in Release

Intuitive knowledge of the Self destroys false knowledge. Consequently, attraction, aversion, stupidity or Moha and other faults vanish. Then activity also disappears. Then birth due to action does not take place. Consequently, pain connected with birth also disappears.

THE SANKHYA

INTRODUCTION

Obeisance to Sri Kapila Muni, the founder of the Sankhya system of philosophy, the son of Brahma, the Avatara of Vishnu.

The word 'Sankhya' means 'number'. The system gives an enumeration of the principles of the universe, twenty-five in number. Hence the name is quite appropriate. The term 'Sankhya' is used in the sense of 'Vichara' or 'philosophical reflection' also.

In the Sankhya system, there is no analytical enquiry into the universe as actually existing, arranged under topics and categories. There is a synthetical system, starting from an original primordial Tattva or Principle, called Prakriti, that which evolves or produces or brings forth (Prakaroti) everything else.

Perception (Pratyaksha), inference (Anumana) and right affirmation (Apta Vakya) are the three Pramanas or proofs in the Sankhya system. The word Apta means fit or right. It is applied to the Vedas or inspired teachers. The Naiyayikas have four kinds of proofs, viz., perception, inference, comparison and verbal authority. The Mimamsakas recognise six kinds of proofs.

Dual Concept of Purusha and Prakriti

The Sankhya system is generally studied next to the Nyaya. It is a beautiful system of philosophy. The western philosophers also have great admiration for this system. It is more categorically dualistic. It denies that anything can be produced out of nothing. It assumes the reality of Purusha and Prakriti, the knowing Self and the objects known.

Prakriti and Purusha are Anadi (beginningless) and Ananta (infinite). Non-discrimination between the two is the cause for birth and death. Discrimination between Prakriti and Purusha gives Mukti (salvation). Both Purusha and Prakriti are Sat (real). Purusha is Asanga (unattached). He is consciousness, all-pervading and eternal. Prakriti is doer and enjoyer. Souls are countless.

Non-acceptance of Isvara or God

The Sankhya system is called Nir-Isvara (Godless) Sankhya. It is atheistical. The Sankhyas do not believe in Isvara. They do not accept Isvara (God). The creation produced by Prakriti has an existence of its own, independent of all connection with the particular Purusha to which it is united. So the Sankhyas say that there is no need for an intelligent Creator of the world, or even of any superintending power.

This is a mistake; according to the Vedanta, Prakriti is always under the control of the Lord. It cannot do anything by itself. The Lord gazes at Prakriti. Then alone it is put in motion, and it begins to create. Prakriti is non-intelligent. An intelligent Creator alone can have a thought-out plan for the universe. Prakriti is only a helper (Sahakari). This is the theory of Vedanta.

Theory of Evolution and Involution

The Sankhya adopts the theory of evolution and involution.

The cause and effect are the undeveloped and developed states of one and the same substance. There is no such thing as total destruction. In destruction, the effect is involved into its cause. That is all.

There cannot be any production of something out of nothing. That which is not cannot be developed into that which is. The production of what does not already exist potentially is impossible like a horn on a man, because there must, of necessity, be a material out of which a product is developed, and because everything cannot occur everywhere at all times, and also because anything possible must be produced from something competent to produce it.

That which does not exist cannot be brought into existence by an agent. It would be useless to grind ground-nut, unless the oil existed in it. The same force applied to sand or orange would not express groundnut oil. The manifestation of the oil is a proof that it was contained in the groundnut and consequently, a proof of the existence of the source from which it is derived.

The effect truly exists beforehand in its cause. This is one of the central features of the Sankhya system of philosophy. Cause is a substance in which the effect subsists in a latent form. Just as the whole tree exists in a latent or dormant state in the seed, so also the whole world exists in a latent state in Prakriti, the Avyakta (unevolved), or the Avyakrita (undifferentiated). The effect is of the same nature as the cause. The effect or product is not different from the material of which it is composed.

Fourfold Classification of the Twenty-five Tattvas

The Sankhya gives a description of categories based on their respective productive efficiency, viz., (i) Productive (Prakriti), (ii) Productive and Produced (Prakriti-Vikriti), (iii) Produced (Vikriti) and (iv) Neither Productive nor Produced (Anubhavarupa). This fourfold classification includes all the twenty-five principles or Tattvas. Prakriti or Nature or Pradhana (chief) is purely productive. It is the root of all. It is not a product. It is a creative force, evolver, producer. Seven principles—intellect (Buddhi), egoism (Ahankara) and the five Tanmatras (subtle rudiments)—are productions and productive. Buddhi is productive, as Ahankara is evolved out of it. It is produced also, as it itself is evolved out of Prakriti. Egoism is a production, as it is derived from intellect. It is productive, as it gives origin to the five subtle rudiments or Tanmatras. The subtle rudiments are derived from egoism. Hence they are productions. They give origin to the five elements. Hence they are productive. The sixteen principles, the ten organs, the mind and the five elements, are productions only. They are unproductive, because none of them can give birth to a substance essentially different from itself. The Purusha or Spirit is neither a production, nor is it productive. It is without attributes.

The Object of the Sankhya Philosophy

The enquiry into this system of philosophy is to find out the means for eradicating the three sorts of pain, viz., internal or Adhyatmika (e.g., fever and other diseases), celestial or Adhidaivika (thunder, cold, heat, rain, etc.), and external or Adhibhautika (pain from animals, scorpion, etc.), and the disease of rebirths. Pain is an embarrassment. It stands in the way of doing Yoga Sadhana and attaining Moksha or release. Kapila Muni imparted a knowledge of the twenty-five principles which annihilates this pain. According to the Sankhya philosophy, he who knows the twenty-five principles attains liberation. The ultimate cessation of the three kinds of pain is the final goal of life.

PRAKRITI

'Prakriti' means that which is primary, that which precedes what is made. It comes from 'Pra' (before) and 'Kri' (to make). It resembles the Vedantic Maya. It is the one root of the universe. It is called Pradhana or the chief, because all effects are founded on it and it is the root of the universe and of all objects.

Characteristics of Prakriti

Pradhana or Prakriti is eternal, all-pervading, immovable. It is one. It has no cause, but is the cause of all effects. Prakriti is independent and uncaused, while the products are caused and dependent. Prakriti depends only on the activity of its own constituent Gunas (metaphysical properties).

Prakriti is destitute of intelligence. It is like a string of three strands. The three Gunas form the three strands. Prakriti is mere dead matter which is equipped with certain potentialities due to the Gunas.

The Modifications of Prakriti

Crude matter is without form. Mahat or the Cosmic Intelligence is its first form. Intellect is the matter for egoism. Egoism is a form of intellect. It is the matter from which the senses and the rudimental elements are formed. The senses and the rudimental elements are forms of egoism. The gross elements are forms of the rudimental elements.

Intellect, egoism and the five subtle rudiments or Tanmatras are the effects of Prakriti. This creation, from intellect down to the elements, is brought about by the modifications of Prakriti. Having observed the effects, the cause (Prakriti) is inferred. It is imperceptible from its subtlety. It must, therefore, be inferred from its effects.

The Function of Prakriti

Prakriti is the basis of all objective existence. Prakriti does not create for itself. All objects are for the enjoyment of the spirit or soul. Prakriti creates only when it comes into union with Purusha, like a crystal vase with a flower. This work is done for the emancipation of each soul. As it is the function of milk to nourish the calf, so it is the function of Prakriti to liberate the soul.

THE GUNAS

According to the Sankhya philosophy, Prakriti is composed of three Gunas or forces, called Sattva (purity, light, harmony), Rajas (passion, activity, motion) and Tamas (inertia, darkness, inertness, inactivity).

Guna means a cord. The Gunas bind the soul with a triple bond. These Gunas are not the Nyaya-Vaiseshika Gunas. They are the actual substances or ingredients, of which Prakriti is constituted. They make up the whole world evolved out of Prakriti. They are not conjoined in equal quantities, but in varying proportions, one or the other being in excess. Just as Sat-Chit-Ananda is the Vedantic trinity, so also the Gunas are the Sankhyan trinity.

Interaction Between the Gunas Leads to Evolution

The three Gunas are never separate. They support one another. They intermingle with one another. They are intimately related as the flame, the oil and the wick of a lamp. They form the very substance of Prakriti. All objects are composed of the three Gunas. The Gunas act on one another. Then there is evolution or manifestation. Destruction is only non-manifestation.

The Gunas are the objects. Purusha is the witness-subject. Prakriti evolves under the influence of Purusha. Mahat or the Great (Intellect), the Cause of the whole world, is the first product of the evolution of Prakriti. Ahankara arises after Buddhi. Agency belongs to Ahankara. It is the principle that creates individuality. Mind is born of Ahankara. It carries out the orders of the will through the organs of action (Karma Indriyas). It reflects and doubts (Sankalpa-Vikalpa). It synthesises the sense-data into percepts. The mind takes part in both perception and action. There is no separate Prana Tattva in the Sankhya system. The Vedanta system has a separate Prana Tattva. In the Sankhya system, mind, with the organs, produces the five vital airs. Prana is a modification of the senses. It does not subsist in their absence.

Characteristics of the Three Gunas

Sattva is equilibrium. When Sattva prevails, there is peace or tranquillity. Rajas is activity which is expressed as Raga-Dvesha, likes or dislikes, love or hatred, attraction or repulsion. Tamas is that binding force with a tendency to lethargy, sloth and foolish actions. It causes delusion or non-discrimination.

When Sattva is predominant, it overpowers Rajas and Tamas. When Rajas is dominant, it overpowers Sattva and Tamas. When Tamas is predominant, it overpowers Rajas and Sattva.

How Man Is Affected by the Three Gunas

There are three Gunas in every man. Sometimes, Sattva prevails in him. Then he is calm and tranquil. He reflects and meditates. At other times, Rajas prevails in him and he does various sorts of worldly activities. He is passionate and active. Sometimes, Tamas prevails. He becomes lazy, dull, inactive and careless. Tamas generates delusion.

Again, one of these Gunas is generally predominant in different men. A Sattvic man is virtuous. He leads a pure and pious life. A Rajasic man is passionate and active. A Tamasic man is dull and inactive.

Sattva makes a man divine and noble, Rajas makes him thoroughly human and selfish, and Tamas makes him bestial and ignorant. There is much Sattva in a sage or saint and there is much Rajas in a soldier, politician and businessman.

THE PURUSHA

Characteristics of the Purusha

The Purusha or the Self is beyond Prakriti. It is eternally

separate from the latter. Purusha is without beginning or end. It is without attributes and without qualities. It is subtle and omnipresent. It is beyond mind, intellect and the senses. It is beyond time, space and causality. It is the eternal seer. It is perfect and immutable. It is pure consciousness (Chidrupa).

The Purusha is not the doer. It is the witness. The Purusha is like a crystal without any colour. It appears to be coloured by the different colours which are placed before it. It is not material. It is not a result of combination. Hence it is immortal. The Purushas or souls are infinite in number, according to the Sankhya. There are many Purushas. If the Purushas were one, all should become free if any one attained release.

The different souls are fundamentally identical in nature. There is no movement for the Purusha. It does not go anywhere when it attains freedom or release.

Souls exist eternally separate from each other and from Prakriti. Each soul retains its individuality. It remains unchanged through all transmigrations. Each soul is a witness of the act of a separate creation, without taking part in the act. It is a looker-on uniting itself with the unintelligent Prakriti, like a lame man mounted on a blind man's shoulders, in order to behold the phenomena of creation, which Prakriti herself is not able to observe.

The Purusha or the Self is the witness (Sakshi), a spectator (Drashta), a by-stander (Madhyastha), solitary (Kaivalya), passive and indifferent (Udasina).

Inference of the Existence of the Purusha

Intelligence cannot belong to the intellect, because the intellect is material and is the effect of Prakriti which is non-intelligent. If intelligence is absent in the cause, it cannot manifest itself in the effect. Therefore, there must be a distinct principle of intelligence and this principle is Purusha or the Self.

The insentient body seems sentient on account of its union

with the Self, and the Self appears as the agent. Just as a pot with cold water appears to be cold, with hot water seems to be hot, so intellect and the rest seem to be sentient on account of union with the Purusha. This mutual transfer of properties is like that of fire and iron, or that of the sun and water.

There must be a Supervisor over and above the Pradhana or Prakriti. The Supervisor is Purusha or the Self.

Prakriti and its products are objects of enjoyment. There must exist an enjoyer who must be an intelligent principle. This intelligent enjoyer is Purusha or the Self.

Just as chair and bench are for the use of another, so also this body, senses and mind are for the use of the Self which is immaterial, as it is destitute of attributes and as it is beyond the Gunas. The Purusha is the witness of the Gunas. The Gunas are the objects. Purusha is the witness-subject. Hence, it is not affected by pleasure, pain and delusion which are attributes of the three Gunas, Sattva, Rajas and Tamas, respectively. If pain is natural to the Purusha and if the Purusha is not naturally free from the action of the Gunas, no salvation from rebirth is possible.

Purusha and Prakriti—A Contrast

The characteristics of Prakriti and Purusha are contrary in nature. Purusha is consciousness, while Prakriti is non-consciousness. Purusha is inactive (Akarta), while Prakriti is active. Purusha is destitute of the Gunas, while Prakriti is characterised by the three Gunas. Purusha is unchanging, while Prakriti is changing. The knower is Purusha. The known is Prakriti. The knower is the subject or the silent witness. The known is the visible object.

THE UNIVERSE

The world is evolved with its different elements when the equilibrium in Prakriti is disturbed. The countless Purushas exert on Prakriti a mechanical force which distracts the equipoise of Prakriti and produces a movement. Then the evolution of the universe starts.

The Process of Evolution and Involution

Prakriti is the root of the universe. Prakriti is both the material and the efficient cause of the universe. From this Prakriti emanates the cosmic Buddhi or Mahat. From Mahat proceeds the cosmic Ahankara or the principle of egoism. From this egoism emanate the ten senses and the mind on the subjective side, and the five subtle Tanmatras of sound, smell, taste, colour and touch on the objective side. From these Tanmatras proceed the five gross elements—earth, water, fire, air and ether.

Akasa (ether) has the property of sound which is the Vishaya or object for the ear. Vayu (air) has the property of touch which is the Vishaya for the skin. Tejas (fire) has the property of form or colour which is the Vishaya for the eye. Apas (water) has the property of taste which is the Vishaya for the tongue. Prithvi (earth) has the property of odour which is the Vishaya for the nose. Each of these elements, after the first, has also the property of the preceding besides its own.

During dissolution of the world, the products return by a reverse movement into the preceding stages of development, and ultimately into Prakriti. Earth merges in its cause, water, water in fire, fire in air, air in Akasa; and Akasa in Ahankara, Ahankara in Mahat, and Mahat in Prakriti. This is the process of involution. There is no end to Samsara or the play of Prakriti. This cycle of evolution and involution has neither a beginning nor an end.

THE PROCESS OF KNOWLEDGE

An object excites the senses. The mind arranges the sense-impressions into a percept. Egoism refers it to the Self. Intellect forms the concept. It converts the percept into a concept and presents it to the Purusha. Then there is knowledge of the object.

Before you engage in any matter, you first observe or consider, then you reflect, and then determine: "This must be done by me;" and then you proceed to act. This ascertainment: "Such act is to be done by me," is the determination of the intellect (Adhyavasaya). The intellect is an instrument which receives the ideas or images conveyed through the organs of sense and the mind, constructs them into a conclusive idea, and presents this idea to the Self. The function of the intellect is determination (Nischaya).

The mind is both an organ of sensation and of action. The senses receive simple impressions from without. The mind cooperates with the senses, and then the impressions are perceived. The mind ponders, the intellect determines, and egoism becomes conscious.

Agency belongs to egoism—the Ahankara or the I-maker—which is itself a product of Prakriti, but not to the Purusha or Self who is always a silent witness.

Intellect, egoism, mind and the eye see a form at once, in one instant, and come immediately to the conclusion, say, "This is a jar." The same three, with the tongue, at once relish taste; with the nose smell; and so with the ear and the skin. The function is also occasionally gradual. A man going along a road sees an object at a distance. A doubt arises in his mind whether it is a post or a man. He then sees a bird sitting on it. Then the doubt is removed by the reflection of the mind. The intellect makes a determination that it is a post only. Then the egoism say: "I am certain it is a post only." In this way, the functions of the mind, intellect, egoism and the eye are gradual, also. There is leisure for the eye to see, for the mind to reflect or consider, for egoism to apply, and for the intellect to conclude. There is another example. The ear hears the twang of a bowstring; the mind reflects that this must be for the shooting of an arrow; egoism says: "It is aimed at me;" and the intellect determines: "I must run at once."

The intellect, the mind and egoism are the door-keepers. The five senses of perception or Jnana-Indriyas are the gates. The intellect is the instrument or organ which is the medium between the senses and the Self.

THE INTELLECT AND ITS FUNCTIONS

The intellect or the Buddhi is the most important of all the products of Prakriti. The senses present their objects to the intellect. The intellect exhibits them to the Purusha. The intellect discriminates the difference between Purusha and Prakriti.

The intellect is the instrument or organ which is the medium between the other organs and the Self. All ideas derived from sensation, reflection, or consciousness are deposited in the chief or great instrument, intellect, before they can be made known to the Self for whose use and advantage alone they have assembled. They convey impressions or ideas with the properties or effects of pleasure, pain and indifference, accordingly as they are influenced by the qualities of Sattva (purity), Rajas (passion) or Tamas (darkness).

Just as the headman of a village collects the taxes from the villagers and pays them to the collector of the district, just as the local collector pays the amount to the minister, and the minister receives it for the use of the state, so also the mind receives the ideas from the external organs, transfers them to egoism, and egoism delivers them to the intellect which is the general superintendent and takes charge of them for the use of the Sovereign Self.

The intellect is the prime minister of Purusha. It brings for Purusha the fruition of all that is to be experienced. It appears to be intelligent on account of the reflection of Purusha which is very near to it, though, by itself, it is really non-intelligent.

The Jiva is the soul in union with the senses. It is limited by the body. It is endowed with egoism. The reflection of Purusha in the Buddhi or intellect appears as the ego or the empirical soul. It is associated with ignorance and Karma. It is subject to pleasure and pain, action and its fruits, and rotates in the cycle of births and deaths.

The Jiva must realise the perfection of the Purusha. It must attain to the status of the Purusha. Every Jiva has in it the higher Purusha hidden within. It must become conscious of the real nature of the higher Purusha. Freedom or perfection is a return into one's true Self. It is the removal of an illusion which conceals one's true nature.

RELEASE

Bondage belongs to Prakriti, but is attributed to Purusha. Purusha is eternally free. Union of Purusha with Prakriti due to non-discrimination is bondage; the failure to discriminate between Purusha and Prakriti is the cause of Samsara or bondage; and disunion of Purusha and Prakriti due to discrimination is emancipation. Release is not merging in the Absolute, but isolation from Prakriti.

The object of the Sankhya system is to effect the liberation of the Purusha or Self from the fetters which bind it on account of its union with Prakriti. This is done by conveying the correct knowledge of the twenty-four constituent principles of creation, and rightly discriminating the Self from them.

In the Sankhya system, the Pramanas or means of obtaining the correct measure of existing things, are three, viz., Pratyaksha or perception by the senses, Anumana (inference) and Apta-Vachana (trustworthy testimony).

How Release Is Effected

When the separation of the soul from the body takes place by destruction of the effects of virtue, vice and the rest, and

Prakriti ceases to act in respect to it, then there is the final and absolute emancipation or the final beatitude.

When the fruits of acts cease, and body—both gross and subtle—dissolves, Nature does not exist with respect to the individual soul. The soul attains the state called Kaivalya. It is freed from the three kinds of pain.

The Linga-Deha or subtle body which migrates from one gross body to another in successive births, is composed of intellect, egoism, mind, the five organs of knowledge, the five organs of action and the five Tanmatras. The impressions of actions done in various births are imbedded in the subtle body. The conjunction of the Linga-Deha with the gross physical body constitutes birth and separation of the Linga-Deha from the gross physical body is death. This Linga-Deha is destroyed by the knowledge of the Purusha.

When one attains perfect Knowledge, virtue and vice become destitute of causal energy, but the body continues for some time on account of the previous impulse, just as after the action of the potter has stopped, the wheel continues to revolve owing to the momentum given to it.

Release Is Nothing but Termination of the Play of Prakriti

The union of the Self with Nature or Prakriti is like the association of a lame man with a blind man. A lame man and a blind man were deserted by their fellow-travellers in a forest. They agreed to divide between them the duties of walking and of seeing. The lame man mounted himself on the shoulders of the blind man and directed the blind man. The blind man was able to pursue his route by the directions of his friend. Even so, the Self is like the lame man. The faculty of seeing is in the Self, not that of moving. The faculty of moving, but not of seeing, is in Prakriti. Prakriti is like the blind man. The lame man and the blind man separated when they reached their destination. Even so, Prakriti, having effected the liberation of the

Self, ceases to act. The Self obtains Kaivalya or the final beatitude. Consequently, their respective purposes being effected, the connection between them terminates. The Self attains liberation by knowledge of Prakriti.

Prakriti's performances are solely for the benefit and enjoyment of the Self. Prakriti takes hold of the hand of the Self and shows it the whole show of the universe, and makes it enjoy everything which this world can give, and lastly helps it in its liberation.

In truth, the Self is neither bound nor released, nor does it migrate, but Nature alone in relation to various beings is bound, is released, and migrates.

As a dancing girl, having exhibited herself on the stage to the spectators, stops dancing, so also Nature ceases to function when she has made herself manifest to the Purusha or the Self. Nothing is more modest than Prakriti, when she becomes conscious that she has been seen by the Purusha. She does not again expose herself to the gaze of the Purusha.

THE YOGA

INTRODUCTION

Prostrations to Sri Patanjali Maharshi, the exponent of the Raja Yoga system of philosophy, the first systematiser of the Yoga school, whose 'Yoga Sutras' is the basic text.

The word Yoga comes from the root *Yuj* which means to *join.* Yoga is restraint of the activities of the mind, and is the union of the individual soul with the Supreme Soul.

Hiranyagarbha is the founder of the Yoga system. The Yoga founded by Patanjali Maharshi is a branch or supplement of the Sankhya. It has its own charm for students of a mystic temperament and of a contemplative type. It claims greater orthodoxy than the Sankhya proper by directly acknowledging the existence of a Supreme Being (Isvara).

The God of Patanjali is a Special Purusha or Particular Soul unaffected by afflictions, works, fruition and vehicles. In Him is the highest limit of the seed of omniscience. He, being unconditioned by time, is the Teacher of even the ancients. He is ever free.

The sacred syllable Om is the symbol of God. Repetition of Om and meditation on Om, should be practised. This will remove all obstacles and will lead to the attainment of God-realisation.

The Yoga Sutras

The 'Yoga Sutras' of Patanjali form the oldest text-book of the Yoga school. It has four chapters. The first chapter, Samadhi Pada, deals with the nature and aim of Samadhi. The second chapter, Sadhana Pada, explains the means of attaining this end. The third chapter, Vibhuti Pada, gives a description of the supernatural powers or Siddhis that can be achieved through the Yoga practices. The fourth chapter, Kaivalya Pada, describes the nature of salvation.

Raja Yoga and Hatha Yoga

Patanjali's Yoga is Ashtanga-Yoga or Yoga with eight limbs. This Yoga deals with the discipline of the mind and its psychic powers. Hatha Yoga treats of the methods of bodily control and regulation of breath. The culmination of Hatha Yoga is Raja Yoga. A progressive Sadhana in Hatha Yoga leads to the accomplishment of Raja Yoga. Hatha Yoga is a ladder to ascend to the stage or summit of Raja Yoga. When the movement of breath is stopped by means of Kumbhaka, the mind becomes supportless. Purification of the body and control of breath is the direct aim of Hatha Yoga. The Shat-Karmas or six acts of purification of the body are Dhauti (cleansing of the stomach), Basti (natural form of enema), Neti (cleansing of the nostrils), Trataka (unwinkingly gazing at some object), Nauli (churning of the belly) and Kapalabhati (removal of the phlegm through a certain kind of Pranayama). The body is rendered healthy, light, strong and steady by the practice of Asanas, Bandhas and Mudras.

Yoga—A Methodical Effort to Control the Mind

Yoga is a method of strict discipline. It imposes restrictions on diet, sleep, company, behaviour, speech and thought. It should be practised under the careful supervision of an expert and illumined Yogi.

Yoga is a methodical effort to control the mind and attain perfection. Yoga heightens the power of concentration, arrests the wanderings and vagaries of the mind, and helps to attain the superconscious state or Nirvikalpa Samadhi. The practice of Yoga removes restlessness of body and mind. It removes the impurities of the mind also and steadies it. The aim of Yoga is to teach the means by which the individual soul may attain complete union with the Supreme Soul. This fusion or blending of the individual soul with the Supreme Purusha is effected by controlling the Vrittis or thoughts of the mind. This is a state which is as clear as crystal, since the mind is not coloured by contact with worldly objects.

THE YOGA AND THE SANKHYA

Kapila's system is Nirisvara Sankhya, as in it there is no Isvara or God. The system of Patanjali is Sa-Isvara Sankhya, because there is Isvara or Special Purusha in it, who is untouched by afflictions, works, desires, etc. Patanjali built his system on the background of the metaphysics of the Sankhya. Patanjali accepts the twenty-five principles of the Sankhya. He accepts the metaphysical view of the Sankhya system, but lays great emphasis upon the practical side of self-discipline for the realisation of the absolute unity of the Purusha or true Self.

Sankhya is a system of metaphysics. Yoga is a system of practical discipline. The former lays emphasis upon investigation and reasoning, and the latter upon concentration of the will-power.

The individual soul in the Yoga has greater freedom. It can attain salvation with the help of God. The Sankhya maintains that knowledge is the means to salvation. The Yoga holds that concentration, meditation and Samadhi will lead to Kaivalya or Independence. The Yoga system holds that the Yogic process consists in the suppression of the diversities of mental functions and the concentration of the mental energy on the self-luminous Purusha.

THE EIGHT LIMBS OF RAJA YOGA

Raja Yoga is known by the name Ashtanga-Yoga or the Yoga with Eight Limbs. The eight limbs are: (i) Yama (restraint), (ii) Niyama (observances), (iii) Asana (posture), (iv) Pranayama (control of breath), (v) Pratyahara (withdrawal of the senses), (vi) Dharana (concentration), (vii) Dhyana (meditation), and (viii) Samadhi (superconscious state). The first five of these form the external limbs (Bahir-anga) of Yoga. The last three form the internal limbs (Antar-anga) of Yoga.

Yama and Niyama

The practice of Yama and Niyama constitutes ethical discipline. It prepares the Yogic student for the real practice of Yoga. The Yogic student should practise non-violence, truthfulness, continence, non-stealing, and non-acceptance of gifts which are conducive to luxurious living; and practise purity, contentment, austerity, sacred study and surrender to God. The chief of them is non-violence (Ahimsa). All other virtues are rooted in Ahimsa. Non-violence is abstinence from malice towards all living beings—in every way and at all times. It is not merely non-voilence, but non-hatred. The Yamas or restraints are the great universal vows (Mahavrata), not limited by caste, place or country, time or circumstances. They must be practised by all. There are no exceptions to these principles. Not even self-defence can justify murder for one who is practising the vow of non-violence. He should not kill even his enemy if he is to practise Yoga rigorously.

Asana, Pranayama and Pratyahara

Asana is steady, comfortable posture. Asana or posture is a physical help to concentration. When one obtains mastery over the Asana, he is free from the disturbance of the pairs of opposites. Pranayama or regulation of breath leads to tranquillity and steadiness of mind, and good health. Pratyahara is introversion. It is withdrawal of the senses from their objects. Yama, Niyama, Asana, Pranayama and Pratyahara are accessories to Yoga.

Dharana, Dhyana and Samadhi

Dharana, Dhyana and Samadhi are the three consecutive stages of the same process of mental concentration and are thus parts of an organic whole. Dharana is the effort to fix the mind steadily upon an object. Dhyana is continuous and unbroken fixity of the mind upon the object. Samadhi is fixity of the mind upon the object with such intensity of concentration as to become the object itself. The mind is wholly merged in and identified with the object upon which it is fixed.

Samyama or concentration, meditation and Samadhi are one and the same, that gives a knowledge of supersensual objects. Siddhis are by-products of concentration. The supernatural powers are really obstacles to Samadhi or freedom.

YOGA SAMADHI AND ITS CHARACTERISTICS

Dhyana or meditation culminates in Samadhi. The object of meditation is Samadhi. Samadhi is the goal of Yoga discipline. Body and mind become dead, as it were, to all external impressions. The connection with the outer world is broken. In Samadhi, the Yogi enters into Supreme Silence which is untouched by the ceaseless noises of the outer world. The mind ceases its functioning. The senses are absorbed in the mind.

When all the modifications of the mind are controlled, the Seer, the Purusha, rests in his own Self. Patanjali speaks of this in his Yoga Sutras as *Svarupa-Avasthanam* (establishment in one's true Self).

There are kinds or degrees of concentration or Samadhi, viz., Samprajnata or conscious and Asamprajnata or superconscious. In Samprajnata Samadhi, there are definite objects of concentration for resting. The mind remains conscious of the object. Savitarka (with deliberation), Nirvitarka (without deliberation), Savichara (with reflection), Nirvichara (without reflection), Sananda (with joy), and Sasmita (with the sense of personality) are forms of Samprajnata Samadhi. In Samprajnata Samadhi, there is a clear consciousness of the object meditated upon, as distinct from the subject. In Asamprajnata Samadhi, this distinction vanishes, it being transcended.

CONDITIONS FOR SUCCESS IN RAJA YOGA

The Importance of Yama and Niyama

Aspirants who desire to attain God-realisation should practise all the eight limbs of Yoga. On the destruction of the impurities through the practice of the eight limbs—or accessories—of Yoga, arises the light of wisdom leading to the discriminative knowledge.

For the attainment of Samadhi or union with the Divine, the practice of Yama and Niyama is an indispensable necessity. The Yogic student should practise Yama and observe Niyama side by side. It is not possible to attain perfection in meditation and Samadhi without the observance of the practice of Yama and Niyama. You cannot have concentration of mind without removing falsehood, deceit, cruelty, lust, etc., within. Without concentration of mind, meditation and Samadhi cannot be attained.

THE FIVE MENTAL PLANES ACCORDING TO THE SCHOOL OF PATANJALI

Kshipta, Mudha, Vikshipta, Ekagra and Niruddha are the

five mental planes according to the Raja Yoga school of Patanjali. The Kshipta plane is that wherein the mind wanders amongst various sensual objects. The mind is filled with Rajas. The Mudha plane is that wherein the mind is in a state of sleep and impotence on account of Tamas. The Vikshipta plane is that wherein Sattva preponderates, and the mind oscillates between meditation and objectivity. The rays of the mind are slowly collected and gathered. When Sattva increases, you will have cheerfulness of mind, one-pointedness of mind, conquest of the senses and fitness for the realisation of the Atman. The Ekagra plane is that wherein the mind is one-pointed. There is deep meditation. Sattva is free from Rajas and Tamas. The Niruddha plane is that wherein the mind is under perfect control. All the Vrittis of the mind are annihilated.

A Vritti is a whirlpool or thought-wave in the mind-lake. Every Vritti or mental modification leaves behind a Samskara or impression or latent tendency. This Samskara may manifest itself as a conscious state when the occasion arises. Similar Vrittis strengthen similar dispositions. When all the Vrittis are arrested, the mind is in a balanced state (Samapatti).

Disease, langour, doubt, carelessness, laziness, worldliness, erroneous perception, failure to attain concentration and instability in it when attained, are the main obstacles to concentration.

THE FIVE KLESAS AND THEIR REMOVAL

According to Patanjali, Avidya (ignorance), Asmita (egoism), Raga-Dvesha (desire and aversion, or likes and dislikes) and Abhinivesa (clinging to mundane life) are the five great Klesas or afflictions that assail the mind. These are alleviated by means of continued Yogic practice, but not uprooted totally. They remain hidden in the from of seed. They sprout out again the moment they find an opportunity and favourable surroundings. But Asamprajnata Samadhi (Absolute-Experience) destroys even the seeds of these evils.

Avidya is the main cause of all our troubles. Egoism is the immediate result of Avidya. It fills us with desires and aversions, and veils the spiritual vision. The practice of Yoga-Samadhi uproots Avidya.

Practice of Kriya-Yoga

Kriya-Yoga purifies the mind, attenuates or thins out the five afflictions, and leads to Samadhi. Tapas (austerity), Svadhyaya (studying and understanding of scriptures) and Isvarapranidhana (worship of God and surrendering the fruit to God) constitute Kriya-Yoga.

Cultivation of friendliness (Maitri) towards equals, compassion (Karuna) towards inferiors, cheerfulness (Mudita) towards superiors and indifference (Upeksha) towards wicked people (or with regard to things pleasant and painful, good and bad) produce tranquillity of mind (Chitta-Prasada).

One can attain Samadhi through devotion to God. Devotion to God gives freedom. By Isvarapranidhana, the Yogic student obtains the grace of God.

Abhyasa and Vairagya

Abhyasa (practice) and Vairagya (dispassion, non-attachment) help in steadying and controlling the mind. The mind should be withdrawn again and again and brought back to the centre, whenever it goes out towards sensual objects. This is Abhyasa Yoga. Practice becomes fixed and steady, when pursued for a long time without any break and with perfect devotion.

The mind is a bundle of Trishnas (cravings). Practice of Vairagya will destroy all Trishnas. Vairagya turns the mind away from the objects. It does not allow the mind to go outwards (Bahirmukha action of the mind), but promotes its Antarmukha (inward-going) action.

THE STATE OF KAIVALYA OR ABSOLUTE INDEPENDENCE

The goal of life is the absolute separation of Purusha from

Prakriti. Freedom in Yoga, is Kaivalya or absolute independence. The soul is freed from the fetters of Prakriti. The Purusha is in its true form or Svarupa. When the soul realises that it is absolutely independent, and that it does not depend on anything else in this world, Kaivalya or Isolation comes in. The soul has removed the Avidya through discriminative knowledge (Viveka-khyati). The five Klesas or afflictions are burnt by the fire of Knowledge. The Self is not touched by the conditions of the Chitta. The Gunas retire to rest and the Self abides in its own divine essence. Even if one becomes a Mukta (liberated Soul), Prakriti and its modifications exist for others. This, the Yoga system holds, in agreement with the Sankhya.

THE PURVA MIMAMSA

INTRODUCTION

Adorations to Sri Jaimini, the founder of the Purva Mimamsa system, the disciple of Sri Vyasa Bhagavan!

Purva Mimamsa or Karma-Mimamsa is an enquiry into the earlier portion of the Vedas, an enquiry into the ritual of the Vedas or that portion of the Vedas which is concerned with the Mantras and the Brahmanas only. The Purva Mimamsa is so called, because it is earlier (Purva) than the Uttara Mimamsa, not so much in the chronological as in the logical sense.

Mimamsa—A System of Vedic Interpretation

Mimamsa is not a branch of any philosophical system. It is rather a system of Vedic interpretation. Its philosophical discussions amount to a kind of critical commentary on the Brahmana or ritual portion of the Veda. It interprets the Vedas in the literal sense. The central problem of Purva Mimamsa is ritual. Jaimini has systematised the rules of Mimamsa and established their validity in his work. The rules of Mimamsa are very important for the interpretation of the Hindu Law.

The Mimamsa Sutras of Jaimini give a detailed description

of the different sacrifices and their purposes, the doctrine of Apurva, and also some philosophical propositions. There are twelve chapters.

Sabara is the author of the chief commentary or Bhashya on the work of Jaimini. Kumarila, the Guru of Bhavabhuti, commented on the Sutra and the Bhashya. He proved the eternal character of the Vedas and the efficiency of Vedic ceremonials. Prabhakara was a pupil of Kumarila. He wrote a commentary on the Bhashya of Sabara.

Jaimini accepts the three Pramanas of perception (Pratyaksha), inference (Anumana) and authoritative testimony (Sabda or Veda). Jaimini holds that there is a perpetual connection between a word and its sense and that sound is eternal.

THE ETERNAL, SELF-EXISTENT VEDA

Jaimini was an opponent of rationalism and theism. The Veda was practically the only God for him. The eternal Veda needs no other basis to rest on. There is no divine revealer. The Veda itself is authoritative. It is the only source of our knowledge of Dharma. God was not necessary for him and his system. He said that Veda was itself the authority. His first aphorism 'Athato Dharma-Jijnasa' states the whole aim and object of his system, viz., a desire to know Dharma or duty, which consists in the performance of the rites and sacrifices prescribed by the Veda. Dharma itself bestows the rewards. The aim of Purva Mimamsa is to investigate into the nature of Dharma.

The Purva Mimamsa has a number of deities. The offerings may be made to them. The practice of Vedic Dharma is not in need of any Supreme Being or God. Vedic religion does not require the assistance of God. The eternal self-existent Veda serves all the purposes of Jaimini and the Purva Mimamsakas. Jaimini does not so much deny God as ignore Him.

PRACTICE OF VEDIC DHARMA—THE KEY TO HAPPINESS

Dharma is enjoined by the Vedas, known as the Sruti. Its practice leads to happiness. If the Smriti does not agree with the Sruti, the former is to be ignored. The practice by virtuous men or custom comes next to the Smriti. A Hindu should lead his life in accordance with the rules of the Vedas. A Hindu must perform Nitya Karmas like Sandhya, etc., and Naimittika Karmas during proper occasions, to get salvation. These are unconditional duties. If he fails to do these, he incurs the sin of omission (Pratyavaya Dosha). He performs Kamya Karmas to attain *special* ends. If he avoids prohibited actions (Nishiddha Karmas), he will avoid hell. If he performs the unconditional duties, he will attain salvation.

Some later Mimamsakas maintain that all works ought to be performed as an offering to God or the Supreme Being. Then they become the cause or means of emancipation.

If works or sacrifices are done in a mechanical way without feeling, Sraddha (faith) and devotion, they cannot help one to attain salvation. One may perform any number of sacrifices; and yet, there may not be any change in the heart, if they are performed without the right spirit or right mental attitude and right will. What is really wanted is not the ceremonial sacrifice, but the sacrifice of selfishness, egoism and Raga-Dvesha (likes and dislikes).

THE DOCTRINE OF APURVA

The fruits or rewards of sacrifices are not dispensed by any beneficient God. *Apurva* bestows the reward on the sacrificer. *Apurva* is the link or necessary connection between work and its fruit or result. Apurva is Adrishta. It is a positive, unseen force created by an act, which leads to the attainment of the fruit of the action. This is the view of Jaimini.

Others thinkers criticised severely that the unconscious or non-intelligent Apurva could not bestow the rewards. The Mimamsa system could not satisfy the intelligent, thoughtful men. Hence, the later Mimamsakas slowly introduced God. They declared that if sacrifices were performed in honour of the Supreme Being, it would lead to the achievement of the Supreme Good. Apurva cannot act, unless it is moved by God or the Supreme Being. He who makes the Apurva function is God.

THE SELF AND ITS CHARACTERISTICS

The self is distinct from the body, the senses and the intellect. The self is the experiencer or enjoyer. The body is the abode of experiences. The senses are the instruments of experience. The self perceives when it is in union with the mind. It experiences internally pleasure and pain; and externally, objects such as trees, rivers, plants, etc.

The self is not the senses, because it persists even when the senses are injured or destroyed. The body is made up of matter. The perceiver is distinct from the body. The self directs the body. The body is a servant of the self. There is some being which systhesises the various sense-data. That being or entity is the self. The self is all-pervading and imperishable. Selves are countless.

The real self survives the annihilation of the body. The performer of a sacrifice goes to heaven. Jaimini does not believe in Moksha. He believes in the existence of Svarga (heaven) attainable through Karma or sacrifice. The Veda promises rewards to the sacrificer to be enjoyed in another world.

THE LATER MIMAMSAKAS
Prabhakara and Kumarila

Jaimini showed the way to attain happiness in Svarga or heaven, but he did not tell anything about the problem of the final emancipation. The later writers like Prabhakara and Kumarila, however, could not avoid this problem of final salvation as it engaged the attention of the thinkers of other schools. Prabhakara says that the absolute cessation of the body caused by the total disappearance of Dharma and Adharma, whose operation is the cause of rebirth, is ultimate release or liberation. Man abandons prohibited acts, and the deeds which lead to happiness in heaven. He does the necessary expiations for exhausting the previously accumulated Karmas. He practises self-restraint and disciplines himself. He develops virtuous qualities. He frees himself from rebirths by a true knowledge of the self. One cannot attain release by *mere* knowledge. Exhaustion of Karmas only can bring about release. Knowledge prevents further accumulation of virtue and vice. Karma *by itself* cannot lead to the attainment of the final emancipation. Raga-Dvesha (likes and dislikes), which lead to the performance of actions, must be destroyed if one wants to attain Moksha. Moksha is the cessation of pleasure and pain. It is not a state of bliss, as the attributeless soul cannot have even bliss. It is simply the natural form of the soul.

The view of Kumarila comes very near to the view of Advaita Vedantins. Kumarila maintains that the Veda is composed by God and is Brahman in the form of sounds. Moksha is a positive state for him. It is the realisation of the Atman. He is of opinion that knowledge is not sufficient for salvation. He thinks that final emancipation can be attained through Karma (action) combined with Jnana (knowledge).

JAIMINI'S PHILOSOPHY IN A NUT-SHELL

According to Jaimini, performance of the actions that are enjoined in the Vedas is the Sadhana or means for attaining heaven. Karma-Kanda is the chief section of the Vedas. The cause of bondage is the performance of Nishiddha Karmas or prohibited actions. The self is Jada-Chetana, a combination of insentiency and intelligence. Souls are countless. The soul is doer and enjoyer. It is all-pervading. Jaimini does not believe in the creation of the world. He believes in grades of happiness in heaven and in Sadachara or right conduct, viz., *Satyam Vada* (Speak the truth), *Dharmam Chara* (Perform duty).

CRITICISM OF JAIMINI'S PHILOSOPHY

The Purva Mimamsa system of philosophy is said to be unsatisfactory and incomplete, inasmuch as it does not deal with the problems of the Ultimate Reality and its relation to soul and matter. There is no philosophical view of the world. The central feature is the performance of the sacrifices. This is the most essential or fundamental thing. "Perform sacrifices and enjoy in Heaven"—this is the sum and substance of Jaimini's teaching. This is his Moksha or the final goal. This cannot give satisfaction to the thinkers who know that the enjoyment in heaven is transitory, imperfect, sensual and worldly.

THE VEDANTA PHILOSOPHY

INTRODUCTION

Prostrations and adorations to Sri Vyasa, the founder of Uttara Mimamsa or the Vedanta system of philosophy, Avatara of Lord Vishnu, son of Sri Parasara Rishi.

Uttara Mimamsa or the Vedanta philosophy of Vyasa or Badarayana is placed as the last of the six orthodox systems, but, really, it ought to stand first.

The Uttara Mimamsa conforms closely to the doctrines propounded in the Upanishads. The term *Vedanta* means literally *the end or essence of the Veda*. It contains the doctrines set forth in the closing chapters of the Vedas. The closing chapters of the Vedas are the Upanishads. The Upanishads really form the essence of the Vedas.

THE BRAHMA SUTRAS OF BHAGAVAN VYASA

Sri Vyasa wrote the Brahma Sutras or the Vedanta Sutras which explain the doctrine of Brahman. Brahma Sutras are also known by the name Sariraka Sutras, because they deal with the embodiment of the Supreme Nirguna Brahman. 'Brahma Sutras' is one of the three books of the Prasthana Traya, the three authoritative books on Hinduism, the other two being the Upanishads and the Bhagavad-Gita. Sri Vyasa has systematised the principles of Vedanta and removed the apparent contradictions in the doctrines. The Brahma Sutras are 555 in number. Sri Sankara, Ramanuja, Madhva, Nimbarka, Vallabha, Bhaskara, Yadavaprakasa, Kesava, Nilakantha, Baladeva and Vijnana Bhikshu are the chief commentators on the Brahma Sutras. Each has commented in his own way and built his own philosophy. The most reputed teacher of this school of philosophy was Sri Sankaracharya.

Sri Vyasa has criticised the doctrines of the Vaiseshika system and the Sankhya system. The several schools of Buddhism and the Bhagavata doctrines are also discussed.

There are four chapters, viz., Samanvaya, Avirodha, Sadhana and Phala. In the first chapter, an account of the nature of Brahman and of its relation to the world and the individual soul, is given. In the second chapter, the rival theories, viz., Sankhya, Yoga, Vaiseshika, etc., are criticised. Suitable answers are given to the objections levelled against this view. In the third chapter, the means of attaining Brahma-Vidya are treated. In the fourth chapter, there is a description of the fruits of Brahma-Vidya. There is also a description of how the individual soul reaches Brahman through the Devayana or the path of the Devas, whence there is no return. The characteristics of the Jivanmukta or liberated soul are also discussed in this chapter. Each chapter has four parts (Padas). The Sutras in each part form Adhikaranas or topics.

The first five Sutras of the first chapter are very important. The first Sutra is: *"Athato Brahma-Jijnasa*—Now, therefore, the enquiry into Brahman." The first aphorism states the object of the whole system in one word, viz., Brahma-Jijnasa, the desire of knowing Brahman. The second Sutra is: *"Janmadyasya Yatah*—Brahman is the Supreme Being from whom proceeds the origin, sustenance and dissolution of the world." The third Sutra is: *"Sastra-Yonitvat*—The scriptures alone are the means of right knowledge. The omniscience of Brahman

ALL ABOUT HINDUISM

follows from Its being the source of the scriptures." The fourth Sutra is: *"Tat Tu Samanvayat*—That Brahman is to be known only from the scriptures and not independently by any other means is established, because it is the main purport of all Vedanta texts." The fifth Sutra is: *"Ikshater Na Asabdam*—On account of 'thinking,' Prakriti or Pradhana not being the first cause." Pradhana is not based on the scriptures. The last Sutra of the fourth chapter is: *"Anavrittih Sabdat, Anavrittih Sabdat*—There is no return for the released souls, on account of scriptural declaration to that effect."

BRAHMAN, MAYA AND JIVA

Brahman

Brahman, the Absolute, after creating the elements, enters them. It is the Golden Person in the sun. It is the Light of the soul. It is ever pure. It is Sat-Chit-Ananda, one without a second. It is Bhuma (infinite, unconditioned). It dwells in the heart of man. It is the source of everything.

Brahman is the material cause, as well as the instrumental cause, of the universe. Brahman and the universe are not different, just as the jar is not different from clay. Brahman develops Itself into the universe for Its own Lila or sporting, without undergoing the least change, and without ceasing to be Itself.

Brahman is without parts, without qualities, without action and emotion, beginningless, endless and immutable. It has no consciousness, such as is denoted by 'I' and 'Thou'. It is the only Reality. Brahman is to the external world what yarn is to cloth, what earth is to jar and what gold is to a ring.

Brahman is Paramarthika Satta (Absolute Reality). The world is Vyavaharika Satta (relative reality). The dream object is Pratibhasika Satta (apparent reality).

Maya

Maya is the Sakti (power) of God. It is the Karana Sarira

(causal body) of God. It hides the real and makes the unreal appear as real. It is neither Sat nor Asat nor Sat-Asat. It is Anirvachaniya (indescribable). Maya has two powers, viz., the power of veiling or Avarana Sakti and the power of projecting or Vikshepa Sakti. Man has forgotten his essential divine nature on account of the veiling power of Maya. This universe is projected owing to the Vikshepa Sakti of Maya.

Jiva

The Jiva or the individual soul is enclosed within five sheaths (Kosas), which are like the sheaths of an onion. The five sheaths are food-sheath (Annamaya Kosa), vital sheath (Pranamaya Kosa), mental sheath (Manomaya Kosa), intellectual sheath (Vijnanamaya Kosa) and the bliss-sheath (Anandamaya Kosa). The first sheath constitutes the physical body. The next three sheaths form the subtle body. The last sheath forms the causal body. The individual soul should transcend all its sheaths through meditation and become one with the Supreme Soul which is beyond the five Kosas. Then only it will attain liberation or freedom.

There are three states of consciousness for the individual soul, viz., the waking state, the dreaming state and the deep sleep state. Turiya or the fourth state is the superconscious state. Turiya is Brahman. Turiya is the silent witness of the three states. The individual should transcend the first three states and identify himself with the Turiya or the fourth state. Then only he can attain oneness with the Supreme Soul.

Avidya is the causal body of Jiva or the individual soul. The Jiva identifies itself with the body, mind and the senses on account of Avidya. It has the erroneous notion that the body is the soul, just as one has the wrong notion that the rope is the serpent, in twilight. The moment the individual soul is freed from the self-imposed ignorance by a proper understanding of the Truth through the Vedanta philosophy, Vichara (enquiry), reflection and meditation.on the Supreme Brahman, all the illusion disappears. The identity of the Jivatman and of the entire phenomenal world with the Supreme Soul or Brahman is re-established. The Jiva attains immortality and eternal bliss. It merges itself in Brahman or the Ocean of Bliss.

Badarayana believes in *Jivanmukti* or *Liberation While Living*.

CELEBRATED VEDANTIC FORMULAE

The following are the celebrated formulae of Vedanta:—

Ekam Eva Advitiyam—The Reality is One alone without a second.

Brahma Satyam Jagan Mithya, Jivo Brahmaiva Na Aparah—Brahman only exists truly, the world is false, the individual soul is Brahman only and no other.

Sarvam Khalvidam Brahma—All this is, indeed, Brahman.

Satyam Jnanam Anantam Brahma—Brahman is Truth, Knowledge and Infinity.

Brahmavid Brahmaiva Bhavati—The knower of Brahman becomes Brahman.

Santam, Sivam, Advaitam—Brahman is Peace, Auspiciousness and Non-duality.

Ayam Atma Santah—This Atman is Silence.

Asango Ayam Purusha—This Purusha is unattached.

Santam, Ajaram, Amritam, Abhayam, Param—This Brahman is Peace, without old age, Immortal, fearless and Supreme.

May you all understand the truths of Vedanta philosophy. May you all realise the bliss of oneness. May you all become Jivanmuktas while living.

CHAPTER 12

HINDU PHILOSOPHY—II

(THE SCHOOLS OF VEDANTA)

INTRODUCTION

The Sutras or aphorisms of Vyasa are the basis of the Vedanta philosophy. These Sutras have been variously explained by different commentators. From these interpretations have arisen several schools of philosophy, viz., Kevala Advaita philosophy of Sri Sankaracharya, the philosophy of Qualified Monism or Visishtadvaita of Sri Ramanujacharya, the Dvaita philosophy of Sri Madhvacharya, the Bhedabheda philosophy of Sri Nimbarkacharya, the Suddha Advaita philosophy of Sri Vallabhacharya, the Achintya Bhedabheda philosophy of Sri Chaitanya and the Siddhanta philosophy of Sri Meykandar.

Each system of philosophy treats of three main problems, viz., God, world and soul. The several schools of philosophy are only different attempts at discovering the Truth.

The different Acharyas, belonging to distinctly different cults, became founders of sects and great system-builders. The followers of these schools sought to prove their orthodoxy by interpreting the Vedanta Sutras in accordance with their own tenets, showing their claim to be based on, and regularly evolved from, ancient tradition.

SRUTI—THE COMMON BASIS OF ALL SCHOOLS

The Vedanta schools base their doctrines on the Upanishads. The Upanishads, the Vedanta Sutras and the Bhagavad-Gita are regarded as the authoritative scriptures. They are called Prasthana-Traya Granthas. Different commentators of the Vedanta Sutras have formed different views on the true nature of Brahman, but they all base their theories on the supreme authority of the

Sruti. To reject any one of these views is to reject the Sruti it-self.

THE THREE MAIN SCHOOLS OF METAPHYSICAL THOUGHT

Dvaita, Visishtadvaita and Advaita

Sri Sankara, Sri Ramanuja and Sri Madhva are the most illustrious commentators on the Vedanta Sutras. These commentators have tried to establish theories of their own, such as Advaita-Vada (unqualified non-dualism or uncompromising or rigorous monism), Visishtadvaita-Vada (differentiated or qualified monism) and Dvaita-Vada (strict or rigorous dualism). Sankaracharya had in view, while preparing his commentary, chiefly the purpose of combating the baneful effects which blind ritualism had brought to bear upon Hinduism.

Dualism (Dvaita), Qualified Monism (Visishtadvaita) and Monism (Advaita) are the three main schools of metaphysical thought. They are all stages on the way to the Ultimate Truth, viz., Para-Brahman. They are rungs on the ladder of Yoga. They are not at all contradictory. On the contrary, they are complimentary to one another. These stages are harmoniously arranged in a graded series of spiritual experiences. Dualism, Qualified Monism, Pure Monism—all these culminate eventually in the Advaita Vedantic realisation of the Absolute or the transcendental Trigunatita Ananta Brahman.

Madhva said: "Man is the servant of God," and established his Dvaita philosophy. Ramanuja said: "Man is a ray or spark of God," and established his Visishtadvaita philosophy. Sankara said: "Man is identical with Brahman or the Eternal Soul," and established his Kevala Advaita philosophy.

A Dvaitin wants to serve the Lord as a servant. He wishes to play with the Lord. He wishes to taste the sugar-candy. A Visishtadvaitin wants to become like Lord Narayana and enjoy the divine. He does not wish to merge himself or become identical with the Lord. He wishes to remain as a spark. A Jnani merges himself in Brahman. He wishes to become identical with Brahman. He wants to become the sugar-candy itself.

People have different temperaments and different capacities. So, different schools of philosophy are also necessary. The highest rung is Advaita philosophy. A dualist or qualified monist eventually becomes a Kevala Advaitin.

DIFFERENT CONCEPTIONS OF BRAHMAN ONLY DIFFERENT APPROACHES TO THE REALITY

Nimbarkacharya reconciles all the different views regarding the Lord taken up by Sankara, Ramanuja, Madhva and others, and proves that their views are all true with reference to the particular aspect of Brahman dealt with by them, each in his own way. Sankara has taken Reality in Its transcendental aspect, while Ramanuja has taken It in Its immanent aspect, principally; but, Nimbarka has adjusted different views taken by the different commentators.

Sri Sankaracharya, Sri Ramanujacharya, Sri Madhvacharya, Sri Vallabhacharya and Sri Nimbarkacharya—*all* were great souls. We cannot say that Sri Sankara was greater than Sri Ramanuja, or Sri Vallabha was greater than Nimbarka, etc. All were Avatara Purushas. Each one incarnated himself on this earth to complete a definite mission, to preach and propagate certain doctrines which were necessary to help the growth of a certain type of people, who flourished at a certain period, who were in a certain stage of evolution. All schools of philosophy are necessary. Each philosophy is best suited to a certain type of people. The different conceptions of Brahman are but different approaches to the Reality. It is extremely difficult, rather impossible, for the finite soul to get—all at once—a clear conception of the Illimitable or Infinite Soul, and more so, to express it in adequate terms. All cannot grasp the highest Kevala Advaita philosophy of Sri Sankara all at once.

The mind has to be disciplined properly before it is rendered as a fit instrument to grasp the tenets of Sri Sankara's Advaita Vedanta.

Salutations and adorations to all Acharyas! Glory to the Acharyas! May their blessings be upon us all.

THE ADVAITA PHILOSOPHY OF SRI SANKARA

INTRODUCTION

The first systematic exponent of the Advaita is Gaudapada, who is the Parama-Guru (preceptor's preceptor) of Sri Sankara. Govinda was the disciple of Gaudapada. He became the preceptor of Sankara. Gaudapada has given the central teaching of Advaita Vedanta in his celebrated Mandukya Karikas. But it was Sankara who brought forth the final beautiful form of Advaita philosophy, and gave perfection and finishing touch to it. Carefully go through Sri Sankara's commentaries on the principal Upanishads, the Brahma Sutras and the Bhagavad-Gita. You will clearly understand his Advaita philosophy. The commentary on the Vedanta Sutras by Sankara is known as Sariraka Bhashya.

The teachings of Sankara can be summed up in half a verse: "*Brahma Satyam Jagan Mithya Jivo Brahmaiva Na Aparah—* Brahman (the Absolute) is alone real; this world is unreal; and the Jiva or the individual soul is non-different from Brahman." This is the quintessence of his philosophy.

The Advaita taught by Sri Sankara is a rigorous, absolute one. According to Sri Sankara, whatever is, is Brahman. Brahman Itself is absolutely homogeneous. All difference and plurality are illusory.

BRAHMAN—THE ONE WITHOUT A SECOND

The Atman is self-evident (Svatah-siddha). It is not established by extraneous proofs. It is not possible to deny the Atman, because It is the very essence of the one who denies It. The Atman is the basis of all kinds of knowledge, presuppositions and proofs. Self is within, Self is without; Self is before, Self is behind; Self is on the right, Self is on the left; Self is above and Self is below.

Brahman is not an object, as It is Adrisya, beyond the reach of the eyes. Hence the Upanishads declare: "*Neti Neti*—not this, not this, not that." This does not mean that Brahman is a negative concept, or a metaphysical abstraction, or a non-entity, or a void. It is not another. It is all-full, infinite, changeless, self-existent, self-delight, self-knowledge and self-bliss. It is Svarupa, essence. It is the essence of the knower. It is the Seer (Drashta), Transcendent (Turiya) and Silent Witness (Sakshi).

Sankara's Supreme Brahman is impersonal, Nirguna (without Gunas or attributes), Nirakara (formless), Nirvisesha (without special characteristics), immutable, eternal and Akarta (non-agent). It is above all needs and desires. It is always the Witnessing Subject. It can never become an object as It is beyond the reach of the senses. Brahman is non-dual, one without a second. It has no other beside It. It is destitute of difference, either external or internal. Brahman cannot be described, because description implies distinction. Brahman cannot be distinguished from any other than It. In Brahman, there is not the distinction of substance and attribute. Sat-Chit-Ananda constitute the very essence or Svarupa of Brahman, and not just Its attributes.

The Nirguna Brahman of Sankara is impersonal. It becomes a personal God or Saguna Brahman only through Its association with Maya.

Saguna Brahman and Nirguna Brahman are not two different Brahmans. Nirguna Brahman is not the contrast, antithesis or opposite of Saguna Brahman. The same Nirguna Brahman appears as Saguna Brahman for the pious worship of devotees. It is the same Truth from two different points of view. Nirguna Brahman is the higher Brahman, the Brahman from the transcendental viewpoint (Paramarthika); Saguna

Brahman is the lower Brahman, the Brahman from the relative viewpoint (Vyavaharika).

THE WORLD—A RELATIVE REALITY

The world is not an illusion according to Sankara. The world is relatively real (Vyavaharika Satta), while Brahman is absolutely real (Paramarthika Satta). The world is the product of Maya or Avidya. The unchanging Brahman appears as the changing world through Maya. Maya is a mysterious indescribable power of the Lord which hides the real and manifests itself as the unreal. Maya is not real, because it vanishes when you attain knowledge of the Eternal. It is not unreal also, because it exists till knowledge dawns in you. The superimposition of the world on Brahman is due to Avidya or ignorance.

NATURE OF THE JIVA AND THE MEANS TO MOKSHA

To Sankara, the Jiva or the individual soul is only relatively real. Its individuality lasts only so long as it is subject to unreal Upadhis or limiting conditions due to Avidya. The Jiva identifies itself with the body, mind and the senses, when it is deluded by Avidya or ignorance. It thinks, it acts and enjoys, on account of Avidya. In reality it is not different from Brahman or the Absolute. The Upanishads declare emphatically: "*Tat Tvam Asi*—That Thou Art." Just as the bubble becomes one with the ocean when it bursts, just as the pot-ether becomes one with the universal ether when the pot is broken, so also the Jiva or the empirical self becomes one with Brahman when it gets knowledge of Brahman. When knowledge dawns in it through annihilation of Avidya, it is freed from its individuality and finitude and realises its essential Satchidananda nature. It merges itself in the ocean of bliss. The river of life joins the ocean of existence. This is the Truth.

The release from Samsara means, according to Sankara, the absolute merging of the individual soul in Brahman due to dismissal of the erroneous notion that the soul is distinct from

Brahman. According to Sankara, Karma and Bhakti are means to Jnana which is Moksha.

VIVARTA VADA OR THE THEORY OF SUPERIMPOSITION

To Sankara the world is only relatively real (Vyavaharika Satta). He advocated Vivarta-Vada or the theory of appearance or superimposition (Adhyasa). Just as snake is superimposed on the rope in twilight, this world and body are superimposed on Brahman or the Supreme Self. If you get knowledge of the rope, the illusion of snake in the rope will vanish. Even so, if you get knowledge of Brahman or the Imperishable, the illusion of body and world will disappear. In Vivarta-Vada, the cause produces the effect without undergoing any change in itself. Snake is only an appearance on the rope. The rope has not transformed itself into a snake, like milk into curd. Brahman is immutable and eternal. Therefore, It cannot change Itself into the world. Brahman becomes the cause of the world through Maya, which is Its inscrutable mysterious power or Sakti.

When you come to know that it is only a rope, your fear disappears. You do not run away from it. Even so, when you realise the eternal immutable Brahman, you are not affected by the phenomena or the names and forms of this world. When Avidya or the veil of ignorance is destroyed through knowledge of the Eternal, when Mithya Jnana or false knowledge is removed by real knowledge of the Imperishable or the living Reality, you shine in your true, pristine, divine splendour and glory.

THE ADVAITA—A PHILOSOPHY WITHOUT A PARALLEL

The Advaita philosophy of Sri Sankaracharya is lofty, sublime and unique. It is a system of bold philosophy and logical subtlety. It is highly interesting, inspiring and elevating. No other philosophy can stand before it in boldness, depth and subtle thinking. Sankara's philosophy is complete and perfect.

Sri Sankara was a mighty, marvellous genius. He was a

master of logic. He was a profound thinker of the first rank. He was a sage of the highest realisation. He was an Avatara of Lord Siva. His philosophy has brought solace, peace and illumination to countless persons in the East and the West. The Western thinkers bow their heads at the lotus-feet of Sri Sankara. His philosophy has soothed the sorrows and afflictions of the most forlorn persons, and brought hope, joy, wisdom, perfection, freedom and calmness to many. His system of philosophy commands the admiration of the whole world.

THE VISISHTADVAITA PHILOSOPHY OF SRI RAMANUJA

INTRODUCTION

The Visishtadvaita is so called because it inculcates the Advaita or oneness of God, with Visesha or attributes. It is, therefore, qualified monism. God alone exists. All else that is seen are His manifestations or attributes. God or Lord Narayana of Sri Ramanuja is a complex organic whole—Visishta—though it is one. Hence the name Visishtadvaita.

According to Sri Sankara, all qualities or manifestations are unreal and temporary. They are a result of Avidya or ignorance. According to Sri Ramanuja, the attributes are real and permanent. But, they are subject to the control of the one Brahman. God can be one despite the existence of attributes, because they cannot exist alone; they are not independent entities. They are Prakaras or the modes, Sesha or the accessories, and Niyama or the controlled aspects, of the one Brahman.

Ramanuja's celebrated system of philosophy known as Visishtadvaita or qualified monism is Advaita or non-dualism with a qualification or Visesha. It admits plurality. Sri Ramanuja's Brahman or Lord Narayana subsists in a plurality of forms as souls (Chit) and matter (Achit). Hence it is called Visishtadvaita or qualified non-dualism. Visishtadvaita philosophy is Vaishnavism. The Sampradaya of Ramanuja's cult or creed is known as Sri Sampradaya. His followers are Vaishnavas. Ramanuja systematised the philosophy of Vaishnavism. Ramanuja's religion is called Sri Vaishnavism, because 'Sri' or the Goddess Lakshmi is made to have an important function to perform in the salvation of the soul.

Sri Sankara's philosophy is too high, subtle and abstract for the vast majority of persons. But Sri Ramanuja's philosophy is suitable for those in whom the devotional element preponderates. In Sri Ramanuja's system of philosophy, the Lord (Narayana) has two inseparable Prakaras or modes, viz., the world and the souls. These are related to Him as the body is related to the soul. They have no existence apart from Him. They inhere in Him as attributes in a substance. Matter and souls constitute the body of the Lord. The Lord is their indweller. He is the controlling Reality. Matter and souls are the subordinate elements. They are termed Viseshanas, attributes. God is the Viseshya or that which is qualified.

THE VISISHTADVAITA SYSTEM—THE STORY OF ITS EVOLUTION

The Visishtadvaita system is an ancient one. It was originally expounded by Bodhayana in his Vritti, written about 400 B.C. It is the same as that is expounded by Ramanuja. Ramanuja followed Bodhayana in his interpretation of the Brahma Sutras.

The Bhakti school worships a personal God. The devotees develop devotion to Vasudeva or Narayana. Those who worship the personal God are called Bhagavatas. They have their own scriptures, called the Pancharatra Agamas which are regarded by them as equal to the Upanishads. The Bhakti movement was further strengthened in South India by the work of the twelve Alvar saints. The hymns composed by the Alvar saints were called collectively by the name Nalayira-Prabandham, a series of four thousand poems.

Afterwards came the Vaishnava Acharyas—Natha Muni, Yamunacharya and Ramanujacharya. They were great scholars. They gave a philosophical basis and colouring to their beliefs and practices. The Alvars solely relied on Bhakti, but these Acharyas combined Jnana and Karma with it for the realisation of God. They regarded Jnana and Karma as means for realising God. Their object was to reconcile the Vedas, the Upanishads and the Gita with the Tamil Prabandha. They interpreted the Tamil Prabandha in terms of the Upanishads and the Gita. Therefore, they were called by the name Ubhaya-Vedantins. Ramanuja accepts the Vedas, the Upanishads and the Tamil works of the Alvars also as the source of authority for his philosophy. Therefore, his system is known as Ubhaya-Vedanta.

Natha Muni raised the Prabandha to the level of the Vedas. Yamunacharya laid the foundations on which Ramanuja, his successor, built his philosophy. Ramanuja wrote the commentaries on the Brahma Sutras known as the Sri Bhashya. He wrote a commentary on the Bhagavad-Gita also. He wrote also three other books—Vedanta Sara, Vedartha Sangraha and Vedanta Dipa. These are the chief texts of the Visishtadvaita system of philosophy.

Ramanuja accepts perception, inference and scripture as valid sources of knowledge. The Vedas and the Smritis are the sole and independent authority for the knowledge of Brahman. He adopts the theories of Satkarya-Vada and Parinama-Vada, i.e., the doctrine of a real effect proceeding from a cause.

RAMANUJA'S BRAHMAN—A PERSONAL GOD WITH ATTRIBUTES

According to Ramanuja, whatever is, is Brahman; but, Brahman is not of a homogeneous nature. It contains within Itself elements of plurality on account of which It truly manifests Itself in a diversified world. Ramanuja's Brahman is essentially a Personal God, the all-powerful and all-wise Ruler of a real world, permeated and animated by His spirit. There is thus no room for the distinction between Param Nirguna and an Aparam Saguna Brahman, between Brahman and Isvara.

Ramanuja's Brahman is Savisesha Brahman, i.e., Brahman with attributes.

Ramanuja's Brahman is not the Impersonal Absolute, but He is a Personal God, with the qualities of omnipotence, omniscience and infinite love. God is Saguna. When the Vedic texts declare that He is Nirguna, it means that there are no base or lower qualities such as sorrow, pain, mortality, change and old age in Him.

The Lord is interpenetrating everything. He is the essence of the soul. He is the Antaryamin or the Inner Ruler. He is one with the soul. He is all-pervading (Vibhu). He is the Supreme Being. He is full of auspicious attributes. He is of the nature of Satya (Truth), Jnana (Intelligence) and Ananda (Bliss). Matter and soul depend on Him. He is the Adhara or support for this world and all souls. God is the Governor or Controller (Niyanta or Seshin) of the world. Jiva or soul is Niyama or Sesha (one who is being controlled).

The Lord is immanent. He is also transcendent. He is unchanging. The entire universe is latent in Him during Pralaya. The world is projected during creation, but this does not touch His essence. Ramanuja's Brahman has internal difference (Svagata Bheda). It is a synthetic whole, with souls and matter as Its modes (Chit-Achit-Visishta). Para, Vyuha, Vibhava, Archa and Antaryamin, i.e., the transcendent, the group, the incarnation, the image and the immanent are the five forms of the Lord.

Ramanuja identifies God with Narayana who dwells in Vaikuntha with His Sakti or consort, Lakshmi. Lakshmi is the Goddess of Prosperity. She is the Divine Mother. She pleads with Her husband on behalf of man. She introduces the devotee to Her Lord and obtains for him salvation. Lakshmi occupies a pre-eminent place in Vaishnavism.

THE WORLD—A REAL PART OF BRAHMAN'S NATURE

The world, with its variety of material forms of existence

and individual souls, is not an unreal Maya, but a real part of Brahman's nature. It is the body of the Lord. Matter is real. It is Achit or non-conscious substance. It undergoes a real Parinama or evolution. Matter exists in a subtle state as the Prakara of God during Pralaya. Hence it is eternal, but ever dependent. It is controlled by the will of God. It is neither good nor bad. It becomes a source of pleasure or of pain according to the nature of the Karma of souls. It forms the object of experience for the souls.

Prakriti has three Gunas: Sattva, Rajas and Tamas; but, Suddha-Tattva has only Sattva. It is pure matter. Suddha-Tattva is the substance which constitutes the body of God and is called His Nitya-Vibhuti. The manifested world is His Lila-Vibhuti.

THE SOUL—A DISTINCT INDIVIDUAL ENTITY

The soul is a higher Prakara of God than matter, because it is a conscious entity. It is of the essence of God. According to Ramanuja, God, soul and Nature are three eternal entities. The soul is self-conscious, unchanging, partless and atomic (Anu). The souls are infinite in number. The individual soul of Ramanuja is really individual. It is absolutely real and eternally distinct from God. It has indeed, sprung from Brahman, and is never outside Brahman; nevertheless, it enjoys a separate personal existence and will remain a personality forever.

Three Classes of Souls

According to Ramanuja, there are three classes of souls, viz., Nitya (eternal), Mukta (free) and Baddha (bound). The eternal souls have never been in bondage. They are eternally free. They live with God in Vaikuntha. The freed souls were once subject to Samsara, but have attained salvation now and live with God. The bound souls are caught up in the meshes of Samsara and are striving to be released. They wander from life to life till they are redeemed.

Man or the individual soul is a particle of which God is the whole. The individual soul is like a spark of that mass of fire. The whole pomegranate fruit represents the Brahman of Ramanuja, each seed corresponding to the individual soul.

THE EVOLUTION OF THE SOUL AND ITS FINAL EMANCIPATION

When the individual soul is immersed in worldliness or Samsara, its knowledge is contracted. It gets its body according to its past Karma, and goes from birth to death and from death to birth, till it attains Moksha or the final emancipation. When it attains Moksha, its knowledge expands. It knows everything. "Every action that contracts the heart of the soul is bad, and every action that expands the heart of the soul is good"—this is the statement of Ramanuja. The soul is marching on in this Samsara, expanding or contracting through its good and evil actions, till it attains the final emancipation through the grace of Lord Narayana. The grace descends on those souls who are pure and struggling for the divine grace.

Emancipation or Passing into Paradise

According to Ramanuja, Moksha means the soul's passing from the troubles of mundane life into a kind of heaven or paradise (Vaikuntha) where it will remain forever in undisturbed personal bliss in the presence of God. The liberated soul attains to the nature of God. It never becomes identical with Him. It lives in fellowship with the Lord, either serving Him or meditating on Him. It never loses its individuality. There is no such thing as Jivanmukti, according to Ramanuja. Salvation comes when the soul leaves the body.

Bhakti—The Means to Emancipation

The final emancipation can be obtained only through Bhakti and the grace of the Lord. The grace of the Lord comes through devotion and Prapatti or absolute self-surrender. Karma and Jnana are only means to Bhakti.

THE DVAITA PHILOSOPHY OF SRI MADHVACHARYA

INTRODUCTION

Sri Madhvacharya evolved a dualistic system of philosophy out of the Prasthana-Traya, viz., the Upanishads, the Bhagavad-Gita and the Brahma Sutras. It is an unqualified dualism. Madhva's Vaishnavism is called Sad-Vaishnavism, in order to distinguish it from the Sri Vaishnavism of Ramanujacharya.

Madhva makes an absolute distinction between God, and animate and inanimate objects. God is the only independent Reality. The animate and inanimate objects are dependent realities. Madhva's Vedanta is the doctrine of absolute differences. It is an Atyanta-Bheda-Darsana. He insists on five great distinctions (Pancha-Bheda), viz., (i) the distinction between God and the individual soul, (ii) the distinction between God and matter, (iii) the distinction between the individual soul and matter, (iv) the distinction between one soul and another and (v) the distinction between one material thing and another. Madhva's philosophy is a philosophy of distinction. Every follower of the Madhva school should have a firm belief in this fivefold distinction, known as the Pancha-Bheda.

You can clearly grasp Sri Madhvacharya's philosophy if you study his commentary on the Brahma Sutras and Anu-Vyakhyana, his commentaries on the Upanishads and the Bhagavad-Gita, and his glosses on the Mahabharata (Bharata-tatparya-nirnaya) and on the Bhagavata Purana.

Madhva's philosophy has many points in common with those of Ramanuja. In Madhva's system of philosophy, Hari or Vishnu is the Supreme Being. The world is real. Difference is true. All the Jivas are dependent on Hari, the Lord. There are grades of superiority and inferiority among the individual souls. Liberation is the individual soul's enjoyment of its innate bliss. This is Moksha or the final emancipation. Bhakti, or devotion, without faults, is the means of attaining Moksha.

Perception, inference and the scriptures are the three Pramanas, or ways of knowledge. Hari is knowable only through the Vedas. Worship of Lord Krishna as taught in the Bhagavata Purana is the centre of his religion. This is the quintessence of Madhva's teachings.

THE CATEGORIES

According to Madhva, Padartha or objective reality is of two kinds—independent (Svatantra) and dependent (Paratantra). God, the Supreme Being, is the only independent Reality. The soul and the world are dependent realities. God rules them. The dependent beings are of two varities—positive and negative. Conscious souls (Chetana), and unconscious entities like matter and time (Achetana), are the two varieties of the positive. Unconscious entities are either eternal like the Vedas, or eternal and non-eternal like Prakriti, time and space or non-eternal like the products of Prakriti.

THE SUPREME BEING AND HIS CONSORT

The Supreme Being is Vishnu or Narayana. He is the *personal* first cause. He is the Intelligent Governor of the world. He lives in Vaikuntha along with Lakshmi, His consort. He and His consort Lakshmi are real. Brahma and Vayu are two of His sons. One can know His nature through a study of the Vedas. He manifests Himself through various Vyuhas or Group-forms, and through Avataras. He is present in the sacred images. He is also the Antaryamin or the Inner Controller of all souls. He creates, maintains and destroys the world.

God is free from Doshas or faults. He is endowed with all auspicious qualities. He is omnipresent or all-pervading and independent. He is beyond time and space. He is greater than Lakshmi. There is no other who is greater than Lakshmi. She is the foremost of the dependents. Lakshmi is the Lord's Sakti or energy. She is the personification of His power or creative energy. Lakshmi can put on various forms without a material body. She is co-eternal with Vishnu and all-pervading. She beholds the glory of Her Lord through eternity. She is Nitya-Mukta, i.e., eternally free from Samsara. She is not affected by sorrow and pain. She is intelligent.

PRAKRITI—THE MATERIAL CAUSE OF THE WORLD

God is the efficient—but not the material—cause of the world, because Prakriti which is the world-stuff is different from Him. Prakriti is the material cause of the world. It evolves into the visible world. All the objects, bodies, and organs of the souls are made out of Prakriti. God energises Prakriti through Lakshmi. Then there is creation.

The three aspects of Prakriti are presided over by the three Powers: Lakshmi, Bhu and Durga. Avidya is a form of Prakriti. It obscures the spiritual powers of the individual soul. It forms a veil which hides the Supreme from the vision of the individual soul.

Mahat, Ahankara (egoism), Buddhi, mind, the ten senses, the five sense-objects, and the five great elements are the modifications of Prakriti. These exist in the primordial Prakriti in subtle forms before their evolution.

THE WORLD—A REALITY DISTINCT FROM GOD

According to Madhva, the world is not an illusion. It is not also a transformation of God, as curd is of milk. Madhva does not admit that the world is the body of God. The distinction between God and the world is absolute and unqualified. Hence the system of Madhva is called Dvaita or unqualified dualism.

THE INDIVIDUAL SOUL—A DISTINCT ENTITY

Plurality of Souls

There is plurality of Jivas. They are all of atomic size. The entire universe is filled with Jivas or individual souls. Every atom of space is filled up with Jivas. Madhva says in his 'Tattvanirnaya': "Infinite are the souls dwelling in an atom of space."

No two Jivas are alike in character. They are essentially different from one another. There are different grades amongst them even in their enjoyment of bliss after salvation.

A REAL DISTINCTION BETWEEN JIVA AND BRAHMAN

The Jivas are different from God, and from matter. Madhva regards the distinction between Brahman and Jiva as real.

Though the Jiva is limited in size, it pervades the body owing to its quality of intelligence. The Jivas are active agents, but they depend on the guidance of the Lord. The Lord impels the Jivas to action in accordance with their previous conduct. They are eternal, and by nature, blissful. But, the connection with material bodies due to their past Karma makes them suffer pain and undergo transmigration. So long as they are not freed from their impurities, they wander about in the Samsara. They pass from birth to death, and from death to birth. When their impurities are removed, they attain salvation. The natural bliss of the soul becomes manifest at the time of Moksha or salvation.

Salvation Does Not Entitle the Soul to Equality With God

The soul does not attain equality with God. It is entitled only to serve Him.

Even in heaven, there are essential differences among the Jivas. The classes of souls in the realm of bliss are various. There are different grades also. The liberated souls are not all equal; but, there is no discord among them, because they all know Brahman and have no faults.

Classification of Souls

Madhva accepts Ramanuja's classification of the souls into Nitya or eternal (like Lakshmi), Mukta or liberated (the gods, men, Rishis, sages and fathers), and Baddha or bound ones. The third group consists of two classes: (i) those who are eligible for Moksha (Mukti-yogya) and (ii) those who are not so eligible. Of those who are not eligible for salvation, there are two classes again: (a) those who are bound to the cycle of Samsara forever (Nitya-samsarins) and (b) those whose destiny is hell, the region of blinding darkness (Tamo-yogya).

Some are pre-ordained for the final emancipation by their inherent aptitude. Some others are eternally destined either to wander in Samsara without end, or to go to the world of darkness. The Sattvika souls go to heaven, the Rajasa souls revolve in Samsara and the Tamasa souls fall into hell.

BHAKTI—THE MEANS TO SALVATION

Bhakti is the means to salvation. Souls attain salvation through the grace of God. That grace comes on the devotee only through the mediator Vayu, the son of Vishnu. God cannot be approached directly. Vayu is the mediator. The grace of the Lord is in proportion to the intensity of devotion.

Worship of God is the indispensable preliminary condition for obtaining the grace of God. The soul is saved by the knowledge that it is dependent on God and is under His control. Correct knowledge results in the love of God. Bhakti is the result of knowledge of the greatness of God.

Ankana, Namakarana, Bhajana and Smarana

The worship of Vishnu consists in: (i) Ankana, marking the body with His symbols, (ii) Namakarana, giving the Names of the Lord to children, (iii) Bhajana, singing His glories, and (iv) Smarana, constant practice of remembrance of God. Madhva says: "Form a strong habit of remembering God. Then only it will be easy for you to remember Him at the moment of death." He pointed out that when the Lord incarnated, no Prakrita Deha or material body was put on by Him. Madhva has prescribed a rigorous kind of fasting to his followers.

Practice of Sadhana

Good moral life is a preliminary for Moksha. The aspirant

should equip himself with the study of Vedas, control of the senses, dispassion and perfect self-surrender, if he wants to have vision of the Lord. Renunciation, devotion and direct cognition of the Lord through meditation, lead to the attainment of salvation. The devotee attains direct intuitive realisation of God through meditation and divine grace. Then he is freed from the round of births and deaths.

These are some of the important teachings of Sri Madhvacharya, the renowned exponent of the dualistic school of philosophy.

THE DVAITADVAITA PHILOSOPHY OF SRI NIMBARKA
INTRODUCTION

This is also known by the name Bhedabheda School of Philosophy or dualistic monism. This system was evolved by Sri Nimbarkacharya. Nimbarka was a Telugu Brahmin of the Vaishnava faith. He lived some time after Ramanuja and prior to Madhva, about the eleventh century A.D. He is regarded as the incarnation of the Sun.

He wrote a short commentary on the Brahma Sutras called Vedanta-Parijata-Saurabha, as well as Dasasloki. His commentary develops the theory of the transformation (Parinama) of Brahman.

Nimbarka's view was largely influenced by the teachings of Bhaskara who flourished in the first half of the ninth century and who interpreted the Vedanta system from the viewpoint of Dvaitadvaita or dualistic non-dualism. This doctrine was not a new discovery of Bhaskara. It was upheld by the ancient teacher Audulomi to which Sri Vyasa himself refers in his Vedanta Sutras.

GOD, SOUL AND WORLD
Identity in Difference

Nimbarka holds that the relation of God to the soul and the world is one of identity in difference. The soul and the world are different from God, because they are endowed with qualities different from those of God. At the same time, they are not different from God, because God is omnipresent and they depend entirely on Him.

Nimbarka's philosophy admits Brahman as the Supreme Reality without a second. The world and the Jivas are only partial manifestations of His Power (Sakti).

Jiva and Brahman are self-conscious. Jiva is limited. Brahman is infinite. Brahman is independent Reality. Jiva and Prakriti are dependent realities. Jiva is the enjoyer (Bhokta). The world is the enjoyed (Bhogya). Brahman is the Supreme Controller (Niyanta).

God, Jiva and the world are not absolutely distinct. If the Supreme Being is absolutely distinct from the individual soul and the world, it cannot be omnipresent. It will be as limited as the individual soul or the world. It cannot, then, be regarded as their Governor. Nimbarka says that both difference and non-difference are real. The soul and the world are different from Brahman, as they are endowed with natures and qualities different from those of Brahman. They are not different, as they cannot exist by themselves and as they depend absolutely on Brahman. Such a relation exists between the sun and its rays, the fire and its sparks. The souls and matter are distinct from God, but they are closely connected with Him—as waves with water, or coils of a rope with the rope itself. They are both distinct and non-distinct from Brahman.

THE SUPREME BEING AND ITS CHARACTERISTICS

In this school, Brahman is regarded as both the efficient and the material cause of the world. Brahman is both Nirguna and Saguna, as It is not exhausted in the creation but also transcends it.

The Four Forms of the Ultimate Reality

The Ultimate Reality exists in four forms. In Its primary

form, It is the unconditioned, immutable, Supreme Brahman. In Its second form, It is Isvara, the Lord of the Universe. In the third form, It is called Jiva or the individual soul. In Its fourth form, It is manifested as the universe of names and forms. The phenomenal universe is a part of Brahman. It has no existence separate from, and independent of Brahman. The relation between the world and Brahman is also one of Bhedabheda. The universe is not different from Brahman.

Krishna—The Supreme Being

The Supreme Being is absolutely free from all defects. He is full of all auspicious qualities. He has a divine body. He is full of beauty, love, sweetness and charm.

Nimbarka identifies the Supreme Brahman with Krishna. He is endowed with all auspicious qualities. He is free from egoism, ignorance, passion and attachment. He has the four forms (Vyuhas), viz., Vasudeva, Sankarshana, Pradyumna and Aniruddha. He also manifests Himself as the Avataras (incarnations).

In Nimbarka, Krishna and Radha take the places of Narayana and Lakshmi. Radha is not simply the chief of the Gopis, but is the eternal Consort of Lord Krishna.

How Brahman Is Both the Material and the Efficient Cause of the World

Brahman is the material and the efficient cause of the universe. His powers of Chit and Achit in their subtle forms manifest themselves as the universe. Hence He is the material cause. He causes the union of the individual souls with their respective Karmas and their fruits. He provides them the proper instruments for their experience. Hence He is the efficient cause.

Brahman does not want raw materials in order to create the universe. Also, He does not need hands or any other instruments. He is omnipotent. He simply wills and the whole world comes into being. His Satsankalpa objectifies or materialises as this universe. Just as a spider spins a cobweb out of itself, so also Brahman has evolved the universe out of Himself. This is the declaration of the Upanishads. In thus evolving the universe, Brahman is both its material and the efficient cause. As Brahman is all-powerful. it is perfectly within His power to be so evolved, and at the same time, to remain beyond such evolution. This is supported by the Upanishads and the Brahma Sutras. Brahman has transformed Himself into this world, without His noumenal aspect being affected. This is due to the inscrutable creative power inherent in the nature of Brahman.

RELATION BETWEEN THE INDIVIDUAL SOUL AND THE SUPREME SOUL

Formal Difference and Essential Identity

The individual soul is a *part of* the Supreme Soul. It is also *identical with*, or the same as, the Supreme Soul. Just as a wave is both different from the ocean (being only a part of the ocean), and identical with it (both being water), so also is the individual soul both different from (being a part of the Supreme Soul), and identical with (both being of the nature of Chaitanya or Consciousness), the Supreme Soul. The relation between the individual soul or Jiva and the Supreme Soul or Brahman is one of formal difference and essential identity. There is no difference between Jiva and Brahman in kind. The difference is only in degree.

The Jiva is different from Brahman with reference to the phenomenal aspect or the body-idea. It is identical with, or the same as, Brahman with reference to the noumenal aspect as the indivisible whole. This is what is called Bhedabheda.

A strong wind perturbs the sea and a wave is formed. The wave is different from the ocean, though it is a part of it. The wind passes away and the wave subsides. Now it cannot be distinguished from the sea. Even so, the mind is agitated by desires and cravings. It runs towards the objects along with

the senses and becomes conscious of a distinctive individuality. The ego or the finite self beholds the relative
world with its phenomena, and gets experiences. When the
mind becomes calm and serene by eradication of desires, it
ceases to function and all the Vrittis or waves subside. The
phenomenal world vanishes and the finite self realises the
Infinite Self or Brahman.

THE JIVA AND ITS ATTRIBUTES

Souls are infinite in number and are atomic in size. The Jiva
is minute (Anu). It is of the form of knowledge (Jnanas-
varupa), though not in the sense of Sankara. The Jiva is
knowledge and it is the possessor of knowledge also, just as
the sun is light and the source of light also. The relation of the
soul to its attribute is like that of the Dharmin (the qualified)
to the Dharma (the attribute). It is one of difference and non-
difference (Bhedabheda).

Though the Jiva is atomic in size, it experiences the
pleasures and pains throughout the body owing to its
omnipresent quality of knowledge. It is everlasting. It
continues to exist in deep sleep and the final state of emancipation. In Pralaya or dissolution, the individual souls and the
world merge in the Lord in subtle form. Births and deaths concern the body, but not the Self.

The individual soul is the agent of activity (Karta). It has no
independent knowledge or activity. The individual souls and
the world are not self-sufficient. They are guided by the Lord.
They are all sustained and governed by God. Each soul is a
ray of Brahman individualised. Ananda or bliss belongs to the
individual soul in all its states.

Two Classes of Jivas

Jivas are of two classes: (i) Jivas who have knowledge of
the all-pervading indwelling spirit and who have realised that
the appearances are non-separate from Brahman. They are

called liberated souls (Mukta). They are free from ignorance. (ii) Jivas who only behold the appearances, but have no knowledge of the all-pervading indwelling spirit, the support of these names and forms. They are called bound souls (Baddha).

THE WORLD—A TRUE MANIFESTATION OF BRAHMAN

The world is not an illusion for Nimbarka, as it is a manifestation (Parinama) of what is contained subtly in God.

The world is not unreal or illusory, but is a true manifestation or Parinama of Brahman. It may, however, be said to be unreal only in the sense that the present state of its existence is not self-sufficient and it has no separate existence from Brahman. The world is identical with as well as different from Brahman, just as a wave or bubble is the same as, and at the same time different from, water.

There are three principal Tattvas or principles: (i) Aprakriti, which is not derived from the primordial Prakriti, which is the stuff of the divine body of the Lord (which is similar to the Suddha-Sattva of Ramanuja), and which is the basis of the Nitya-Vibhuti (eternal glory) of Isvara; (ii) Prakriti with its three Gunas, Sattva, Rajas and Tamas; and (iii) Kala or time. These three Tattvas or principles are also eternal like the individual souls.

According to Nimbarka, the Sakti of Brahman is the material cause of the world. The changes of Sakti do not affect the integrity of Brahman. The 'Body of Brahman' of Ramanuja is the 'Sakti' of Nimbarka.

SALVATION

Avidya is beginningless. The purity of the individual soul is obscured by its Karma which is the result of Avidya. This Avidya can be put an end to by the grace of the Lord.

True Devotion and Real Knowledge Lead to Release

Prapatti or complete surrender to God is the way to release.

God showers His grace on His devotees who make complete self-surrender. The grace of God lifts up the devotees to have Brahma-Sakshatkara. The Lord generates devotion in them which results in God-realisation.

Bhakti involves a knowledge of Brahman, of the nature of the Jiva, of the fruit of the Lord's grace or Mukti, and of the nature of the impediments to God-realisation such as the wrong identification of the soul with the body, the senses and the mind.

Salvation is attained by real knowledge (Jnana) and true devotion (Bhakti). Real knowledge reveals the true nature of the all-pervading Brahman. True devotion leads to total self-surrender to the Lord. The individual soul retains its individuality with reference to divine enjoyment (Bhoga-samyatvam), but its will is subservient to that of Brahman. The individuality of the soul is not dissolved even in the state of Moksha or the final emancipation. Even in the state of release, the individual soul is different from, as well as identical with, Brahman. This is identity with difference, Bheda-abheda.

Salvation—A State of Full Awareness of Identity With the Lord

Brahman is revealed to the liberated soul in Its pristine glory, but not in the form of a deity. The soul realises itself now as an inseparable part of Brahman. It no longer feels that it is a separate or distinct individual, as it felt in bondage. It is released from its previous state of bondage. It abides now in the glory of its own true Self which is Brahman Itself. It is in full awareness or consciousness of being one with the Lord. It will not return to the world. It is freed from the round of births and deaths. As it is in union with Brahman, it attains the same status as that of Brahman, but it has no power over creation, preservation and dissolution of the world.

THE SUDDHADVAITA PHILOSOPHY OF SRI VALLABHA

INTRODUCTION

The philosophy of Sri Vallabhacharya is Suddha-Advaita or pure monism, because he does not admit Maya like Sankara, and believes that the whole world of matter and souls is real and is only a subtle form of God. Those who bring Maya for the explanation of the world are not pure Advaitins, because they admit a second to Brahman. Vallabha holds that Brahman can create the world without any connection with such a principle as Maya, but Sankara traces the universe to Brahman through the power of Maya. Hence the philosophy of Vallabha is called pure monism or Suddhadvaita. Vallabha expounded that system in the Anu-Bhashya, his commentary on the Brahma Sutras. He called it Suddha-Advaita or pure monism as against Sankara's Kevala Advaita and Ramanuja's Visishta-Advaita. Vallabha was a Telugu Brahmin of South India. He migrated to the north and developed the views of Vishnuswamin who belonged to the thirteenth century. His system of thought is known by the name Brahma-Vada.

Vallabha says that the entire universe is real and is subtly Brahman. The individual souls and the world are, in essence, one with Brahman. Jiva, Kala (time) and Prakriti or Maya are eternal existences, but they have no separate existence apart from Brahman.

Vallabha was a great Sanskrit scholar. He settled down first at Mathura and then at Varanasi. He preached with great zeal the Vaishnava cult and philosophy. He was the founder of the great Vaishnava Mutts of Rajasthan and Gujarat. His followers are found in great numbers in Nathdwara.

Important Works of Vallabha

Vallabha accepts the authority not only of the Upanishads, the Bhagavad-Gita and the Brahma Sutras, but also of the Bhagavata Purana. The important works of Vallabha are

Vyasa-Sutra Bhashya (Anu-Bhashya), Jaimini Sutra Bhashya, Bhagavata-Tika Subodhini, Pushti-Pravaha-Maryada and Siddhanta-Rahasya. All these books are in Sanskrit. He has written many books in Braj Bhasha also. The scriptures are the final authority for Vallabha.

Stress on Worship and Grace

Vallabha's religion is a religion addressed to the worship of Vishnu in the form of Krishna. It was derived chiefly, like the system of Chaitanya, from the Vaishnava philosophy propounded by Ramanuja. It is centred round the conception of a personal and beneficent God who is Sat-Chit-Ananda. Lord Krishna is the highest Brahman. His body consists of Sat-Chit-Ananda. He is called Purushottama.

Vallabha's followers worship Bala-Krishna (Krishna as a lad). They have Vatsalya-Bhava (the attitude which regards God as a child). Vallabha lays great stress on Pushti (grace) and Bhakti (devotion). Maha-Pushti is the highest grace or Anugraha which helps the aspirants to attain God-realisation.

GOD—THE ONLY BEING

According to Vallabha, God is the Absolute or the Purushottama. He is perfect. He is Sat-Chit-Ananda. He is infinite, eternal, omnipresent, omniscient and omnipotent. He has all the auspicious qualities also. The Sruti texts which say that He has no attributes, mean only that He has not the ordinary qualities.

God is *real*. There is no other reality besides Him. He is the *only* Being. He is the source for this universe and all souls. He is the first cause and the only cause. God is the material as well as the efficient cause of the universe. He creates the world by the mere force of His Will. Brahman manifests Himself, of His own Will, as the universe and the individual souls, but He does not undergo any change in His essential nature. Things come out of the Akshara (Sat-

Chit-Ananda), like sparks from fire. Brahman is the Creator of the world. He is also the world itself.

God is personified as Krishna, when He possesses the qualities of wisdom and action. He appears in various forms to please His devotees.

THE WORLD OF NATURE AND THE WORLD OF FALSE RELATIONS

Creation is manifestation of Brahman. The universe is the effect of Brahman. The universe is as eternal and real as Brahman Himself. The inanimate universe is filled with Brahman. The world is not an illusory appearance. It is not different from Brahman in essence.

Jagat is the world of Nature. It is not illusory. It is real. It is God Himself in one form. But, the Samsara or temporal involvement is illusory. This is created by the soul around its 'I-ness' and 'mine-ness'. The separation from God on account of egoism makes the soul forget its original, true, divine nature. Samsara is a product of the soul's imagination and action which play round its 'I-ness' and 'mine-ness'. On account of its selfishness, it puts itself in wrong relations with other souls and with the objective universe. It creates a web of its own and gets itself entangled in it. This is an illusion, because the web has no reality. This Samsara, the world of false relations created by the soul, is alone Maya. Samsara or Maya rises because the soul, which is not apart from God, tries to set itself up as an independent reality or entity in its own right. The self which is something apart from God is illusory. Its body is illusory and its world also is illusory. All this is Samsara. It is very different from the world of Nature.

JIVA AND BRAHMAN

Analogy of the Spark and the Fire

The Jivas are not effects. They are Amsas or parts of God. They issue from Him spontaneously as sparks from fire. Brahman is the whole. The Jiva or the individual soul is part; but, there is no real difference between Brahman and the individual soul, because the individual soul is of identical essence with Brahman.[*] The soul is one with Brahman. It is as real and eternal as Brahman.

The individual soul is not Brahman screened by the veil of Avidya. It is itself Brahman, with the attribute 'bliss' being obscured or suppressed. Ananda or bliss is suppressed or obscured in the individual soul. Ananda and consciousness are suppressed or obscured in matter or the inanimate world. When the soul attains bliss, and the inanimate world attains both consciousness and bliss, the difference between Brahman and these vanishes.

The soul is both a doer and an enjoyer. It is atomic in size, but it pervades the whole body by its quality of intelligence, just as sandalwood pervades even the places where it does not exist by its sweet fragrance and just as a lamp, though confined only to a part of a room, illuminates the whole room.

CLASSIFICATION OF SOULS

There are three kinds of souls: (i) The pure (Suddha) Jivas. The divine qualities (Aisvarya) are not obscured in these souls by ignorance. (ii) The worldly Jivas (Samsarin). These souls are caught in the net or clutches of Avidya or ignorance. They experience births and deaths on account of their connection with gross and subtle bodies. (iii) Mukta Jivas or liberated souls. These souls are freed from the bonds of Samsara through Vidya or Knowledge. When the soul attains the final emancipation, it recovers its suppressed qualities and becomes one with God or Brahman. The world appears as Brahman to one who has realised the Truth or Brahman.

There is another classification of souls, viz., Pushti souls, Maryada souls and Pravahika souls. All these are different

---

[*] According to Ramanuja, the parts are really different from the whole.

from one another in their origin, nature and final end. They all issue from God with their differences.

The Pushti souls are the highest, as they issue from the Ananda-Kaya or the bliss-body of God. These souls are the Amsa (parts) of His body. God is the Amsi (the whole). These are the souls of grace. They have the divine seed in them which bears fruit in the end. They ultimately reach the goal through the grace of the Lord. They have communion and fellowship with Lord Krishna. They develop Bhakti through the grace of the Lord. Bhakti is the means and the end in itself.

The Maryada souls are generated from the Vak or the Word of God. They are governed by law, not by grace. They perform their ritualistic duties, at first with selfish interests. Later on, they develop Nishkama-Bhava (unselfish attitude) and do their ritualistic routine without any self-interest. This purifies their mind. They reach the Akshara, which is a kind of vestibule to the abode of God. Afterwards they attain the supreme abode of God.

The Pravahika souls issue from the mind of God. They are the Samsaric Jivas. They are souls neither of grace nor of law. They are in continuous motion (Pravaha).

These three kinds of souls have further sub-divisions and cross-divisions into Pushti-Pushti, Pushti-Maryada, Pushti-Pravahika, Maryada-Maryada, Maryada-Pushti, Maryada-Pravahika, Pravahika-Pravahika, Pravahika-Pushti and Pravahika-Maryada.

PUSHTI MARGA OR THE WAY OF GRACE

The way of life and salvation preached by Vallabha is called Pushti Marga. The soul of man has become weak and lean on account of sin. It is, therefore, in dire need of the grace of God for its upliftment and emancipation. God's grace gives Pushti (nourishment) and Poshana (strength); and hence the name Pushti Marga or the Way of Grace.

The individual soul can attain the final emancipation only through the grace of God. Bhakti is the chief means of salvation. Jnana is useful. Maha Pushti or the highest grace removes great obstacles and helps in the attainment of God. The Bhakti generated by special grace is known as Pushti Bhakti.

The Four Kinds of Bhakti

This Pushti-Bhakti is of four kinds: (i) Pravaha Pushti-Bhakti, (ii) Maryada Pushti-Bhakti, (iii) Pushti Pushti-Bhakti and (iv) Suddha Pushti-Bhakti. Pravaha Bhakti is the path of those who while leading the worldly life, perform works which will lead to the attainment of God-realisation. Worldly life is compared to the flow of a river (Pravaha). Maryada Bhakti is the path of those who are rendered fit to attain knowledge which is useful for worship, through the grace of the Lord. They know all about the ways of God. They depend upon their own efforts to obtain knowledge. In Pushti Bhakti, the devotees lead a life of self-restraint. They hear discourses about the Lord. They do Kirtana and sing His Name. They do Japa of Mantra.

Suddha Pushti-Bhakti or the Purest Type of Devotion

In Suddha Pushti-Bhakti, the devotees do Kirtana and sing the Lord's Name. They praise God. They develop a strong passion for doing these. This kind of devotion is generated by the Lord Himself. The Lord's grace descends on the devotees. Then they develop a liking for God. This liking grows into Prema Bhakti (taste for God). The devotees acquire knowledge about God. Then they get attachment to God (Asakti). Then they develop a strong passion for attaining God. This is the ripe condition of love and Asakti. It is called Vyasana. This strong passion, or Vyasana, leads to the attainment of the highest bliss, the *summum bonum* or the end.

When love for Sri Krishna becomes intense, the devotee

sees Lord Krishna everywhere. Hence everything becomes an object of love for him. He identifies himself with everything. The Gopis had this experience. They saw Krishna everywhere. They saw themselves also as Krishna. This is Para Bhakti or supreme devotion which becomes akin to the knowledge or Brahman-Jnana of the Vedantins or Jnanins. The inner and outer world is full of Krishna or Purushottama for such devotees. The fruit of this devotion is admission to the eternal sports or Lilas of Sri Krishna.

The supreme goal is not Mukti or emancipation. The highest goal is eternal service of Lord Krishna and participation in His sports in the celestial Vrindavana. Those who have developed Vyasana, or strong passion for God, reject with scorn the four kinds of Mukti. The Maryada-Bhaktas attain Sayujya Mukti, i.e., they become one with Sri Krishna. The Pushti-Bhaktas reject Mukti and take part in the sports or Lilas of Sri Krishna. They choose with intense delight the eternal service of Sri Krishna. The Bhaktas assume the forms of cows, birds, trees and rivers and enjoy the company of Sri Krishna, which bestows infinite joy. These sports are similar to those which Sri Krishna did in Vraja and Vrindavana. Some of the devotees become Gopas and Gopis and join the sports in the celestial Vrindavana.

Different Kinds of Liberated Souls

The liberated souls are of different kinds. Some have freed themselves like Sanaka. Some dwell in the city of God and attain salvation through the grace of the Lord. Some others develop perfect love and become the associates of God.

THE ACHINTYA BHEDABHEDA PHILOSOPHY
OF SRI CHAITANYA

INTRODUCTION

Sri Chaitanya or Lord Gauranga may be regarded as the

greatest Vaishnava teacher of the North. He gave a new form to the Vaishnava faith. He was born in 1486 A.D., in Bengal.

Chaitanya had a very large heart. He accepted converts from Islam freely. His disciple Haridas was a Muslim Fakir. Nityananda spread far and wide the Chaitanya movement. Rupa and Sanatana who descended from a prince of Karnataka and settled in Bengal, and their nephew Jiva Goswami, were great Sanskrit scholars and were really the fathers of the Chaitanya movement. Jiva Goswami and Baladeva furnished the philosophical basis for the school. The philosophical classics of the school are Jiva's Sat-sandarbha, and his own commentary on it, Sarva-Samvadini, and Baladeva's Govindabhashya on the Brahma Sutras. Baladeva's Prameyaratnavali is also another popular book. Jiva and Baladeva were greatly influenced by the views of Ramanuja and Madhva. They admit God, souls, Maya or Prakriti, Suddha Sattva and Kala or time.

The world and souls depend on God, though they are separate and distinct from Him. They are neither one with God nor different from Him. There is an incomprehensible difference—non-difference (Achintya Bhedabheda).

Chaitanya insisted on the unity of Godhead which underlies the multitude of idols of popular worship.

THE ULTIMATE REALITY

The Ultimate reality is Vishnu. He is the God of love and grace. He is one without a second. He is Sat-Chit-Ananda. He is Nirguna in the sense that He is free from the qualities of Maya. He is Saguna as He is endowed with the attributes of omnipotence and omniscience. He is the material and the efficient cause of the world. He is the source, support and end of this universe. He is the efficient cause through His higher energy (Para-Sakti). He is the material cause through His other energies (Apara-Sakti and Adya-Sakti).

Mysterious and Incomprehensible Saktis of the Lord

Just as the sun has its light and the fire its heat, so the supreme God, Krishna, has naturally His energies or Saktis which are mysterious and incomprehensible. These Saktis have no independent existence. They depend upon God. God and His powers are either identical or different.

These energies are of three kinds, viz., Chit-Sakti, Jiva-Sakti and Maya-Sakti. They are also called Antaranga, Tatastha and Bahiranga, respectively. Jiva-Sakti is called Tatastha, because it occupies an intermediate place between Chit-Sakti and Maya-Sakti.

The Process of Creation

Chit-Sakti created Vaikuntha. There is only pure Sattva in Vaikuntha. Maya has no access here. Kala (Time) cannot execute its destructive power.

The souls are created by the Tatastha Sakti or Jiva-Sakti of the Lord. The Lord's Svarupa-Sakti supports His Jiva-Sakti.

The Lord creates the universe from the great principle of Mahat. He manifests the Vedas and communicates them to Brahma. The work of creating other stages of creation is given to Brahma. The souls and matter are the manifestations of God's energy according to Jiva Goswami and Baladeva. Maya is set in vibration by the mere gazing of the Lord.

The Lord Who Appears in Different Forms

The Supreme Lord Krishna manifests Himself as Brahman to Jnanins; as Paramatman to Yogins; and as Bhagavan full of all glories, all beauties, all sweetness and all attributes, to Bhaktas. Lord Krishna is the Soul of all souls and the Lord of all that is. A Bhakta only has full knowledge of the Supreme Personal God with all His divine attributes. Krishna's form is unique. He assumes endless forms.

Matsya, Kurma, Varaha, Narasimha, Vamana, Rama, Krishna, etc., are Lila-Avataras. There are Gunavataras and

Manvantaravataras. The four Sanakas, Narada, Prithu, Parasurama, Brahma, Sesha in Vaikuntha and Ananta who supports the earth are the chief Avestavataras of the major type who have direct power from God. In Sanaka, Jnana-Sakti; in Narada, Bhakti-Sakti; in Brahma, creative Sakti; in Ananta, the earth-supporting Sakti; in Sesha, God-serving Sakti; in Prithu, the power of preserving people; and in Parasurama, the power of destroying the wicked prevailed.

Radha-Krishna

The Avataras are one with the Supreme. They are not parts like the individual souls. God assumes infinite forms of which the chief is that of Krishna. Radha is the essence of the delight-giving power of Lord Krishna (Hladini). The Lord is the ruler of all souls. He is omnipresent or all-pervading.

THE JIVA

The Jiva is of atomic size. He is the eternal servant of God. He bears the same relation to God as the sun's rays bear to the sun and as a spark bears to the mass of fire from which it flits out. The ray, although it radiates from the sun and is part and parcel of the sun, is not the sun. So also, the Jiva, who is partly similar to God in respect of his spirituality or Chaitanya and partly dissimilar on account of his animal nature and susceptibility to the influence of Maya, is not God Himself.

The soul is bound by the power of Maya. Maya makes him forget his real, essential, divine nature. The Jiva, illumined and infatuated by Maya, can naturally have no knowledge of Lord Krishna. Lord Krishna has, therefore, out of His infinite mercy, created the Vedas; and reveals Himself to the Jiva through the media of scriptures, Guru and intuition. Then the Jiva is convinced that Lord Krishna is his Lord and saviour.

The Jiva can have God-realisation through spiritual love or Prema to Lord Krishna. Bhakti overcomes the force of Karma.

Bhakti is the way to the final emancipation. Through Bhakti the soul attains to a status of equality with God, but he is never absorbed in Him. He is freed from the round of births and deaths.

THE CULTURE OF BHAKTI

Chaitanya taught that God could be realised only by means of ardent and all-absorbing love. He wrote to a royal minister who had asked if there was any path of salvation for a man leading an active life: "As an immoral woman constantly thinks of her illicit lover while living in the midst of her family, so do thou silently and ceaselessly meditate on Hari while doing your worldly activities."

According to Chaitanya, ardour is born from the culture of Bhakti and when ardour deepens, it is called love (Prema).

From taste (Ruchi) comes strong inclination (Aasakti) which generates the sprout of passion (Rati) for Krishna. When this emotion deepens, it becomes Prema. This is the permanent form of Bhakti in Krishna.

When love grows, it is successively called Sneha, Pranaya, Anuraga, Bhava and Mahabhava, just as we have successively cane-seed, sugar-cane juice, molasses, sugar and fine sugar-candy.

When the permanent emotion (Bhava) is mingled with Rasa, it is changed into Vibhava, Anubhava, Sattvika and Vyabhichari; just as curd, when being mixed with black sugar, black pepper and camphor, becomes a thing of extreme deliciousness named Rasala. Vibhava is of two kinds: (i) Alambana, which is kindled by Krishna, etc., and (ii) Uddipana, by the notes of His flute, etc. Anubhava is stimulated by smile, dance and song. Stupor and other sensations are included in Sattvika Anubhava. Vyabhichari is of thirty-three kinds, such as delight, rapture, etc.

Rasa is of five kinds—Santa, Dasya, Sakhya, Vatsalya and

Madhurya. In the Santa Rasa, Rati advances to the stage of Prema and in the Dasya, to Raga. Sakhya and Vatsalya attain to the limit of Anuraga.

KRISHNA-PREMA—THE SUPREME ATTAINMENT

That devotee who has developed Prema always communes with Lord Krishna. No mundane sorrow or affliction can perturb his mind. He has no attraction for earthly objects. He has no fear. He never cares for material success. He intensely longs for union with Lord Krishna.

Love of Krishna is the highest thing worth attaining. Bhakti is the means of attachment. Krishna-prema is, indeed, the highest achievement of life. This Prema makes the devotees serve Krishna in a selfless spirit and enjoy the Rasa or sweetness of the Lord. Bhakti is the only means of attaining Krishna and is, therefore, spoken of as Avidhaya or means. Just as wealth gives comforts, and with the enjoyment of comforts all worldly miseries disappear of their own accord, so also, Bhakti generates Krishna-prema, and with the enjoyment of Prema, the cycle of births and deaths comes to an end. Escape from the effects of privations and the stoppage of rebirths are not, however, the *fruits* of Prema. Beatitude or Moksha is Prema's *handmaid*. Therefore, this Krishna-prema is regarded as the supreme attainment.

OTHER TEACHINGS OF SRI CHAITANYA

Veneration for the preceptor is a fundamental feature of Sri Chaitanya's teachings. Study of the Vedas, the Bhagavata Purana, etc., is inculcated. Practice of ethics and development of ethical virtues such as mercy towards all creatures, humility, purity of heart, freedom from mundane desires, serenity and truthfulness are essential. The distinctions of caste have to be ignored. Anyone can obtain the grace of the Lord.

The following qualities makes a Vaishnava. He is compassionate, truthful, saintly, innocent, charitable, gentle, pure, spiteless, humble, serene, tender, friendly and silent. He is a universal benefactor. He solely depends upon Lord Krishna. He is desireless. He is abstemious in diet and self-controlled. He has mastery over the six enemies. He honours others and does not care for honour from others.

Sankirtana—The Supreme Healer

The supreme healer in this iron age is Sankirtana of the Name. It is equivalent to the Vedic sacrifice. The true sacrifice is rewarded with Krishna's feet. Sankirtana enables you to conquer sin and the world. It creates purity of soul and all kinds of Bhakti. It is not restricted to a particular place or time. It works everywhere. It bears the name of Sarva-sakti (omnipotence).

Hari's Name should always be chanted by him who must be humbler than a blade of grass (which is trodden upon); who is more patient, forbearing and charitable than a tree (which does not cry out even when it is cut down and which does not beg for water even when scorched to death, but on the contrary, offers its treasure to whosoever seeks it, bears the sun and rain itself, but protects those who take shelter under it from rain and sunshine); who, however worthy of esteem should, instead of claiming respect for himself, give respect to all (from a sense of God's immanency in all beings). He who thus takes Krishna's Name gets Divine Love (Prema).

CHAPTER 13

HINDU PHILOSOPHY—III

(SAIVA SIDDHANTA AND SAKTAISM)

THE SAIVA SIDDHANTA PHILOSOPHY

INTRODUCTION

In the books which treat of Saivism, there is a reference to four schools, viz., the Nakulisapasupata, the Saiva, the Pratyabhijna and the Rasesvara.

Saiva Siddhanta is the philosophy of Southern Saivism. It owes its origin to no single author. It is midway between Sankara's Advaita and Ramanuja's Visishtadvaita. Its literature consists chiefly of: (i) the twenty-eight Saivite Agamas, (ii) the collection of Saivite hymns known as Tirumurai,* (iii) the collection of the lives of the Saivite saints, known as Periyapuranam, (iv) Meykandar's Sivajnanabodham, (v) Arulnandi's Sivajnanasiddhiar, and (vi) the works of Umapati. Tirumular's work 'Tirumantiram' is the foundation upon which the later structure of Saiva Siddhanta philosophy was built.

The central doctrine of the Saiva Siddhanta philosophy is that Siva is the Supreme Reality, and that the Jiva or the individual soul is of the same essence as Siva, but not identical. Pati (God), Pasu (soul) and Pasa (the bonds), and the thirty-six Tattvas or principles which constitute the world, are all real.

The Saiva Siddhanta system is the distilled essence of the Vedanta. It prevailed in Southern India even before the Christian era. Tirunelveli and Madurai are the centres of the Saiva

---

* Compiled by Nambi Andar Nambi, the Tirumurai includes the Tirumantiram of Tirumular, the Tevaram of Appar, Sundarar and Sambandhar, and the Tiruvachakam of Manikkavachagar.

Siddhanta school. Even now, Saivism is a very popular creed in South India. It is a rival school of Vaishnavism.

CHARACTERISTICS OF THE SUPREME REALITY

The Supreme Reality is called Siva. He is infinite consciousness. He is eternal, changeless, formless, independent, omnipresent, omnipotent, omniscient, one without a second, beginningless, causeless, taintless, self-existent, ever-free, ever-pure and perfect. He is not limited by time. He is infinite bliss and infinite intelligence. He is free from defects, the all-doer and the all-knower.

Lord Siva is the God of love. His grace is infinite. His love is infinite. He is the saviour and Guru. He is engaged in freeing the souls from the thraldom of matter. He assumes the form of a Guru out of His intense love for mankind. He wishes that all should know Him and attain the blissful Siva-Pada. He watches the activities of the individual souls and helps them in their onward march. He liberates the individual souls from their fetters or bonds.

The Five Activities of the Lord

The five activities of the Lord (Pancha-Krityas) are: Srishti (creation), Sthiti (preservation), Samhara (destruction), Tirobhava (veiling) and Anugraha (grace). These, separately considered, are the activities of Brahma, Vishnu, Rudra, Mahesvara and Sadasiva.

SIVA, SAKTI AND MAYA

The Lord Siva pervades the whole world by His Sakti. He works through His Sakti. Sakti is the conscious energy of Lord Siva. She is the very body of Lord Siva. The potter is the first cause for the pot. The stick and the wheel are the instrumental causes. The clay is the material cause of the pot. Similarly, Lord Siva is the first cause of the world. Sakti is the instrumental cause. Maya is the material cause.

Sakti is not the material cause of the universe, because she is of the nature of consciousness (Chaitanya). Siva is pure consciousness, but matter is pure unconsciousness. Sakti is the intermediate link between the two.

Sakti is the reflex of Siva. It has no independent existence. Siva assumes this form out of His great love for mankind. Siva wishes that all should know Him.

EVOLUTION OF THE TATTVAS FROM SUDDHA-MAYA

The world undergoes evolution for the benefit of the souls. The whole process of creation is for the sake of the salvation of the souls. The world is real and eternal. The world of matter and souls forms the body of the Lord.

The Saiva Siddhanta analyses the universe into thirty-six Tattvas or principles, as against the twenty-five of the Sankhya. The thirty-six Tattvas arise from Maya, the material cause of the world. Suddha-Maya is Maya in its primal state. From it arise the five pure principles called Siva Tattva, Sakti Tattva, Sadasiva Tattva, Isvara Tattva and Suddhavidya Tattva. Siva functions through these five pure principles.

Maya evolves into the subtle principles and then into the gross. Siva Tattva is the basis of all consciousness and action. It is undifferentiated (Nishkala Suddha Maya). The Sakti of Siva starts her activity. Then Siva becomes the experiencer. Then He is called Sadasiva, known also by the name Sadakhya, who is not really separate from Siva. The Suddha Maya becomes active. Then Siva, the experiencer, becomes the ruler. He is then Isvara, who is not really separate from Sadasiva. Suddhavidya is the cause of true knowledge.

THE BONDS THAT BIND THE SOUL

Anava, Karma and Maya

Souls (Pasu) are by nature infinite, all-pervading, eternal and all-knowing like Lord Siva (Pati). Yet they think that they are finite, limited and little-knowing, ignorant and temporary. This is due to their bonds (Pasa), viz., Anava, Karma and

Maya which are called the three Malas or impurities. Anava is the impurity which makes the all-pervading Jiva think itself to be atomic (Anu). It produces the erroneous notion of finiteness. The second impurity or bond is Karma. The soul acts in certain ways on account of its limitation and does good and evil actions. Karma brings about the conjunction of the soul with its body. The results of the Karma have to be worked out in the world. There should be worlds and bodies, in order to experience the fruits of actions and acquire knowledge. These are provided by Maya, the third Mala or bond. Maya is the material cause of the world. The soul gets experience and limited knowledge through Maya.

The soul learns, by long experience, that this Samsara is full of pains and is transitory, and that he can attain eternal bliss and immortality only by attaining Sivatva or the nature of Siva or God-realisation. He develops Vairagya (dispassion), and Viveka (discrimination between the real and the unreal, the permanent and the impermanent).

Three Orders of Jivas

The Saiva Siddhantins divine Jivas or Pasus into three orders, viz., Vijnanakalas, Pralayakalas and Sakalas. Vijnanakalas have only the Anava Mala (egoism). Maya and Karma have been resolved. Pralayakalas are those who are free from Maya alone, in the stage of Pralaya. Sakalas have all the Malas (defects), viz., Anava, Karma and Maya.

The Malas affect only the Jivas and not Siva. Those who are freed from the Malas or impurities attain Sivatva or the nature of Siva. They are Siddhas or perfected beings.

THE WAY TO THE ATTAINMENT OF SIVATVA OR GOD-REALISATION

You must free yourself from the three bonds, if you want to attain salvation. You must annihilate Maya which is the root of all sins. You must destroy all Karmas which produce rebirth. You must remove the erroneous notion of a finite self.

The three bonds can be removed only through rigorous Tapas, proper discipline, the help of a Guru, and above all, the grace of Lord Siva. Charya (observance), Kriya (rites) and Yoga (Yama, Niyama, etc.) constitute the discipline. When the aspirant practises in right earnest Charya, Kriya and Yoga, he obtains the grace of Lord Siva. Then the Lord instructs the soul, reveals Himself and illumines him. Then the soul realises its nature as Siva (Jnana).

Discipline and grace culminate in Jnana. Jnana is the supreme means of salvation or the attainment of the final beatitude. Karma and other means are only subsidiary to it. They are only auxiliaries.

The attainment of Sivatva or Siva-nature does not mean complete merging of the soul in Siva. The liberated soul does not lose its individuality. It continues to exist as soul in God. Sivatva is the realisation of an identity of essence in spite of difference. The soul attains the nature of Siva or God, but it is not itself Siva or God.

THE SAKTI YOGA PHILOSOPHY

INTRODUCTION

In this system of Sakti Yoga philosophy, Siva is omnipresent, impersonal and inactive. He is pure consciousness. Sakti is dynamic. Siva and Sakti are related as Prakasa and Vimarsa. Sakti or Vimarsa is the power that is latent in the pure consciousness. Vimarsa gives rise to the world of distinctions. Siva is Chit, Sakti is Chidrupini. Brahma, Vishnu and Siva do their functions of creation, perservation and destruction in obedience to Sakti. Sakti is endowed with Ichha (will), Jnana (knowledge) and Kriya (action). Siva and Sakti are one. Sakti-Tattva and Siva-Tattva are inseparable. Siva is always with Sakti.

Siva-Tattva and Sakti-Tattva

The creative aspect of the Supreme Siva is called Siva-Tattva. Sakti-Tattva is the will of Siva. It is the seed and womb of the entire world.

Siva has two aspects. In one aspect, He is the supreme, changeless One who is Satchidananda. This is Para Samvit. Nishkala Siva is Nirguna Siva. He is not connected with the creative Sakti. In the other aspect, He changes as the world. The cause of the change is Siva-Tattva. Sakti-Tattva is the first dynamic aspect of Brahman. This Siva-Tattva and Sakti-Tattva are inseparable.

Sakti—The Ruler of Maya

Maya or Prakriti is within the womb of Sakti. Maya is the matrix of the world. Maya is potential in the state of dissolution. She is dynamic in creation. Maya evolves into several material elements and other physical parts of all sentient creatures, under the direction of Sakti.

There are thrity-six Tattvas or principles in the Sakti philosophy.

SAKTI—THE ACTIVE ASPECT OF THE IMMANENT GOD

The power or active aspect of the immanent God is Sakti. Siva or Brahman is the unchanging consciousness. Sakti is His changing Power which appears as mind and matter. Sakti is the embodiment of power. She runs this world-show. She maintains the sportive play or Lila of the Lord. She is the supporter of the vast universe. She is the supreme Power by which the world is upheld. She is the Universal Mother. She is Durga, Lakshmi, Sarasvati, Kali, Chandi, Chamundi, Tripurasundari and Rajarajesvari. She is Lalita, Kundalini and Parvati. There is no difference between God and His Sakti, just as there is no difference between fire and its burning power.

Devi is Sakti of Lord Siva. She is Jada Sakti and Chit Sakti. Prakriti is Jada Sakti. Suddha Maya is Chit Sakti. Nada, Bindu and the rest are only names for different aspects of Sakti. Sakti is Prakriti, Maya, Mahamaya and Sri Vidya. Sakti is Brahman Itself. Sakti manifested Herself to Lord Siva in the ten forms as the Dasa-Maha-Vidyas, viz., Kali, Bagalamukhi, Chhinnamasta, Bhuvanesvari, Matangi, Shodasi, Dhumavati, Tripurasundari, Tara and Bhairavi.

Sakti is Chidrupini. She is pure, blissful Consciousness. She is the Mother of Nature. She is Nature Itself. She is Jagat-Janani, Creatrix of the world; Mahishasuramardini, destroyer of Mahishasura; Bhrantinasini, destroyer of illusion or Avidya; and Daridryanasini, destroyer of poverty.

The world is a manifestation of Sakti. The countless universes are only dust of Divine Mother's holy feet. Her glory is ineffable. Her splendour is indescribable. Her greatness is unfathomable. She showers Her grace on Her sincere devotees. She leads the individual soul from Chakra to Chakra, from plane to plane, and unites him with Lord Siva in the Sahasrara.

MANIFESTATIONS OF THE DIVINE MOTHER

The Supreme Lord is represented as Siva and His power is represented as His consort—Sakti, Durga or Kali. Just as the husband and wife look after the well-being of the family, so also Lord Siva and His Sakti are engaged in looking after the affairs of this world.

Divine Mother is everywhere triple. She is endowed with the three Gunas, viz., Sattva, Rajas and Tamas. She manifests Herself as Will (Ichha Sakti), Action (Kriya Sakti) and Knowledge (Jnana Sakti). She is Brahma-Sakti (Sarasvati) in conjunction with Brahma, Vishnu-Sakti (Lakshmi) in conjunction with Vishnu and Siva-Sakti (Gauri) in conjunction with Siva. Hence She is called Tripurasundari.

Radha, Durga, Lakshmi, Sarasvati and Savitri are the five primary forms of Prakriti or Devi. Durga destroyed Madhu and Kaitabha through Vishnu. As Mahalakshmi, She

destroyed the Asura Mahisha; and as Sarasvati, she
destroyed Sumbha and Nisumbha with their companions
Dhumralochana, Chanda, Munda and Raktabija.

THE ABODE OF THE DIVINE MOTHER

The abode of Tripurasundari, the Divine Mother, is called
Sri-Nagara. This magnificent abode known as Mani-Dvipa,
is surrounded by twenty-five ramparts which represent the
twenty-five Tattvas. The resplendent Chintamani Palace is in
the middle. The Divine Mother sits in the Bindu-Pitha in
Sri-Chakra in that wonderful palace. There is a similar abode
for Her in the body of man also.

The body is Sakti. The needs of the body are the needs
of Sakti. When man enjoys, it is Sakti who enjoys
through him. She sees through his eyes, works through
his hands and hears through his ears. Body, mind, Prana,
egoism, intellect, organs, and all functions are Her
manifestations.

The whole world is Her body. Mountains are Her bones.
Rivers are Her veins. Ocean is Her bladder. Sun and moon
are Her eyes. Wind is Her breath. Agni is Her mouth.

THE INDESCRIBABLE GLORY OF DEVI

The Story of the Yaksha

In the Kenopanishad, it is said that the gods became
puffed up with a victory over the Asuras. They wrongly
took the success to be the result of their own valour and
powers. The Lord wanted to teach them a lesson. He appeared before them in the form of a Yaksha—a huge
form, the beginning and end of which were not visible.
The Devas wanted to find out the identity of this form
and sent Agni for this purpose. The Yaksha asked Agni:
"What is thy name and power?" Agni replied: "I am Agni,
Jatavedas. I can burn up the whole universe in a minute."
The Yaksha placed before Agni a dry blade of grass and

asked him to burn it. Agni was not able to burn it. He ran away from the Yaksha in shame. The gods then sent Vayu to enquire who he was. Vayu approached the Yaksha. The Yaksha asked Vayu: "Who are you? What is your power?" Vayu replied: "I am the wind-god. I can blow the whole world in a minute." The Yaksha then placed a blade of grass before Vayu and challenged him to blow it away. Vayu could not make it move an inch from its place. He, too, left the place in shame. Last of all came Indra himself. When Indra reached the place, he found that the Yaksha vanished.

Then Uma appeared before Indra and revealed to him the real identity of the Yaksha. She said to Indra: "It is the power of the Divine Mother—and not that of the gods—that crowned the gods with victory. It is the Sakti of Uma or Haimavati, sister of Krishna, that is the source of the · strength of all the gods." Sakti is the great Teacher of Jnana. She sheds wisdom on Her devotees.

The Devi Behind the Gods

When Vishnu and Mahadeva destroyed various Asuras, the power of Devi was behind them. Devi took Brahma, Vishnu and Rudra and gave them the necessary Sakti to proceed with the work of creation, preservation and destruction. She is at the centre of the life of the universe. She is in the Muladhara Chakra in our bodies. She vitalises the body through the Sushumna. She vitalises the universe from the summit of Mount Meru.

THE MOTHER THAT PROTECTS

Sakti may be termed as that by which we live and have our being in this universe. In this world, all the wants of the child are provided by the mother. The child's growth, development and sustenance are looked after by the mother. Even so, all the necessities of life, life's activities in this world and the energy needed for it, depend upon Sakti or the Universal Mother.

The first syllable which a child or a quadruped utters is the name of the beloved mother. Is there any child who does not owe its all to the affection and love of its mother? It is the mother who protects you, consoles you, cheers you and nurses you. She is your friend, philosopher, preceptor and guide throughout your life. The human mother is a manifestation of the Universal Mother. All women are forms of the Divine Mother.

THE SCRIPTURES OF THE SAKTA SCHOOL

The Devi-Sukta of the Rig-Veda, Sri-Sukta, Durga-Sukta, Bhu-Sukta and Nila-Sukta, and the specific Sakta Upanishads such as the Tripurasundari Upanishad, Sitopanishad, Devi Upanishad, Saubhagya Upanishad, Sarasvati Upanishad, Bhavanopanishad, Bahvrichopanishad, etc.—all emphatically declare the Mother-aspect of God.

SAKTAISM—A UNIVERSAL CULT

He who worships Sakti, that is, God in Mother-form, as the Supreme *Power* which creates, sustains and withdraws the universe, is a Sakta.

Worship of Sakti, or Saktaism, is one of the oldest and most widespread religions in the world. Everybody in this world wants power and loves to possess power. He is elated by power. He wants to domineer over others through power. War is the outcome of greed for power. Scientists are followers of Saktaism. He who wishes to develop will-power and a charming personality is a follower of Saktaism. In reality, every man in this world is a follower of Saktaism.

Scientists say now that everything is energy only, and that energy is the physical ultimate of all forms of matter. The followers of the Sakta school of philosophy have said the same thing long ago. They further say that this energy is only a limited manifestation of the infinite Supreme Power or Maha Sakti.

VEDANTA AND SAKTAISM

The basis of Saktaism is the Veda. Saktaism upholds that the only source and authority (Pramana) regarding transcendental or supersenual matters such as the nature of Brahman, etc., is the Veda. Sakti Vada or Sakta Darsana is a form of monism or Advaita Vada. Saktaism is only Vedanta. The Saktas have the same spiritual experiences as those of a Vedantin.

Saktaism speaks of the personal and impersonal aspects of Godhead. Brahman is Nishkala or without Prakriti, and Sakala or with Prakriti. The Vedantins speak of Nirupadhika Brahman (pure Nirguna Brahman without Maya), and Sopadhika Brahman (with Upadhi or Maya) or Saguna Brahman. It is all the same. Names only are different. It is a play of words or Sabda Jala. People fight on words only and carry on lingual warfare, hair-splitting, logical chopping and intellectual gymnastics. In reality, the essence is One. Clay only is truth; all modifications such as pot, etc., are in name only. In Nirguna Brahman, Sakti is potential; whereas, in Saguna Brahman, Sakti is dynamic.

SAKTI-YOGA SADHANA

Saktaism is not mere theory or philosophy. It prescribes systematic Sadhana of Yoga, regular discipline according to the temperament, capacity and degree of evolution of the Sadhaka. Sadhana means unfolding, rousing up or awakening of the power of Sakti. Saktaism helps the aspirant to arouse the Kundalini and unite Her with Lord Siva and to enjoy the supreme bliss or Nirvikalpa Samadhi. A Sakta does Sadhana which helps the union of Siva and Sakti through the awakening of the forces within the body. He becomes a Siddha in the Sadhana when he is able to awaken Kundalini and pierce the six Chakras. The mode of Sadhana depends upon the tendencies and capacities of the Sadhaka.

Bhava or Attitude

The aspirant thinks that the world is identical with the Divine Mother. He moves about thinking his own form to be the form of the Divine Mother and thus beholds oneness everywhere. He also feels that the Divine Mother is identical with Brahman.

The advanced Sadhaka feels: "I am the Devi and the Devi is in Me." He worships himself as Devi instead of adoring any external object. He says: *"Saham*—I am She (Devi)."

The Awakening of Kundalini

The Sakti must be awakened by Dhyana, Bhava, Japa and Mantra Sakti. The Mother, the embodiment of the fifty letters, is present in the various letters in the different Chakras. When the chords of a musical instrument are struck harmoniously, fine music is produced. Even so, when the chords of the letters are struck in their order, the Mother who moves in the six Chakras and who is the very Self of the letters, awakens Herself. The Sadhaka attains Siddhi easily when She is roused. It is difficult to say when and how She shows Herself, and to what Sadhaka.

When Kundalini sleeps, man is awake to the world. He has objective consciousness. When She awakes, he sleeps. He loses all consciousness of the world and becomes one with the Lord. In Samadhi, the body is maintained by the nectar which flows from the union of Siva and Sakti in the Sahasrara.

Pasu Bhava and Divya Bhava

Physical contact with a female is gross Maithuna. This is due to Pasu-Bhava or animal attraction or brutal instinct. Mother Kundalini Sakti unites with Lord Siva in the Sahasrara during Nirvikalpa Samadhi. This is real Maithuna or blissful union. This is due to Divya-Bhava or divine disposition. You must rise from Pasu-Bhava to Divya-Bhava through Satsanga, service of Guru, renunciation, dispassion, discrimination, Japa and meditation.

Indispensability of Guru's Guidance and Mother's Grace

Sakti Yoga Sadhana is to be practised in a perfect, practical way under the guidance of a Guru who has become perfect. Guru is indispensable for the practice of Sakti Yoga Sadhana. He initiates the aspirant and transmits the divine Sakti.

No one can free himself from the thraldom of mind and matter without Mother's grace. The fetters of Maya are too hard to break. If you worship Her as the great Mother, you can very easily go beyond Prakriti through Her benign grace and blessings. She will remove all obstacles in the path, lead you safely into the illimitable domain of eternal bliss, and make you absolutely free. When She is pleased and bestows Her blessings on you, then alone you can free yourself from the bondage of this formidable Samsara.

Knowledge of Sakti Leads to Salvation

Knowledge of Sakti leads to salvation. *"Sakti-Jnanam Vina Devi Nirvanam Naiva Jayate—O Devi!* Without the knowledge of Sakti, Mukti cannot be attained"—says Siva to Devi. The Jiva or the individual soul thinks, when he is under the influence of Maya, that he is the doer and the enjoyer and identifies himself with the body. Through the grace of Sakti and through Sadhana or self-culture, the individual soul frees himself from all fetters and attains spiritual insight and merges himself in the Supreme.

Worship of the Divine Mother, intense faith and perfect devotion and self-surrender, will help you to attain Her grace. Through Her grace alone you can attain Knowledge of the Imperishable.

Glory to Sri Tripurasundari, the World-Mother, who is also Rajarajesvari and Lalita-Devi. May Her blessings be upon you all. May you all obtain the grace of Sakti, the Universal Mother and enjoy the supreme bliss of final emancipation.

CHAPTER 14

EPILOGUE

Man has forgotten his true divine nature. He has degraded himself through selfishness, passion and greed. He is swayed by the two currents of love and hatred.

This is a world of struggle and strife. This is a relative plane of three Gunas. There is ceaseless fight between good and evil, Devas and Asuras, Sattva and Tamas.

Therefore, consolidation of people is an imperative need of the hour. In union lies our strength. People should abandon all petty differences and unite their minds, hearts and souls for the solidarity and the well-being of the nation and the world.

UNITY—THE NEED OF THE HOUR

O my friends! You are weak. You have neither unity nor organisation among you. You are scattered like pebbles on the bank of a river. The sub-castes are countless. Sects, cults and creeds are numberless. Their large number in the population will not in anyway help you. Most of the people are selfish. They have not got the spirit of self-sacrifice and service. This is a most deplorable state. If there is organisation, then only there will be strength and security for you or for any nation.

O my friends! You are all scattered like particles of sand or mercury. When you are all united only, you will have proper strength to defend yourself and do good to the country. United you will stand; divided you will fall. Open your eyes now. Shake off your lethargy, inertia and indifferent nature. There is the clarion call for united action. Do not wait even for a single second. Be up and doing. Stand on your own legs.

Become true Hindus, true Christians and true Muslims. Let

the flame of true love fire your soul. Stand up. Gird up your loins. Strengthen yourself. Unite. Become an indivisible Body.

Do you remember the story of an old man, his sons and the bundle of sticks? The sons were not able to break the whole bundle, but they broke each stick very easily to pieces. Even so, if you are united, you can become very strong. You will be invincible. You can work wonders.

Be prepared to sacrifice everything. Be of one mind. Speak with one voice. Have common aspiration. Act in perfect union. Cultivate immense love for your religion. The flame of love must burn in your hearts steadily. Love one and all. There is no religion greater than love.

WHO IS QUALIFIED TO SERVE RELIGION EFFICIENTLY

Those who want to serve their religion should possess virtuous qualities such as courage, mercy, simplicity, broad tolerance, adaptability, self-restraint, cosmic love, equal vision, humility, equanimity of mind, truthfulness, patience, forbearance, forgiveness and honesty. They will have to cultivate these virtues.

They should have knowledge of Karma Yoga. They should study the second and third chapters of the Gita again and again. They should not expect any fruits of their actions. They should consecrate all actions unto the Lord. They should kill the idea of agency or actorship. They should entertain the Nimitta-Bhava. They should feel that God works through them. Then only they will have purification of heart. God is the foundation of society. God is the substratum for the world. No atom can move without Him. In Him we live and move and have our very being.

Those young men who want to dedicate their lives for the service of religion, can do better service if they remain as Brahmacharins or celibates. They will then have no selfish interests. Fresh flowers should be offered to the Lord. A fresh, vigorous, untainted body and mind should be offered to the Lord.

You may ask: "Why should I practise Karma-Yoga and self-restraint? Why should I kill egoism? Why should I develop renunciation and Vairagya? Why should I serve the country? Why should I control the mind?" I say, all these will help *you* to attain freedom and perfection and to free yourself from pain, sorrow and death.

EDUCATION AND NATION-BUILDING

India, the sacred land of Rishis and sages, is still sunk in the mire of ignorance, from the point of view of the great ideal that is ahead. There is much illiteracy among the masses. Professors, teachers and students should go to the villages during holidays and educate the masses. They should organise night schools for them. Rich persons should give them much help and support. Compare India with Europe or America. The number of illiterates is more in India than in any other civilised country.

SPIRITUAL VALUES—THE BASIS OF TRUE EDUCATION

National schools and colleges for boys and girls, and universities, must be opened. Boys and girls should get the right type of education. Then only the national spirit can be kept up. The education which makes you tread the path of truth and righteousness, which moulds your character, which helps you to attain freedom, perfection and knowledge of the Self, and at the same time enables you to eke out an honest living, can be called as true education.

IMPORTANCE OF PHYSICAL CULTURE

Sabhas, Seva-Dals or Samitis, and physical culture institutions should be founded in all parts of the country. They should be properly organised. It is your duty to serve heart and soul through these institutions. You will develop the true spirit. Your heart will be purified quickly.

The world needs good healthy mothers, healthy, strong boys and girls. What do we find in these days in India? India, the land which produced Bhishma, Drona, Bhima, Arjuna, Asvatthama, Kripa, Parasurama, and countless other chivalrous warriors, the soil which contained numberless Rajput chiefs of undaunted intrepidity, unparalleled chivalry and matchless strength, abounds now with effeminate weaklings dependent on hundreds of external factors for their sustenance. All these people should emulate the example of the few great heroes and geniuses who are still the glory of India. The world requires numberless brave, moral, Adhyatmic soldiers, who are equipped with the five virtues, viz., Ahimsa, Satya, Asteya, Brahmacharya and Aparigraha. Those who are endowed with the above virtues, those who possess health and strength, those who have knowledge of the Self—they alone can secure real freedom for all.

EARLY MARRIAGE—A SOCIAL EVIL

Early marriage is a great social evil. Children beget children. India abounds with weaklings as a consequence. Early marriage should be stopped with a knowledge of the higher laws of life.

NEED FOR ACCENT ON DUTY AND DISCIPLINE

The most wonderful machine in the world is the physical body. It consists of different systems, organs and parts. If all the systems, organs and parts work in harmony, if all the parts are in sound condition, you can enjoy good health. If a single part or system or organ goes out of order, there is disharmony, and you get disease. A vicious circle is created. Even so, the society or the nation consists of different communities and individuals. Every individual should carry out his duty properly. He must be strong and healthy to discharge his duties. Otherwise, the society or the nation will become weak and undergo decay and degeneration.

Mere bubbling juvenile enthusiasm will not do. It will not

serve any purpose. True love must be ingrained in you. Every nerve and every cell should throb with pure love. If you have not got this spirit, you will have to develop it to the maximum degree through service of humanity. Study again and again the lives of great sages and saints who gave their lives for religion. Work under a master for some years. Serve him. Honour him. Obey him. Obedience is better than sacrifice. You will imbibe his spirit and virtues. Do not try to become yourself a leader. If everybody wants to become a leader, if everybody wants to command, the movement will die. Learn to serve. Learn to obey. You can do real service to religion and country.

INDUSTRIAL GROWTH AND ECONOMIC INDEPENDENCE

Use indigenous articles and help the growth of industries. This will lead to our economic independence. Economic independence is indispensable.

Money is wasted in marriage festivals and other ceremonies. Save this money and spend it in building the nation. Every pie spent in this direction is really well-spent. Do not become a slave of social customs. These act as stumbling blocks to progress. They tend to weaken the nation.

Our young graduates should not neglect the industrial and agricultural sides. They should look after their own lands and increase the productive power. There is a great field for work in this direction. They can have independent living. They can make enough money and serve the people by supplying good, unadulterated milk and butter and other food-stuffs which are necessary for keeping up health and strength.

THE POWER THAT COMES FROM A HARD LIFE OF ACTION AND ENDURANCE

Be patient. Persevere and plod on. Do something practical. Herein lies the secret of success. There is no use in making much noise. Everything should be put into practice. Lecture on platform will only create a temporary bubbling of emotion and enthusiasm. This will not help much. Things should take proper shape.

Lead a life of endurance. Bear insult, privations and sufferings. Clean your clothes. Split fuel. Carry water. Do manual labour. Strengthen your body and muscles. Do *Dand, Baithak,* wrestling, Asanas and Pranayama. Swim. Run in open air. Keep a strong and healthy body. Lead a simple and natural life. Preserve Virya. Be a Brahmachari though married. Learn to control the senses.

Luxury and comfort are a curse. That will weaken you. Walk daily three or four miles. The condition of the younger generation is pitiable. They cannot walk even half a mile. They have poor health. They suffer from anaemia, dyspepsia, constipation, debility, etc. In times of danger, they cannot protect their women and children. They have become weak, timid and effeminate. Is this not a lamentable state?

Realise your responsibilities. Face troubles, tribulations and trials. Stand adamant. Be bold. Be cheerful. Draw courage and power from within, through regular meditation on the Immortal Self. Sit alone and peep within for some time. Give up comforts and easy-going life. Work hard. Come out victorious and wear the laurels. Great men have all suffered in order to stick to the path of righteousness and to protect the religion. They still live in our hearts. The glorious lives they led are a source of inspiration for us.

CALL FOR CONSOLIDATION OF THE NATION

O my beloved Sikh brothers! You are chivalrous and bold. The blood of Guru Govind Singh runs through your veins. You are all endowed with a strong physique and sinewy frame. This is due to the grace of the Lord. You are the Kshatriyas of our nation.

O Hindus, O Sikhs, O Maharathas, O Rajputs! Just as the dark unfathomed ocean contains many precious pearls and gems, so also there are many jewels amongst you all; there are many Ranjit Singhs, Shivajis and Rana Prataps. Awaken the dormant faculties. Remember the glory and power of your ancestors. Come forward now. Show your chivalrous nature and undaunted spirit. Work for the consolidation of the nation as a whole.

EXHORTATION TO SADHUS AND SANNYASINS

O Sadhus, Sannyasins, Yogis and Brahmacharins who have attained success in Sadhana! This is my earnest prayer to you all. You will have to come now from your retreats to serve humanity. You need not take any active part in any movement. You can remain like Samartha Ramdas. Ramdas gave wise counsels to Shivaji. Shivaji drew inspiration from his Guru. He hoisted the *Gerua* banner and did all the work. Ramdas's presence was the source of strength to Shivaji. Even so, you can give moral instructions and good counsels to people. You can guide them and give them words of encouragement. You can do everything that is best calculated to unite the nation. As you have no attachment to anybody and as you are endowed with spiritual powers, you can work wonders. You say that the world is your body. In your discourses you say that the whole world is your sweet home—*Vasudhaiva Kutumbakam.* Please show this in action. Kindly put this into practice. Become practical Vedantins.

May the Eternal Dharma be preserved for ever. May all the citizens be consolidated by the bond of true love. May all work together for the well-being and solidarity of the country. May all prosper gloriously both in the material and spiritual planes.

OM SANTI! SANTI! SANTIH!

Appendices

APPENDIX I

THE SIVA-LINGA

A SYMBOL WHICH POINTS TO AN INFERENCE

The popular belief among foreigners is that the Siva-Linga represents the phallus or the virile organ, the emblem of the generative power or principle in nature. This is not only a serious mistake, but a grave blunder. In the post-Vedic period, the Linga became symbolical of the generative power of Lord Siva. Linga is the differentiating mark. It is certainly not the sex mark. You will find in the Linga Purana:

Pradhanam Prakritim Tatcha Yadahur-lingamuttamam
Gandhavarnarasairhinam Sabda-sparsadi-varjitam.

The foremost Linga which is primary and is devoid of smell, colour, taste, hearing, touch, etc., is spoken of as Prakriti (Nature).

Linga means a *mark,* in Sanskrit. It is a symbol which points to an inference. When you see a big flood in a river, you infer that there had been heavy rains the previous day. When you see smoke, you infer that there is fire. This vast world of countless forms is a Linga of the omnipotent Lord. The Siva-Linga is a symbol of Lord Siva. When you look at the Linga, your mind is at once elevated and you begin to think of the Lord.

Lord Siva is really formless. He has no form of His own; and yet, all forms are His forms. All forms are pervaded by Lord Siva. Every form is the form or Linga of Lord Siva.

A POWERFUL AID TO CONCENTRATION

There is a mysterious power or indescribable Sakti in the Linga to induce concentration of the mind. Just as the mind is focussed easily in crystal gazing, so also the mind attains one-pointedness when it looks at the Linga. That is the reason why the ancient Rishis of India and the seers have prescribed Linga for being installed in the temples of Lord Siva.

LINGA REPRESENTS THE FORMLESS SIVA

Siva-Linga speaks to you in unmistakable language of silence: "I am one without a second. I am formless." Pure, pious souls only can understand this language. A curious, passionate, impure foreigner of little understanding or intelligence says sarcastically: "Oh! The Hindus worship the phallus or sex-organ. They are ignorant people. They have no philosophy." When a foreigner tries to learn the Tamil or Hindi language, he first tries to pick up some vulgar words. This is his curiosity-nature. Even so, the curious foreigner tries to find out some defect in the worship of symbols. Linga is only the outward symbol of the formless being, Lord Siva, who is the indivisible, all-pervading, eternal, auspicious, ever-pure, immortal essence of this vast universe, who is the undying soul seated in the chambers of your heart, who is your Indweller, innermost Self or Atman and who is identical with the Supreme Brahman.

SPHATIKALINGA—A SYMBOL OF THE NIRGUNA BRAHMAN

Sphatikalinga is also a symbol of Lord-Siva. This is prescribed for Aradhana or worship of Lord Siva. It is made up of quartz. It has no colour of its own, but takes on the colour of the substances which come in contact with it. It represents the Nirguna Brahman or the attributeless Supreme Self, or the formless and attributeless Siva.

THE MYSTIC SAKTI IN THE BLOCK OF STONE

For a sincere devotee, the Linga is not a block of stone. It is all radiant Tejas or Chaitanya. The Linga talks to him, makes him shed profuse tears, produces horripilation and melting of heart, raises him above body-consciousness, and helps to commune with the Lord and attain Nirvikalpa Samadhi. Lord Rama worshipped the Siva-Linga at Ramesvar. Ravana, a learned scholar, worshipped the golden Linga. What a lot of mystic Sakti there should be in the Linga!

May you all attain the formless Siva through the worship of the Linga, the symbol of Lord Siva which helps concentration of mind and which serves as a prop for the mind to lean upon, in the beginning, for the neophytes.

INDIAN CULTURE BASED ON THE BHAGAVAD-GITA

THE GOSPEL OF NON-ATTACHMENT

The essence of true culture lies in its being based upon a spiritual sense of values and a spiritual outlook on life. The assertion of the essential divinity of man is the heart of Indian culture. The civilisation of India rests on inner refinement, on the nurture and unfoldment of the spiritual spark in man. India is a land of spirituality and the aspiration of every true Indian is for Atma-Svarajya or freedom in the highest divinity of the Self attainable through the conquest of the internal and the external nature. Self-realisation is the goal of the people of India. The Bhagavad-Gita is a universal scripture and it is the true articulate expression of the genuine cultural heritage of India. The Gita is a gospel of non-attachment, the immortality of the Soul and the ultimate freedom of the Self in the Absolute. It is the sacred teachings on the all-inclusive inwardness of the Spirit. The indispensability of non-attachment follows from the fact of the oneness of existence. Sri Krishna asserts that second to Him naught else exists (VII. 7). The truth being an undividedness of life, attachment to outward forms obviously means clinging to falsehood and a breach of truth, the inevitable result of which is misery. "Those pleasures which are contact-born are only wombs of pain" (V. 22). Anaasakti marks the spirit of real renunciation and right activity that does not bind the doer to its fruits. Real culture tends to freedom and it is the glory of the seers of India that with their deep wisdom they realised the freedom of the immortal Self within and proclaimed this truth to the world.

Desirelessness and inward peace mark the distinctive features of culture in India. Knowledge which characterises real culture is not mere learning but wisdom with an ethical background. The extent to which one has succeeded in moral discipline determines the quality of his knowledge. Knowledge does not end with mere understanding but culminates in realising the deepest truth of life. Such a cultured life is not possible without freedom from prejudice and attachment in thought and action. "As the ignorant act with attachment to action, so should the wise act without attachment, with a view to promote the welfare of the world" (III. 25). Perfect detachment is not possible without the knowledge of the ultimate unreality of things which one generally comes in contact with and which act as the causes of attachment towards them. The Indian mind has detected the error in the commonplace view of life held by those who yield to the dictates of their mind and the senses and has brought into light the fact of the transitoriness of physical life amidst the objects of sense. All philosophy starts from the consciousness of pain and suffering and the inadequacy of life in the sense-world. The Viveki seeks emancipation from imprisonment in earthly life and does not pin his faith to things that perish. The Gita points out that this world is 'Anityam', 'Asukham', 'Duhkhalayam' and 'Asasvatam'. When this discrimination dawns in a person, he becomes desireless and is not attached to anything. The fullness of God within reveals the pettiness of life outside, and the seeker of perfection clings not to fleeting appearances. Culture in India is synonymous with the blossoming of the faculty of religious and spiritual consciousness without which man is very little superior to creatures with mere instinct. The Gita enjoins renunciation of belief in and desire for outward forms and exhorts that no man who is mindful of eternal peace should think or act with a selfish motive or with any particular phenomenal end in view. "Established in Yoga, perform actions, casting off attachment" (II. 48). To act, thus, without 'Sanga' and to be inwardly unified with God even while acting in the world is what the Gita stresses upon as the art of right living and the way to peace both here and hereafter. Every bit of effort that is put forth towards the achievement of this end has its own indestructible effect. "There is no destruction of effort here; nor is there the production of contrary result. Even a little (practice) of this Dharma delivers one from great fear" (II. 40). No attempt is a waste; every effort shall lead to a corresponding effect, for the Soul is essentially immortal.

THE IMMORTALITY OF THE SOUL

The great truth to which the Indians hold on and which they can never forget or disbelieve is the immortality of the Soul and the continuance of life after death. The Gita, at the very outset, declares that the Atman cannot be destroyed. "Know That to be indestructible by which all this is pervaded. None can cause the destruction of That, the imperishable. He is not born, nor does He ever die; after having been, He again ceases not to be; unborn, eternal, everlasting and ancient, He is not killed when the body is killed" (II. 17, 20). Nothing can be more glorious than the recognition of this supreme fact. This saving knowledge is the very life-breath of the Indian nation, the solace of mankind and the realisation of which the Absolute in the form of Sri Krishna speaks to Arjuna who is the representative of humanity itself. The culture of India is permeated throughout and thoroughly influenced by the indubitable belief in the immortality and divinity of the Spirit in man. To the Hindus, the world of empirical experience is not the reality, but the Atman or Brahman is the Reality. They have no faith in the unstable universe, but they have full faith in the Eternal Being. God is their aim and the world is only a passage or a step, a mere means and not the end or finality of experience. The Gita is the message of the Life Transcendent which embraces within itself the entire universe which is seen in it in an altogether new light. Every individual can have this experience and even the wicked and the sinner has a hope.

"Even a man of bad conduct, when he worships Me with singular devotion, should be regarded as righteous, for he has rightly resolved" (IX. 30). "Even those who are born in sinful wombs, taking refuge in Me, go to the Supreme Abode" (IX. 32). There is no such thing as 'original sin' or innate evil in man, for the Soul of man is immortal and "even as blazing fire reduces fuel to ashes, so does the fire of knowledge reduce all actions to ashes" (IV. 37). Here knowledge stands for the realisation of the imperishable Self. As the ultimate destiny of man is identity with God, he passes from one life to another, from one body to another, according to his desires and actions, until he exhausts all experiences resulting therefrom, and attains identity with God. Reincarnation cannot stop until Self-realisation is attained, for the immortal Self asserts itself every moment and the individual cannot find rest anywhere except in its realisation, which, again, is not possible unless all Karmas are burnt up or exhausted. The Hindu theory of rebirth and immortality is unparalleled in the religious history of the world, and it is the only scientific and satisfactory explanation of the meaning of life. Without the fundamental acceptance of the immortal Self, no experience can be explained or understood and the theory of Karma is only a corollary to this basic truth which is the central pivot and theme of philosophy and religion.

THE IDEAL OF SOCIAL LIFE

The individual in society has to adapt himself to his environment in the light of the unity of life in the Divine. The stages of life differ in different persons and their Dharmas or duties in life are based on these stages of individual development. The Bhagavad-Gita recognises the temperamental diversities among individuals and the consequent classification of duties suited to their evolutionary stages which determine their Guna and Karma. In all countries there are the philosophical and the spiritual, the active and the militant, and business-loving and the trading, and the work-a-day populace naturally inclined to manual work. These distinctions are not artificially created with any motive behind, but these represent the outward social system revealing the inner aptitudes of human beings. Svadharma is the duty prescribed to a person in accordance with the stage of life in which he is placed, not by any other person or persons, but by his own inner characteristics which he manifests in his daily behaviour and actions. The fourfold social classification is meant to ensure a happy and loving union and fellowship among all people, who, due to their inherent tendencies show their fitness for varying activities in life and not a general equality in thought and deed. It is not possible for all men and all women to think alike and act alike. This kind of equality is not ingrained in the very essence of life *in the world*. Life is a display of heterogeneous species of beings and the fourfold grouping of persons is a broad division of mental dispositions and abilities for knowledge and action. The social good depends upon the proper regulation of the society, not merely by the force of the administrator, but by a loving understanding of one's own position, each for himself, and placing oneself in that particular status for which alone he is meant according to the inner law governing his nature. The members of society are interdependent and their welfare is sought by their social classification relative to the qualities and the actions corresponding to them (Guna-karma-vibhaga). The preservation of the hoary culture of India may be attributed to this wise scheme of life based on natural laws and sanctioned by the promptings of the inner nature in man.

The Gita is, no doubt, a great exponent of the ideal of social and universal brotherhood. It notes, however, in this respect, that individual life, family life, social life, universal life and divine life cannot be ultimately separated from one another, but these represent only the stages of the growth of the individual towards the realisation of Divine Perfection. Brother-hood has a meaning only when it is grounded in Selfhood or oneness. Dharma or righteousness determines the good of the society and the universe is a big society of beings inhabiting its different parts. He who seeks the well-being of the society cannot do so by forgetting the fact that the society is within the universe which is the integral whole, a conforming to the laws of which is necessary both for the individual good and the social good. The universe, too, is not a self-explained truth in itself, but is the expression of the harmony and reality that is in the highest Divine Being. "When one realises that the diversity of beings is centred in the One, and has spread from That alone, then, he attains to Brahman" (XIII. 30). The Dhar-ma of this Reality is the standard with which the Dharmas of the universe, the society, the family and the individual are fixed. As the reality of Brahman is indivisible, universal love and absence of selfishness and attachment become the Dhar-mas of the universe and all its contents. All beings are to be loved impartially and without infatuation, because the fact of the existence of all beings is the one Absolute Self. The vir-tues to be cultivated as enumerated in the Gita, especially in its Thirteenth and Sixteenth Chapters, are the *sine qua non* of leading a happy and good, noble and spiritual life individually as well as socially. Through the possession of divine virtues, more stamina and inner spiritual strength, the brute in man is overcome and the immortal principle within is unveiled.

The ideal of the social ethics of the Gita is Loka-sangraha, the well-being and solidarity of the world. This is brought about by each individual through the performance of Svadhar-ma in the spirit of non-attachment and self-surrender and with the knowledge of the immutable nature of the Atman. Svad-harma aims, at the same time, at Sarvabhutahita or the good of all beings. The fabric of society is to be so constituted as to aid its members to realise the supreme Ideal of life. As all beings share the one Life which is the whole and of which they are parts, their development lies in their being in harmony with that Life. The perfection of the part is the unity of the whole. Mutual love and the execution of duty in loyalty to the whole is the means to the blessedness of the individual and the society. When each one does his own duty without reluctance or desire in his mind, the welfare of the society is ensured, for wherever action commingles with the knowledge of the Divine Purpose that is behind this visible universe, there shall be "prosperity, victory, glory and firm policy" (XVIII. 78). The Gita declares that the Sastras should be taken as the authority in determining human conduct, which shows that society rests on the basis of the eternal principles of morality and spirituality.

Life is essentially a divine worship. Activity in this world is really the adoration of the Virat of the Visvarupa of the Lord. The individuals are 'Nimittamatra' or mere instruments in the fulfilment of the divine Law. Life is a Yajna, a holy sacrifice, and the world which is the Dharmakshetra or the field of righteous action is the altar at which the individual offers himself to God-Being. Dharma which is the ethical value governing the individual exalts him to Moksha which is the Infinite Value and the Goal of life. Everyone should conform to Dharma which supports life and which shall protect him who protects it through dispassionate practice. God Himself is 'Sasvata-dharma-gopta' or the protector of the eternal Dharma. Dharma is the source of material and spiritual good. Artha, Kama and Moksha have their basis in the observance of Dharma. God-realisation is the highest Dharma of all beings and all other Dharmas are subservient to this. This ultimate unity of all in God has to be realised in the entire universe (VI. 29, 30). The whole existence is the one conscious living truth of God who pervades it inside and outside and second to whom nothing can ever be (IX. 4, 5). All thoughts and actions should conform to this absolute ideal. Only when life is lived with this noble spirit of the dedication of the self to the one common and supreme good which is to be realised in God alone and nowhere else, the weal of the society is secure. When the Goal is forgotten, life becomes a misery. When life is founded on virtue and knowledge and the consciousness of the Highest Reality, it becomes Divine Life.

THE MAN OF TRUE CULTURE

The Gita ideal of the man of true culture is the Sthitaprajna, the Bhagavata or the Gunatita. He is the ripe fruit of the fine flower of culture. He is the perfected man who does not follow the course of the senses, but, "casts off all the desires of the mind and is satisfied in the Self by the Self (II. 55). He is the sage of steady wisdom, who has neither love nor hate, whose longings have turned away on account of the vision of the Supreme, whose day is the night of the ignorant, into whom all desires enter as waters enter the ocean which, filled from all sides, remains unmoved, who has attained to Peace and who rests in the Brahmi Sthiti (II. 55, 57, 59, 69, 70, 72). His happiness is within, relaxation within, light within; he sees the One in the all and the all in the One and his equal vision does not make a distinction between high and low. He is ever conscious of the Divine Presence and he is never separated from the Divine. Though he has nothing to achieve for himself, he works for the good of the world, in order to set an example to others. An idea of the goal of culture can be had from the towering example of the man of realisation whose characteristics are described in the Second, the Fifth, the Sixth, the Twelfth and the Fourteenth Chapters of the Gita, and who serves as the pattern into which every man of culture strives to mould himself in order to reach his perfection and blessedness in the homogeneous Brahman (Samam Brahma).

THE MESSAGE OF THE GITA

The Gita is a wonderful message of hope, consolation, peace and above all, the Divinity of man. It solves all problems of life, gives fearlessness to everyone, and lifts the individual from the depth of penury and misery to the height of immortality and eternal bliss. It presents in a concise form the Hindu view of life. In spite of the disturbances that appear on the surface of man's life, India has at its heart a tendency to harmony and unity. The Indians are a peace-loving and God-loving people. The greatest men of India are the saints, the sages and the Avataras who are the great torch-bearers of its culture. All the grand religious ideals that have moulded the character of men, the loftiest tenets of ethics and morality that have raised human beings to the magnanimous height of supreme perfection, and all the sublime truths of spirituality that have raised man to Divinity and directed the spiritual life of nations, first arose in India. India's spiritual culture is that it is responsible for the survival of the Indian nation even in the midst of calamities that have threatened it in the course of history. The Bhagavad-Gita which is the cream of the teachings of the Upanishads is the practical gospel of life of India and India gives this unique recipe to the whole world for the solidarity of all beings. Sri Krishna is the ideal perfect man, God Himself in form, crystallised Satchidananda, the Purna-Avatara, the apex of culture, wisdom, power and delight, and He gives the Gita, the message of the highest culture and realisation. It is to the immortal glory of India and the world at large that the Gita heartens all with the magnificent ideal of the union of man with God even while living in the world and discharging his duties in a spirit of self-sacrifice, non-attachment and surrender to God.